A History
of
Pulaski County
Kentucky

By: Grace Owens Moore

This volume was reproduced from
An 1952 edition located in the
Publisher's private library,
Greenville, South Carolina

All rights reserved. No part of this publication
may be reproduced, stored in a retrieval system,
transmitted in any form, posted on to the web
in any form or by any means without the
prior written permission of the publisher.

Please direct all correspondence and orders to:

www.southernhistoricalpress.com
or
SOUTHERN HISTORICAL PRESS, Inc.
PO BOX 1267
375 West Broad Street
Greenville, SC   29601
southernhistoricalpress@gmail.com

Originally published: Bagdad, KY. 1952
Copyright 1952 by: Grace Owens Moore
Reprinted by:
Southern Historical Press, Inc.
Greenville, SC
ISBN #0-89308-889-7
All rights Reserved.
Printed in the United States of America

. . . . TO MY MOTHER AND FATHER . . .

Whose knowledge of, and interest in,
Pulaski County and its people
inspired me to compile tales they told
their children . . . that you
who, today, live a streamlined life
may appreciate the texture of
the fiber that went into
the warp and woof of the tapestry
of Pulaski County

FOREWORD

This is not meant to be a formal history of Pulaski County. The purpose has been to assemble early records of the organization of the county and to preserve rich fragments of local and personal history, many of which have existed only in oral tradition and among the treasured recollections of aged citizens. These venerable people are rapidly passing away, and with them will be buried the knowledge of much that is interesting about early settlers in Pulaski.

Those resolute men and sacrificing women carved out of a wilderness a place to live and by their heroic deeds and services endeavored to make a way of life. We, their descendants and successors, have a responsibility to bear the high standards they have set and to hold fast to their precepts and principles. They charted the course and made possible the progress later generations have achieved.

Errors there may be in this book, and possibly such a long period of time has not been properly covered. However, had we waited to make this book perfect, it might not have been written at all.

If I have succeeded in accumulating and assembling any portion of early history and interesting facts concerning the people of Pulaski County, my purpose will be accomplished and my efforts rewarded.

A. O. T.

ACKNOWLEDGMENTS

Faded court records, old newspapers, old letters, the memoirs of old citizens, diaries, and old business papers saved by the descendants of early settlers have been invaluable in my endeavor to compile this account. They portrayed the people: who they were; where they came from; where they lived; what their interests and activities were.

I have talked with and interviewed many persons, some of them old residents, and learned—through their recollections of incidents—traditions and stories which were later verified by historical works. To them I wish to express my appreciation.

There are some who contributed written sketches for this volume and whose names have been noted. I gratefully acknowledge their assistance.

Sources of information for this book have been derived from: Pulaski County court records; city clerks' records; photostatic copies of war and post office records from the National Archives; Draper's Manuscripts; Mr. Bayless Hardin, secretary of the Kentucky Historical Society; Collins, *History of Kentucky;* Swigget, *The Rebel Raider;* Basil D. Duke, *History of Morgan's Cavalry;* Eastham Tarrant, *The Wild Riders of the First Kentucky Cavalry;* Ridpath's *History;* Thomas P. Kettell, *History of the Great Rebellion;* Kniffin, Battle, Perrin, *Kentucky, A History of the State;* excerpts from Mrs. Clarice Payne Ramey's thesis, University of Kentucky; office of Assistant to the President of the Southern Railway System, Washington, D. C.; L. L. Waters, division superintendent of the Southern Railway; George Higgins, Gerhard Brown, biographies, church records.

Historical papers have been of help concerning unrecorded facts.

To the following I acknowledge their ready assistance and interest: Bess Hawthorne, La Place, Illinois, for note on Michael Stoner; Mrs. Pearl Catron De Rake, Baltimore, Maryland, notes on the Tate Family; the late Harry Wait whose valued help was cut short by death before this was completed; Lois Reed, research; Joe Parker, Memoirs; J. B. Bobbitt, reminiscences; Mrs. Henry Hail; Mrs. E. B. Hill; Mrs. Hugh Crozier; Maude Girdler; Mrs. Charles Hall; Mrs. O. L. Moore; Mrs. Maggie Owens; William Ramsey; the Reverend Wood; the Reverend Mundy; Mrs. V. D. Roberts; Mrs. Norman Taylor; Mrs. Bettie Tarter Shepard; Mrs. P. H. Hopkins; O'Leary Meece; Ernest Tandy; Mrs. Charles Oatts, Sr.; Mrs. Charles Oatts, Jr.; Mrs. L. E. Brown; Mrs. Elvert Humble; Everett Dagley; W. C. Wilson, Agricultural Department, Lexington, Kentucky; Hugh Hurst; Mrs. Louise Craig; Mrs. Andrew Waddle; Chester Kaiser; Mrs. Ben Adkins; Miss Anice Smith; Lina Porch; Edgar Murrell (booklet); Harold Cain; R. G. Williams; Citizens Bank; Mrs. R. G. Williams; Mrs. Sam F. Parker; Mrs. Robert Richardson; Elizabeth Pettus Meadors; Mrs. Amanda Newell Hicks; Mrs. Harry Wait; Mrs. Ruth Wait Tuttle; Bob Hail; "Park" Hines; Claude Weddle; Mrs. H. C. Kennedy; Mrs. A. S. Fry; Worthington Barnett; Miss Amelia Saunders; Fred Hunt; and O. L. Moore.

. . . . TABLE OF CONTENTS . . . .

FOREWORD vii

ACKNOWLEDGMENTS ix

COUNT CASIMIR PULASKI xv

1. PIONEER DAYS 1

2. PULASKI COUNTY IS FORMED 6
   Organization — Geography — Topography — Natural Resources — First Court — Selection of County Seat — Name — Plan for Town — Courthouse and County Buildings — Pay for Services of County Officers — Officers of Pulaski County.

3. EARLY COURT SESSIONS AND RECORDS......................21
   Early Courts — Early Tax Lists — Deeds — First Marriage Book — Old Records — Military Claims — Members of the Legislature from Pulaski County.

4. EARLY SETTLERS AND FAMILIES....................................34
   Cox — Curd — Denton — Elliot — William Fox — Gastineau — John Gibson — Robert Gibson — Girdler — Jasper — Morrow — Samuel Newell — Owens — Pettus — Porch — Jesse Richardson — Shepperd — Michael Stoner — Tarter — Tate — Cyrenius Wait — John Milton — Weddle — Zachary.

5. EARLY SETTLEMENTS AND VILLAGES........................60
   Incorporations — Woodstock — Burnside — Elihu — West Pulaski County, Old Harrison, Early Churches in West Pulaski County — South of the Cumberland.

6. DEVELOPMENT 69
   Mills — Parker's Mill — Development of Natural Resources; Coal, Timber, Iron, Clay and Limestone — Travel and Transportation; Roads, Stagecoach Days, Steamboats, Conveyances, Railroads — Postal Service — Post Offices in Pulaski County.

7. CHURCHES 88
   Flat Lick Baptist — First (Sinking Creek) Baptist — Fishing Creek Baptist — Hopeful — Baptist, Colored — High Street Baptist — Catholic — Christian — Early Methodist — Methodist — Davis Chapel A. M. E. — Pisgah — First Presbyterian.

8. EDUCATION 111
   Early Education — Early Schools in Somerset — Masonic College — Somerset Public Schools.

9. NEWSPAPERS, BANKS, HOTELS, OLD HOUSES..........119
   Newspapers — Banks — Taverns, Ordinaries, and Hotels — Old Houses and Antique Furniture.

10. AGRICULTURE 135
    Early Agriculture — Improved Methods — Agricultural Extension — From Records of the Extension Service; 1947, 1948 — Home Demonstration — Veterinary Medicine.

11. MEDICINE, ART, MUSIC..145
    Early Medicine — Medical Men; A Tribute to a Family of Doctors — Medical Men in Burnside — Druggists — Art and Handicrafts — Music.

12. THE DEVELOPMENT OF SOMERSET...........................167
    City Services — Hospitals — South Somerset — Somerset — 1949.

13. PULASKI COUNTY CITIZENS...175
    Men — Women — Boy Scouts — Girl Scouts.

14. LOCAL LORE 190
> *The Forty-niners — Deer Hunting Club — County Fair and Circus — Old Swimming Hole — The Johnnycake — Weddings — Disasters — Graham Flour — May Snowfall — Jesse James's Visit — Dr. Kerns's Death — Civil War Stories — A Railroad Legend — A Scrap of Forgotten History.*

15. WARS 203
> *Revolutionary Soldiers — Military of Pulaski County — War of 1812 — Mexican War, 1847 — The Civil War; Battle of Logan's Crossroads, Morgan's Raid through Central Kentucky, Notes and Incidents, Battle of Dutton's Hill, Regiments — Spanish-American War — World War I — World War II — Memorials.*

CONCLUSION 229

ILLUSTRATIONS .... following page 230

INDEX 249

......COUNT CASIMIR PULASKI......

Count Casimir Pulaski, for whom this Kentucky county was named, was a Polish patriot and brigadier general in the U. S. Army during the American Revolution. The second son of Josef and Marjanna Zielinska Pulaski, he was born March 4, 1747, in south central Poland at a time when Poland, although nominally independent, was actually dominated by Russia, Prussia, and Austria. Josef Pulaski, a wealthy nobleman, and his three sons attempted to awaken the Polish people to a desire for true independence and to create a Polish army worthy of the name. He established the Confederation of Bar and the Knights of the Holy Cross, two organizations intended to effect these patriotic purposes. Casimir became the military leader of the Confederation of Bar and proved his capabilities by defeating Russian forces at Berdyczow and Czestochowa. Poland's King Stanislas August Poniatowski, a puppet of Catherine II of Russia, was kidnaped, but released unharmed, by a few renegade members of the Confederation of Bar. King Stanislas and his followers falsely accused Casimir Pulaski of being the perpetrator of this kidnaping, which they enlarged to an attempted regicide. As a result of these accusations and the subsequent loss of prestige, Count Pulaski left Poland to wander about Europe. Once a hero in the courts of western Europe, he found he was now in ill-repute and an unwelcome visitor wherever he went.

While he was living in exile in France, he learned of the American Revolution. The colonists' fight for freedom and liberty fired his imagination, and from Silas Deane and Benjamin Franklin, who were in Paris in behalf of the American cause, he obtained letters of introduction to General Washington. Anxious to get such a controversial character out of France and thereby lessen the danger of his attempting a military venture in eastern Europe, influential Frenchmen arranged for Pulaski to sail for America in 1777.

Pulaski presented himself to General Washington who, in turn, referred him to the Continental Congress for a military commission. While the Congress was considering this request, Pulaski returned to General Washington's headquarters along the Brandywine River about the time General Howe and the British attacked. When the battle was going badly for the Americans, Pulaski proved his mettle by asking General Washington to allow him—even though he had no military commission—to lead thirty of the headquarters' cavalrymen against the British. Pulaski caught the British unawares and delayed the Redcoats sufficiently to permit the bulk of the American forces to withdraw. Casimir Pulaski had established his reputation and on September 15, 1777, the Continental Congress commissioned him a brigadier general in command of cavalry. Although he was not a fluent speaker of English, he did his best to organize an efficient cavalry. He was intensely loyal to General Washington and spent the winter near Valley Forge where he took part in various skirmishes with the British. Early in 1778, the Board of War of the Continental Congress authorized him to recruit and command a Cavalry Legion on his own. He had some disheartening experiences along the frontier in western Pennsylvania as cavalry forces were not adapted to frontier warfare. He had apparently decided to resign his commission and return to Europe when a fresh contingent of British, seizing Savannah and making it their headquarters, attacked through Georgia in 1778.

He was ordered to Charleston, South Carolina, with his cavalry regiment to engage the enemy. Upon his victory at Charleston, he reached a position of real influence for the first time since he came to the United States. He helped drive the British back through Georgia to Savannah where, with a French force which had arrived by sea, the Americans attacked. The battle was going badly; the French commander was wounded; Pulaski started to ride across the British line of fire to rally the French forces when he was struck by a bullet and mortally wounded. The British held their fire while Pulaski was removed from the battlefield. He died October 11, 1779, on board the "Wasp" which was taking him to Charleston for more adequate medical attention. He was truly a soldier of liberty, an excellent military commander, and above dabbling in the political intrigues of the day. His loss was mourned throughout the thirteen states. When he learned of Pulaski's death, Poland's King Stanislas paid him the fitting tribute, "Pulaski died as he lived—a hero—but an enemy of kings."

Count Pulaski's deeds of valor on behalf of the American colonists in their fight for freedom have not gone unnoticed or unsung by subsequent generations of Americans. Seven cities or towns in the United States bear his name, and seven states have Pulaski counties. Fort Pulaski, located on Cockspur Island in the mouth of the Savannah River, is a five-sided fortress of fine masonry which was built between the years 1829 and 1847. It was dedicated a National Monument to this Revolutionary hero in 1924. During World War II the fort served as a Navy and Coast Guard station, and on Pulaski Day, October 11, 1947, it was reopened as a memorial.

A HISTORY

OF

.... *PULASKI COUNTY*

KENTUCKY

Chapter 1

.........PIONEER DAYS..........

Following the Revolution many of the early Americans found their savings were gone, their homes broken, and their hopes dampened. These people were predominantly Scotch, Irish, Welsh, and English, who sought a new start in life.

Word had been brought to them by the Long Hunters, of a land to the west. With this incentive these fearless, hardy men—intrepid pioneers that they were—started the long trek westward. Some of them brought their families and meager possessions in ox carts or by pack horse. Some sickened and died on the way, but they halted only long enough to bury the loved one in a lonely grave, or for a "bornin'."

After weeks of toiling over trackless mountains, through rain and cold and with the constant fear of the Indians and wild animals that were in every mountain fastness, these hardy men and courageous women from the "backwater" section of Virginia and the Carolinas joined the hordes that streamed through Cumberland Gap into this new land. They came over the Wilderness Trail down to the Orchard (Crab Orchard), crossed Rockcastle River and Buck Creek into what was later to be known as "The Glades" in the future Pulaski County of the state of Kentucky. As it was flat, swampy land and held no appeal for the emigrants, they pressed on. Coming at last to a beautiful, rolling, wooded area they stopped. This section which they called "Flat Lick" rivals the central part of the state, and became the site of permanent settlements.

All of the colonists, however, did not remain here. Probably looking for equally desirable locations similar to the valleys of the Holsten and Clinch rivers in Virginia from which they came, they moved on. They scattered: some going to the north, some to the west, and others to the south. Each route took them to streams—which in that early day meant so much to the settlers—providing them with water power for their gristmills and a means of transportation.

Those who came to the bluffs overlooking the Cumberland River stopped and viewed the scene below and it suited them. They thought this was the most fertile land they had yet seen. Undaunted by the trackless hills and tangled growth, these men, who had faced the fire of battle and had so recently crossed the Alleghenies, cut grape vines, tied them to their ox carts and, giving a hitch around trees, let their precious belongings over the bluff. It took days and days to cut through the cane brakes; but here and on some of the high points they took up lands, which were grants from the Governor of Virginia for their services in the Revolution.

Tradition and history agree that this territory was only a part of the Indian hunting ground through which the redskins passed from north to south, leaving trails marked with beds of flint showing where arrowheads were made. One interesting relic is a peace pipe, which was found in a cave in the locality of Burnside and is now the prized possession of the late Dr. Nick Stigall's family.

Below Burnside is a gap in the ridge, known to this day as Double Head's Gap, so called for Chief Double Head of the Cherokees, the last tribe in this part of Kentucky. Legend says he drew his name from the shape of his head which resembled a peanut.

In the month of December, 1786, a body of Indians defeated a party of whites under the command of Captain Hardgrove, at the mouth of Buck Creek. The Indians attacked in the night, killed one man, and wounded Hardgrove. An Indian, at whom Hardgrove had probably fired, made an onset on Hardgrove with his tomahawk and a fierce encounter ensued. Hardgrove finally succeeded in wresting the tomahawk from the hands of the Indian and bore it off.

In May, 1788, a party of Indians stole some horses near Crab Orchard. Nathan McClure, lieutenant to Captain Whitley, with a part of his company pursued the trail to the ridge between Rockcastle and Buck creeks. Here a fierce skirmish took place. Lieutenant McClure was mortally wounded, and died the next night in a cave, where, at his own request, he had been left—knowing he could not live and fearing the others would be killed by the Indians if they remained with him. When his party returned the next day, they found his remains mangled by wild beasts. He was an active officer.[1] His unmarked grave is only a short distance off Highway 80, east of Somerset.

Among the early settlers were, according to Collins' *History of Kentucky,* John Newby, William Owens, Thomas Hansford, Samuel Newell, Charles Neal, Jesse Richardson, the Prathers, Pitmans, and Nicholas Jasper.

The first concern of these people was to establish homes. They made clearings, felled trees, hewed logs, and built one-room cabins. As time went by they added another room, leaving a space between called the "dog trot," though the "breeze way" probably would have been more applicable. It was used as a shelter for sheep whose flesh was so necessary for meat and whose wool provided clothing.

Wild animals abounded. Bear, deer, and wild turkey were all used for meat, their skins for clothing, and feathers for clothing and bedding. There was wood a-plenty for the huge fireplace, which was long enough for the children to stand in and keep warm without crowding the family circle.

The baby was rocked in a hollowed-out log, with one end left open for the warmth from the fire to keep the little one warm. The older children slept in the trundle bed. To conserve room, the quilting frames were attached to pulleys and drawn up to the ceiling when not in use.

The women performed the household duties; the men cleared and cultivated the land and hunted the game to supply the family with meat. Every family raised flax from which their linens were made, and every farm had its patch of cotton which was carded and spun into cloth.

The spinning wheel whirred and the loom creaked day and night. Sewing was all done by hand and with homespun thread. It was not until after the Civil War that the first sewing machine was brought into the county. This machine was an old Wheeler and Wilson (an improved model came later) and unique in the way the material was fed under the presser foot. Instead of the material being fed backward, it passed from left to right. This machine was manufactured and existed before labor was organized and perhaps it held the distinction

---

[1]Information from Collins' *History of Kentucky* (Covington, Ky.: Collins & Co., 1878) II, 685.

of going on the first strike. It is a known fact that it would operate perfectly for several hours and then suddenly stop. No amount of oiling, tinkering, or fuming and fussing had any affect—close it and put it aside until the next day and it would start off and work perfectly for another period of time.

It was late, too, before the first cook stove, hauled from Louisville (no date), attracted the curious who gathered to see it "blow up" when the first fire was built in it.

Food had to be stored for winter use, as there were no fruit jars for canning, no frozen food lockers, no home deep-freezes, no trucks bringing fresh fruits and vegetables. Cabbage, turnips, and potatoes were buried; apples, beans, and pumpkin—which was cut in circles and placed on sticks—rested on the rafters for drying. In addition there were eggs, butter, and famous Kentucky corn bread baked in an iron oven on the hearthstones.

Although limited in variety, the food of the pioneers was wholesome and nutritious. Upon this diet they thrived, being stalwart, robust, and long-lived men. One man, Elijah Denny, a Revolutionary soldier, was 115 years old in 1855 and still active, working on his farm. He drank only one cup of coffee in his lifetime and that was late in 1848. A strict member of the Baptist church, he rode six miles to every service. His grave is on the county line between Pulaski and Rockcastle.

One of the most urgent needs of the settlers was salt. Before they could produce it themselves, men rode horseback or in crude wagons to Middlesboro, a distance of seventy-five miles, and brought back enough to last a community for weeks or perhaps months. They also often rode a great distance to the gristmill to have their corn ground.

Their soap was made from the entrails of hogs. These they cleaned and dried when the hog was butchered and then boiled in lye to produce a strong, soft soap. The lye was made by pouring water over wood ashes in a V-shaped receptacle, called an ash hopper.

The social life of the community in the early days was entirely dependent on the individual and what he could do to entertain himself. It usually took the form of making pleasure in going to the places and doing the things necessary to the everyday life and needs of the people. This may seem very simple to modern children, but it provided human companionship, and, as the early homes were isolated, the great need was to see and know people.

The men had log-rollings, house-raisings, barn-coverings, and corn-shuckings; their wives had apple-peelings, bean-hullings, rag-tackings, and quilting parties. The young people were always ready for a candy-pulling, or to be at a "stirring-off" when sorghum was made. These often ended with the evening spent dancing to the whine of a fiddle played by the neighborhood Negro fiddler.

During their long trek westward and the first years of their settlement these pioneers endured hardships and suffered untold privations. Contemplation of their sturdy qualities and unswerving integrity inspires us to guard their heritage. The study of their lives—their comings and goings as they pushed back primitive civilization for an ordered life—tends to increase one's self-respect and to inspire one to press on to higher goals. Indeed they were goodly, God-fearing people, who knew from whence they came and what they were trying to do.

Chapter 2

.... *PULASKI COUNTY IS FORMED* ....

ORGANIZATION

Pulaski County, located in the south-central part of the state, was the twenty-seventh county formed in Kentucky. It was created by an Act of the General Assembly, December 10, 1798—to begin June, 1799—out of territory belonging to Lincoln and Green counties. It came into existence as an answer to the petitions from citizens, who lived a great distance from the county seats.

The Act passed by the Assembly read:

> That from and after the first day of June next, all that part of the counties of Lincoln and Green, included in the following boundary, to wit,—beginning at the mouth of Rockcastle, thence up the same four miles, where reduced to a straight line, above the reserve line; thence to the dividing ridge between Skegg's Creek and Buck Creek where the road crossing Stephen Lankford's to Buck Creek; thence a straight line to the Round Knobs; thence south forty-five degrees west to the present line between Green and Lincoln; thence to the proposed new county east line taken from Green; thence with the said line to the state line; thence along said line so far that a north line will strike the beginning, shall be one distinct county, and called and known by the name Pulaski; and all the residue of the said counties shall retain the names Lincoln and Green.

The Assembly named the county in honor of Count Casimir Pulaski, a Polish officer who came over to assist our forefathers in their struggle for freedom.

GEOGRAPHY

Since the creation of Pulaski County, several changes have been made in her boundary. The first change was when Wayne

County was formed and part was taken from Pulaski's territory on December 18, 1800. When Rockcastle was created in 1810, another part was taken from it. Then on February 20, 1825, a part of Pulaski was added to Whitley. Again a part of Pulaski was added to Wayne, January 6, 1831. Russell received part of Pulaski territory on February 22, 1839. The last change was in 1912 when McCreary was formed from parts of Pulaski, Wayne, and Whitley.

Pulaski County today is bounded on the east by Rockcastle and Laurel counties, on the south by McCreary and Wayne, on the west by Russell and Casey, and on the north by Lincoln. It lies in the foothills of the Cumberland Mountains and is drained by the Cumberland and South Fork rivers, Pitman, White Oak, Buck, Lyne, Cold Water, and Fishing creeks. When it was created, its southern boundary reached the Tennessee line. In the Thirteenth Biennial Report of the Commission of Agriculture, 1898-99, it was listed as the largest county in the state, with a length of forty miles from north to south and thirty from east to west.

Pulaski is now the third largest county in the state, having an area of 401,920 acres or 628 square miles. Before McCreary was taken off, its area was 1,000 square miles. The following table shows the growth in population:

YEAR	POPULATION
1800	3,161
1850	14,196
1900	31,296
1950	38,591

TOPOGRAPHY

Being off the beaten path of the first people coming into this land, Pulaski County was not among the most favored of Kentucky's counties, but it is rich in natural resources and scenic beauty.

The land is predominantly hilly with valleys lying between the hills; much of the soil is red clay. The valley of the Cumberland River is very fertile. Gorges cut by swift-flowing streams are resplendent with redbud and dogwood in the spring; the rich autumnal colors against a background of pines is a picture no artist can portray. The hillsides are beautiful with rhododendron, mountain laurel, and cucumber (a scion of the magnolia); on the bare and less favored spots are found the mountain violet and Indian pink, the color of which rivals the Kentucky cardinal. Along the creeks are anemones, wild poppies, bloodroot, trilliums, and many more wild flowers.

The soil in the southern part of the county is sandstone; in the northern part, the soil is of limestone with a red clay subsoil, which retains the moisture, enabling this section to withstand the long droughts that often come.

The meandering Cumberland, with its rock-ribbed bluffs in the region above Burnside, is similar to the palisades of the Kentucky River. Just above Burnside there is an unusual rock formation. A perpendicular rock-faced bluff, more than two hundred feet high, is topped with a large plot of irregular, enormous, imbedded limestone formations—many as large as a small house and placed in the manner of a small village. It is called, locally, Rock City.

Just below Burnside on the Cumberland, were the Cascades; a large spring near the top of the bluff spread and fell more than seventy-five feet over moss-covered rocks, finally spilling into the river. At one time it furnished power for a gristmill and water for the village of Bronston; the water was procured for the families by a bucket attached to a car which ran on a wire to the spring, then was drawn up by a hand windlass. This was called a "telegraph."

Underlying the surface of much of the county are many caves; some are irregular passages with no beauty, while others are filled with small streams of water and beautiful rock formations. Worthy of mention is a large one with many passages, which lead to a large opening into the Cumberland River, This cave is near Sloans Valley.

Nine miles east of Somerset is one of nature's freaks. Hidden away from the highway behind a rock-faced ridge is a small stream of water flowing in the curve of one of nature's elbows for one hundred and fifty feet. This is appropriately named Short Creek. It affords enough water for a miniature gristmill before it spills over a natural fall into a cave.

Before the county's boundaries were reduced to their present limits, a natural bridge, a sandstone arch one hundred feet long and sixty feet high connecting the tops of two lofty hills, was in Pulaski County. It is located in a rugged section west of the Cincinnati Southern Railroad, near Parker's Lake station, and lies in Cumberland National Park.

In the upper part of this same territory, where the Cumberland River until 1912 was the boundary line between Pulaski and Whitley counties, is one of Kentucky's most scenic spots—Cumberland Falls—famed for its rare moonbow. Nature was lavish when she endowed this place with so much natural beauty. The river winds between wooded bluffs, flows over shaded shallows and sparkling shoals, spreads over an expanse of sandstone hollowed and fissured from the water of centuries, leaps—roaring, churning, tumbling—over a sixty-eight-foot precipice, and at last spends itself between the bluffs and in the bends below.

NATURAL RESOURCES

There are several veins of coal lying in the eastern part of the county along the Rockcastle, Cumberland, and South Fork rivers, and Buck Creek. Limestone, quarried in enormous quantities, is used for building purposes and making roads. Pulaski County soil contains clay, which was at one time valuable for making brick, and small deposits of iron ore.

Originally the county was covered with timber. Walnut, white oak, black oak, poplar, sugar maple, beech, yellow pine, black pine, cedar, and chestnut trees were plentiful in the forests. A blight, which attacks chestnut trees only, has destroyed that specie in recent years.

FIRST COURT

The section of the Act by the Assembly creating the county has the following provisions for the county courts:

> The courts of Quarter Sessions for said county shall be held on the fourth Tuesday in the months July, October, January, and March in every year, and the County Court of said County shall be held on the fourth Tuesday in every month in which the courts of Quarter Sessions are not hereby directed to be held.[1]

---

[1] Bayless Hardin, secretary and treasurer of Kentucky Historical Society, Frankfort, Kentucky.

The Justices to be named in the commission of the Peace for said County of Pulaski, shall meet at the house of Thomas Hansford upon the first court day after the said division shall take place; and having taken the oath prescribed by law, and a sheriff being legally qualified to act, shall then proceed to fix upon a place to hold courts in said county, in such place as shall be deemed the most central and convenient to the people, and then after the county court shall proceed to erect the public buildings at such place; and until such buildings are completed the Court of Quarter Sessions and County Court may adjourn to such place or places as they may severally think proper.

The first county court was held at the house of Thomas Hansford, June 25, 1799. The location of this house is not very definite, as traditional information does not agree. A published article by George L. Elliot says: "The first court met in the old Prather place, five or six miles south of Somerset. That part of the County was more thickly settled then and court was held there for that fact." The writer's information (from my parents) was the same, yet Judge James Denton says: "If my information is correct the first court was held in a house one-half block of the Hotel Beecher on the opposite side of the street."

The first record of this county court is:

Pursuant to an Act of the General Assembly of Kentucky for erecting a new county out of the counties of Lincoln and Green.[2]

At the house of Thomas Hansford, in the County of Pulaski on Tuesday the 25th of June, 1799, a commission of the peace from his excellancy James Garrard, Esquire, Governor of the Commonwealth aforesaid, where upon the said Samuel Gilmore, Esq. took the oath of office and the oath to support the Constitution of the United States, who, then afterward administered the said oath to the other justices.[3]

After the justices took oath, Samuel Newell I took oath as first sheriff of the county. William Fox was appointed county clerk (which office he held until he resigned in March, 1846); Samuel McKee took oath as first surveyor; Charles Neal was granted an earmark for his livestock. The court then adjourned, agreeing to meet at the next term of court in course, which

[2]Book I Pulaski Court Records.
[3]Book I Pulaski Court Records.

came on August 27, 1799, at the house of Henry Francis. (Henry Francis was owner of considerable land, all of which lay on or near Fishing Creek—this bears out the tradition that the first courts were held southwest of Somerset.)

The first Court of Quarter Sessions was held at the home of Henry Francis in County of Pulaski on Tuesday, the 23rd day of July, one thousand seven hundred and ninety-nine. A commission of the Peace from His Excellancy, James Garrard, Esq. Governor of the Commonwealth of Kentucky, directed to Samuel Gilmore, Joseph McAlister, and John Hardgrove, Gentlemen, appointing them justices of the Court of Quarter Sessions for said County of Pulaski, where upon they produced a certificate of their having taken necessary oaths, and thereupon the court was held for the said County: Present, the worshipful Samuel Gilmore, Joseph McAlister, and John Hardgrove, Gentleman.

The first grand jury was as follows: Henry James (foreman), Thomas Cowan, Joseph Matthews, George Allcorn, Nicholas Alexander, Robert Henderson, Samuel Duncan, Edward Turner, George Smiley, Thomas Sugg, Malikiah Cooper, John Prather, and John Jasper.

The following indictments were returned:

We of the grand jury do present Henry Francis for retailing spirits and no list of his license presented to us. We do present Wiatt Atkins for profane swearing by the name (by God) on this day at Henry Francis. We do present Ephriam Churchwell and John Trap for gambling for one half pint of whiskey. The grand jury having received their charge retired to consider their verdict.

The retiring of the grand jury consisted of going outdoors as there was no room to meet inside.

Both the courts of quarter sessions and county court were held at the house of Henry Francis until 1801.

SELECTION OF COUNTY SEAT

A county court held February 24, 1801, entered the following minutes, which fixed the location of the county seat.

The Court having taken into consideration the business of fixing on the place for erecting the public buildings for this County, after mature deliberation it is ordered that the permanent seat of justice for this County is fixed on a tract of land containing forty acres, this day conveyed by bond to the County Court of this County on land given by William Dodson. He received it as a part of a survey made July 25, 1799, on certificate number seven — this land lying on the waters of Sinking Creek.

On February 24, 1801, William Dodson, Reubin Hill and Moses Hands made bond for $1,000 to justices for Dodson, conveying the forty acres of land to the court on or before March 1, 1802. Dodson made bond to convey all this land except one acre on which the Sinking Creek Baptist Church stood and three lots which he retained for himself. The forty acres were to be laid off into convenient streets and lots, Dodson getting two lots first choice, the court next, and then Dodson third choice. Also, Dodson was to have the same liberty of the use of the water as other persons.

NAME

The name selected for the county seat was Somerset. Concerning the location of the county seat, a legend relates that a group of people from Somerset County, New Jersey, who had settled north of the present site of Somerset (this is said to have been at Mt. Gilead), insisted the county seat be located where they lived. Another story is that another group, who lived south of the Cumberland, wanted it located south of the present site on top of the hill (at Allen's Branch) which commanded a beautiful view of the surrounding country. A duel was almost fought as a climax to this dispute. However, the matter was compromised satisfactorily—so the story goes—with the New Jersey group naming the county seat town for Somerset, England.

PLAN FOR THE TOWN

On February 25, 1801, the day after the site for the county seat was selected, the court appointed commissioners to plan the town, and to select locations of public buildings. Samuel McKee, James Hardgrove, Edward Turner, John Prather, Nicholas Jasper, and William Fox were appointed "to let out and superintend the Publick Buildings," a courthouse, jail, etc., "to lay off forty acres of land yesterday granted to the court by William Dodson, into convenient lots, streets, etc.;

as they think proper." Robert Moderell was added to this commission the same day. However, in the following court the order for the above commissioner was quashed and the following appointed: Jesse Richardson, Nicholas Jasper, James Hardgrove, Phillip A. Sublette, John Prather, and Andrew Russell.

The forty acres making up the town were divided into eighty lots, four of which were set aside for a public square. The plan for the town was not recorded, "owing to neglect," until January 16, 1820. On that plot principal streets were laid off as they exist today.

On this land was a spring, an important factor in the choice of this particular site, and the path by which it was reached became the main street of Somerset. It is remembered as Spring Street, now Vine Street.[4]

COURTHOUSE AND COUNTY BUILDINGS

On June 24, 1801, the court decided to build a temporary courthouse (said to have been built of logs) in the county seat. The court—the first not held in the Henry Francis home—convened at the Baptist meetinghouse, which was on the hill near Sinking Creek west of the Public Square in Somerset.

In less than a year commissioners were appointed to let out and superintend the building of a brick courthouse. This action was taken August 24, 1802. According to tradition it was located in the center of the Public Square and became the seat of justice in 1808. This courthouse served the county for thirty years.

At a court of May 13, 1812, it was decided to build a brick house for a clerk's office. The clerk's office up to this date had been in the home of William Fox. George Allcorn was the contractor for this building which was completed in June, 1816. From references it must have been built of stone rather than brick. This "little stone" clerk's office served until 1829 when it was declared too small for that purpose. At that time the county clerk, William Fox, was authorized to procure a suitable house or room for the office, and again it was moved to his home.[5]

[4]Traditional information by George Elliot.
[5]Order Book I.

According to information given the author by Mrs. E. B. Hill (great-granddaughter of William Fox), her grandfather, Dr. John A. Caldwell, opened an office in a small building, located on the southwest corner of the lot where the present courthouse stands. It had been used by William Fox when he was county clerk.

The court of May 18, 1836, ordered the sheriff to "fend out the old stone Clerk's office," and Bourne Goggin was appointed on August 16, 1836, to sell the rock, lumber, etc., of this little office, since it had to be torn down to make way for building the new courthouse of 1840.

The third courthouse was erected in 1840 on the same site as the present one (corner of Main and West Mt. Vernon Streets). It burned on December 7, 1871, when much of the town was destroyed; but, because the clerk's office was housed separately, none of the records were destroyed.

The erection of a new courthouse presented a problem. Three-quarters of a century had passed since the little log building had served as the Pulaski County courthouse; there were more lawyers who demanded a dignified seat of justice. A commission was appointed to study the matter, and a plan at an estimated cost of $25,000 was submitted. Judge John S. Kendrick, an influential man of that time, opposed such an expenditure, saying, "Our children, our grandchildren and our great-grandchildren will be paying for that indebtedness."

The plan was accepted, however, and the present courthouse, on the same site as the one of 1840, was completed in 1874. The town clock, which still ticks the time and the hours, was hauled by oxen from Stanford (according to old inhabitants), where it had been shipped by rail.

Under the WPA program in President Franklin D. Roosevelt's administration, this courthouse was remodeled. A new wing, built of limestone, was added which provides additional office space and a new jail on the third floor.

The first jail[6] was built in 1802 by Reubin Payne and Joel Jackson and cost $125. Phillip Sublette was appointed the first keeper of this jail. From all available information, its location was southwest of the present jail. This building[7] was constantly out of repair, and in 1815 William Fox, John Tummelson,

[6]A log cabin had actually served as the first jail. See page 23.
[7]Order Book I.

Tunstall Quarles, John Newby, John Gibson, Chrystopher Claunch, and Charles Hays were appointed commissioners to let out and superintend the building of a new jail and to select the proper location for it on the Public Square. This jail, built by Charles Hays, was completed December 25, 1820.[8] Built of brick, it was located on the corner now occupied by the First National Bank. It served the county until 1868, when the building was sold to William Woodcock for a bank.

PAY FOR SERVICES OF COUNTY OFFICERS

William Fox was paid £12 a year for his services as county and circuit clerk, up to the year 1808, when it was changed to $40 a year. He kept the courthouse for £2, 14 shillings, and this was changed in 1808 to $9.00 per year. These salaries remained thus until his resignation in 1846.[9]

The sheriff first drew a salary of £12, then was raised to $40. He received in addition to this the commission for collecting taxes.

Archibald E. Mills, the first attorney for the county court and the circuit court, was paid £9 a year for his services as county attorney and £30 for his services as circuit court attorney. In 1808 Tunstall Quarles, who succeeded Mills, received $50 for services as county attorney and $120 as circuit court attorney.

A levy of November 25, 1800, provided for the cost of surveying the county. Thomas Wiles (Whiles) ran the county line and was paid £12, 11 shillings, and 9 pence. Robert McAllister, Alexander Adams, John Adams, Ansill Stroud, William Roberts, Zacharia Evans, and Thomas Thompson carried the chain for fifty-eight days at six shillings per day.[10]

OFFICERS OF PULASKI COUNTY

Year	Office	Name
1799	Judge	Samuel Gilmore
	Clerk of County Court	William Fox
	Sheriff	Samuel Newell
	Attorney	Archibald Mills

[8]George Elliot, published articles.
[9]Order Book I, Pulaski County Court.
[10]Order Book I, Circuit Court.

Year	Office	Name
	Tax Commissioner	Andrew Evans
	Surveyor	Thomas Wiles (Whiles)
1801	Jailer	Henry Francis
1802	Jailer	Phillip Sublette
	Surveyor	Samuel McKee
1850	Judge	John S. Kendrick
	Clerk	James D. Allcorn
	Sheriff	Thomas Surber
	Attorney	———
	Assessor	William Fitzpatrick
	Jailer	Ezekial Porch
1854	Judge	John Fitzpatrick
	Clerk	William Fox
	Sheriff	Meridith G. Richardson
	Attorney	Dudley Denton
	Assessor	Oliver Jasper
	Jailer	Ezekial Porch
1856	Judge	D. H. Denton (resigned 1861)
		Hiram Gragg (appointed)
	Clerk	James D. Allcorn
	Sheriff	W. D. Black (1856-60)
	Sheriff	Joel W. Sallee (1860-62)
	Attorney	Thomas Z. Morrow (resigned 1861)
		O. B. Bachellor (appointed)
	Assessor	Oliver P. Jasper
	Jailer	Enoch Wesley (resigned)
		Will B. Davis (appointed)
1862	Judge	William H. Pettus
	Clerk	E. D. Porch
	Sheriff	James S. Waddle
	Attorney	D. H. Denton
	Assessor	———
	Jailer	Richard Reynolds
1866	Judge	Charles A. Zachery
	Clerk	E. D. Porch
	Sheriff	Stephen Hail (1863)
		Geo. Hail (1863-68)
		Thomas Ballou (1868-70)
	Attorney	D. H. Denton
	Assessor	William Brent Gragg

Year	Office	Name
1866	Jailer	William S. Shepperd
1870	Judge	Charles A. Zachery
	Clerk	E. D. Porch
	Sheriff	———
	Attorney	Will C. Curd
	Assessor	Dickey F. Cundiff
	Jailer	William S. Shepperd
1874	Judge	John N. Barnett
	Clerk	E. D. Porch
	Sheriff	C. B. Porch (appointed)
	Attorney	George W. Shadoin
	Assessor	F. B. Linville
	Jailer	William S. Shepperd
1878	Judge	J. S. Cosson
	Clerk	C. B. Porch
	Sheriff	Robert Murphy (appointed)
	Attorney	G. W. Shadoin
	Assessor	F. B. Linville
	Jailer	John Silvers
1882	Judge	J. T. Tarter
	Clerk	John S. May
	Sheriff	———
	Attorney	James L. Colyer
	Assessor	A. M. Parsons
	Jailer	William S. Shepperd
1886	Judge	J. T. Tarter (died 1888) succeeded by James Denton
	Clerk	John S. May
	Sheriff	Walter Elrod
	Attorney	George W. Shadoin
	Assessor	James W. Spears
	Jailer	William S. Shepperd
1890	Judge	James Denton
	Clerk	N. L. Barnett
	Sheriff	Walter Elrod
	Attorney	George W. Shadoin
	Assessor	James W. Spears
	Jailer	William S. Shepperd
1894	Judge	William M. Catron
	Clerk	N. L. Barnett

Year	Office	Name
1894	Sheriff	William Cooper
	Attorney	George W. Shadoin
	Assessor	R. J. Shadoin
	Jailer	A. J. Catron
1898	Judge	William M. Catron
	Clerk	N. L. Barnett
	Sheriff	C. B. Langdon
	Attorney	George W. Shadoin
	Jailer	A. J. Catron
	Assessor	A. M. Mounce
1902	Judge	J. S. Cooper
	Clerk	John S. May
	Sheriff	Ben F. Hines
	Attorney	Elbert Wesley
	Assessor	James G. Adams
	Jailer	J. F. Hines
1906	Judge	N. L. Barnett
	Clerk	Daniel Borden
	Sheriff	J. A. L. Jasper
	Attorney	J. W. Colyer
	Assessor	W. R. Price
	Jailer	Frank Hines
1910	Judge	R. C. Tarter
	Clerk	C. W. Langdon
	Sheriff	J. W. Weddle
	Attorney	R. B. Waddle
	Assessor	J. F. Mayfield
	Jailer	Neal Silvers
1914	Judge	R. F. Jasper
	Clerk	C. M. Langdon
	Sheriff	J. D. Jones
	Attorney	George W. Shadoin
	Assessor	W. Dennis Waddle
	Jailer	Moses L. Singleton
1918	Judge	R. C. Tarter
	Clerk	C. M. Langdon
	Sheriff	John M. Weddle
	Attorney	R. B. Waddle
	Assessor	James G. Adams
	Jailer	June Hansford

Year	Office	Name
1922	Judge	R. C. Tarter
	Clerk	C. M. Langdon
	Sheriff	C. I. Ross
	Attorney	C. L. Tarter
	Assessor	N. L. Barnett
	Jailer	V. H. Rexroat
1926	Judge	Napier Adams
	Clerk	C. M. Langdon
	Sheriff	Jack Edwards
	Attorney	George W. Shadoin
	Assessor	N. L. Barnett
	Jailer	George L. Meece
1930	Judge	John Sherman Cooper
	Clerk	O. P. Hamilton
	Sheriff	A. T. Sears
	Attorney	Gladstone Wesley
	Assessor	V. M. Rainwater
	Jailer	John M. Weddle
1934	Judge	John Sherman Cooper, Jr.
	Clerk	O. P. Hamilton
	Sheriff	Clyde Hubble
	Attorney	Gladstone Wesley
	Assessor	Orville Dick
	Jailer	George M. Adkins
1938	Judge	Lawrence Hail
	Clerk	O. P. Hamilton
	Sheriff	James M. Beaty
	Attorney	Russell Jones
	Assessor	Claude Gover
	Jailer	George Jesse
1942	Judge	R. C. Tarter (resigned to become Circuit Judge)
		C. I. Ross (succeeded)
	Clerk	O. P. Hamilton
	Sheriff	James B. Jasper
	Attorney	Russell Jones
	Assessor	Claude Gover
	Jailer	Ted Decker
1946	Judge	C. I. Ross
	Clerk	O. P. Hamilton

Year	Office	Name
1946	Sheriff	Frank Beaty
	Attorney	Homer Neikirk
	Assessor	
	Jailer	Ted Decker
1950	Judge	C. I. Ross
	Clerk	Darrell Hall
	Sheriff	James Jasper
	Attorney	Homer Neikirk
	Assessor	Ernest Farris
	Jailer	Lee Bingham

Chapter 3

EARLY COURT SESSIONS AND RECORDS

EARLY COURTS

As the population grew the assembly allowed a greater number of justices in answer to the petitions of citizens of different parts of the county until they reached twenty in number by 1836.

The following list is in the order they were commissioned:

1800	John James	1801	Ralph Williams
	Thomas Whiles		John Newby
	James Richardson		David McMullins
			John McWhorter
			Drury Lee
1803	William Barnes	1809	Vincent Garner
	Edward Prather		

The county court at this early date had largely the same jurisdiction as county court of today, dealing with matters respecting mills, administration, roads, restraining ordinances, and tippling houses, etc.

From the following entry it is seen that the need for roads and mills was very urgent; pages and pages in Order Book I are given over to recordings of permits for the erection of gristmills and the best places for roads.

December 24, 1799: On motion of Samuel Newell and Henry Francis it is ordered that William Lynch, Andrew Evans, Edward Mobley and Robert Anderson, or any three of them who were first sworn, to view a way for a road from Col. Newell's ferry to Pitman's Creek.

Other orders were for a road from Pitman's Creek to Buck Creek, for a road from the county line to Caney Fork, and a road from there to Fishing Creek and—"report to the next court of the convenience and inconvenience that may attend the same."

At a meeting of the court August 25, 1801, it was ordered that the court be adjourned until court in course, and then to meet in the town of Somerset at a house provided for that purpose.

The order below shows the large territory over which the courts of Pulaski County had jurisdiction, as this location of a mill dam is in Wayne County, near Monticello.

September 24, 1799: on motion of Joshua Jones for leave to erect a dam in the Elk Spring Valley, he owning the land on one side there of the stream and Isaac Crabtree and Robert Beaty the proprietors of the land on the opposite side against which the said Joshua Jones wishes to abut his dam. It is ordered that a writ of adquaddanum issue to the sheriff commanding him to summons a legal jury to meet on the premises aforesaid on the last Friday in October next and then and there to view and examine and lay off the same as the law directs and make return thereof to the next court.

The May court, 1808, shows the following entry:

The persons appointed to view the way for a road from Henry Francis to the County line made report there-of in the words and figures following (to-wit); the subscribers proceeded to view the road according to the order and is of the opinion, the road to begin at Henry Francis, thence to Moses Hanks to Francis McCowan, thense to Arthur Moores, thense to Pitman's Creek, where Mr. Gravery [blurred] was killed by the Indians, thense to McMullins, thense to intersect the old road at Pink Meadows, thense to the County line. We do agree that we believe this to be the best and nearest way to the County line and to the Crab Orchard, and that we know of no injury to any individuals.

Some of the cases found in the early records were interesting—one being that of Joel and Ayers Doss "stealing and carrying away sundry apple trees, of value one dollar." On March 23, 1807, William Woods was given an examining trial for "stealing and carrying away one negro girl, Matilda, six years of age, the value of two hundred dollars."

Archibald Mills, attorney for the circuit court, was fined ten shillings for swearing profanely twice and for contempt of court.

The first mention of a jail for the county was made September 24, 1799. On April 22, 1800, "a small log house" near Henry Francis' home was chosen as the first jail and Henry Francis was appointed as first jailer.

The first license for a ferry was granted to Samuel Newell I, September 24, 1799.[1] The first land grant was to Thomas Hansford in 1801, April 28.[2] The first will was that of John Harper, in 1803.[3] The Reverend Thomas Hill presented his credentials as being in regular communion with the Baptist Church and "leave is granted him to celebrate the rights of matrimony"—this was on February 25, 1800.[4] James Fears, of the Baptist Church, was granted the same on April 22, 1799. The first marriage license was granted July 18, 1799, to William Wade and Sarah Allen.[5]

On February 13, 1800, a grant permitted the erection of a warehouse for inspecting tobacco, hemp, and flour to be shipped down the Cumberland. The first licensed inspection, known as Campbell and Stapp, was established on lands owned by Thomas Cowan. The second licensed inspection, established December 16, 1801, on Samuel Newell's land on the north side of the Cumberland, was known as New Market.

It will be understood shipping, at this early date, was by rafts. Steamboats did not make their appearance until later.

The first stray pen was built by William Roberts for the sum of $15 and received by the court September 22, 1801. The court of June 24, 1801, agreed to pay John James $38 for building the stocks and pillory. For some reason he was discharged and later Anderson Nunnelly was paid $65 for building them. (An Act, passed by the General Assembly December 9, 1850, abolished the stray pen in Pulaski County.)

> John L. Bridges produced license authorizing him to practice law in this court.
>
> Archibald Mills produced license authorizing him to practice law in this court.

---

[1] Order Book I—Circuit Court Book.
[2] Order Book I—Circuit Court Book, page 9.
[3] First Will Book.
[4] Order Book I.
[5] First marriage records.

October 22, 1799—Ordered that William Fox be paid as Clerk of the Court, the sum of one pound, seventeen shillings and six pence for Public Service.

Ordered that Archibald Mills, attorney for the Commonwealth in this County, be allowed seventeen dollars for services in the execution of his office —

(Signed)
JAMES GILMORE

January 29, 1800—John Boyles and William Logan produced authority to practice law in this Court.

March Court, 1804—At a Circuit Court composed of the counties of Pulaski and Wayne at the courthouse in the town of Somerset on Monday the 20th day of March, 1804—present, the Honorable James G. Hunter, John Smith and John Prather, Gent.

At a court on the 27th day of the same month, the same judges were present also, Chrystopher Tompkins and John James, Gent., present.[6]

The following is copied from the Circuit Court *Minute Book*[7] from July 24, 1810, through July 30, 1817.

At a court October 22, 1810—Present Honorable Chrystopher Tompkins, John Prather and John James, Gent.

April 24, 1811—Present Honorable Chrystopher Tompkins and John Prather, Esq.

April 25, 1811—Present the same judges as yesterday, were John James, assistant judges to Tompkins.

October 22, 1810—John January allowed $10.00 by court—he being Jailer, and attended court July 1810 session.

October 22, 1810—Jesse Richardson and John McFall fined for Sabbath breaking.

October 24, 1810—Henry James allowed $100 for keeping John Darus, a person of unsound mind for one year.

October 25, 1810—Ralp Williams, Sheriff.

October 29, 1811—Benjamin Evins indicted for murder. [First reference to a murder]

---

[6]Page copied from Circuit Court, Order Book I.
[7]This book was found by Mrs. Maria Elliot Adkins among old papers, etc., at her father's old home. This must have been recovered by Mr. Elliot just before so much else of value went up in smoke at Mr. Borden's (former county clerk) bonfire of "useless old papers and books" from the clerk's office.

November 1, 1811—T. Quarles, Jr. allowed $120 for service for past year as attorney for the Circuit Court.

November 1, 1811—Gideon Prather deputy for E. Prather, Sheriff.

April 27, 1812—Lewllen Hickman and John Jackson took oaths to practice law before the Court.

April 29, 1812—William J. Sallee fined $3.00 for refusing to attend court as a juror.

April 30, 1812—William Irvine permitted to qualify a deputy to William Fox, Clerk of the Circuit Court.

July 28, 1812 — Baldwin vs. Baldwin — divorce proceedings. [First one referred to]

October 28, 1812—Robert Wells alias Joseph McVey—horse stealing—to jail and penitentiary for two years. (Let sentence stand.)

April 25, 1813—T. Quarles Esq. produced commission from the Governor of Kentucky appointing him Attorney for the Commonwealth in the Eighth Judicial District. [First reference to the Eighth]

October 25, 1813—John Kincaid licensed to practice law.

July 25, 1814—John Farmer licensed to practice law.

July 29, 1814—John Tummelson, Jailer allowed $9.72 for attending on the court.

October 26, 1815—Daniel Claire, Jailer.

October 26, 1815—Josiah Evans, deputy for John Chesney, Sheriff.

October 26, 1815—William Fox, Clerk of Court allowed $16.50 for the purchase of a record book for use in his office.

April 22, 1816—Present Hon'ble Thomas Montgomery, a judge of the 12th Judicial District, having taken the oaths from the Clerk of the Rockcastle Circuit Court, produced same and ordered certified.

April 30, 1817—Present Hon. Thomas Montgomery and John Green, Circuit Attorney commissioned by the Governor of Kentucky for the 12th Judicial District.

EARLY TAX LISTS

The settlement of Lincoln County, from which a part became Pulaski County, had been taken up along water courses now located in Pulaski by that date. From the list of entries describing lands that are almost entirely in Pulaski County, one finds that few names coincide with the first tax list of the county in 1799. This is accounted for perhaps, by the fact that many of these men taking up this land did not live in Kentucky or that they sold their lands and moved farther west before that county was organized.[8]

The first tax list of the early settlers of the county was taken August, 1799, after the county was organized in June, 1799. This list was made by Andrew Evans,[8] the first tax commissioner.

There are listed 383 white males twenty-one years of age and over, 121 slaves, and 886 horses.

Some of the larger landowners as shown by the tax lists of each year are as follows:

1799

Name	Acres	Location
Robert Anderson	279	Pitman Creek
James Gilmore	200	Buck Creek
Andrew Lear	700	Pitman Creek
Andrew Lear	650	Cumberland River
John Prather	204	Pitman Creek
Richard Lee	200	Flat Creek
George Lee	130	Flat Creek
Thomas Lee	130	Flat Creek
James Wiatt	200	South Fork of Cumberland River
Penelope Wiatt	150	South Fork of Cumberland River
William Wiatt	200	South Fork of Cumberland River
Joseph Thomas	200	South Fork of Cumberland River
Thomas Simpson	200	South Fork of Cumberland River
Michael Stoner	100	South Fork of Cumberland River
George Smith	200	South Fork of Cumberland River
Hugh Pierce	200	South Fork of Cumberland River
Sam Newell	350	South Fork of Cumberland River
Benjamin Moberly	200	South Fork of Cumberland River
William Lynch	190	South Fork of Cumberland River
James Hamilton	160	South Fork of Cumberland River
Thomas Cowan	200	South Fork of Cumberland River
John Cowan	200	South Fork of Cumberland River
Jacob Cooper	200	South Fork of Cumberland River
Timothy Dunn	20	South Fork of Cumberland River

[8]Kentucky History, by Mrs. Ramey.

1800

Name	Acres	Location
Jocy Langford	400	Fishing Creek
Jeremiah Dishman	200	Buck Creek
Thomas Owsley	400	Pitman Creek
Sam Owsley	400	Pitman Creek
Sherad Reynolds	346	Fishing Creek
Jesse Richardson	1,500	Pitman Creek
John Beaty	200	Cumberland River
William Gibson	200	Buck Creek
Martin Gibson	118	Pitman Creek
Thomas Wilson	400	Buck Creek

1804

Name	Acres	Location
John Griffin	600	Buck Creek
William Durham	800	Fishing Creek

1806

Name	Acres	Location
George Sanders	850	Buck Creek
George Sanders	300	Buck Creek
William Books	400	Buck Creek
Elizabeth Books	400	Buck Creek
William Zachary	500	Pitman Creek

DEEDS

These records span the early periods of Pulaski County: what was important, how much the early dollars would buy, who earned them, and where they lived. Pulaski streams and woods can be pictured from early surveys.

Christley Tarter, Jr. from Trustees of Somerset Academy, 421 acres on White Oak Creek, also, 145 acres, February 4, 1826 (6-123 and 125.)

Jesse Tarter bought from trustees, February 24, 1826, 67 acres (126.)

This indenture made March 28, 1808 between William Augustus Washington and Sarah his wife, of the District of Columbia, of the one part and Jesse Richardson of the County of Pulaski, and State of Kentucky of the other part, for and in consideration of one thousand dollars—aliened and confirmed and by the presents do grant, bargain and sell unto the said Jesse Richardson and his heirs, a cer-

tain tract of land of 1000 acres lying and being in the County of Pulaski etc. . . .
Signed, WILLIAM AUGUSTUS WASHINGTON   (Seal)
   SARAH WASHINGTON   (Seal)
In the presence of Thomas Peter,
    JOHN———[not legible]
William Fox, Clerk.
  [Deed Book 2 page 97]

DEED FOR ROCKLICK BAPTIST CHURCH[9]

Moses Keeney and Robert McAlister, trustees of the Baptist Church at Rocklick in the County of Pulaski constituted and agreed to an Act of the General Assembly and the rules (?) of the said church, etc.—that the said Jesse Richardson convey to the said trustees, a certain tract of land lying in the county on which a meeting house now stands, known by the name of Rocklick Meeting house containing four acres, for the use of a Baptist Church, provided however, that if the said church should ever be dissolved and be no more—then the tract of ground shall revert to the children of Polly Woods.

Dated December 14, 1822

[Deed Book 5, page 199 or 189. This is an excerpt from the deed.]

DEED 1832

This Indenture of Bargain, sale and conveyance, made and entered into the seventh day of February, 1832, between Benjamin H. Perkins late of Mercer County, Kentucky and John B. Curd of Somerset, Kentucky, of the first part and Cyrenius Wait of the other or second part, Witnesseth that for and in consideration of the sum of three hundred and seventy five dollars, the said Perkins and Curd, the party of the first part, hath this day and doth by their presents bargain, sell [blurred] convey and confirm unto the said Cyrenius Wait and his heirs forever two certain parcels of land, known and designated on the plan of the New Town of Pulaski.

To have and to hold the said two Lotts number 95 and 96 lying and being in the New Town of Somerset, designated on its platt as ——— with all and singular their improvements and appertanances being the land now occupied by Thomas Reynolds, and the said Perkins and Curd doth Covenant and agree to warrent and defend the title and possession of said two lots with all and singular

---

[9]This church exists today—1950.

their improvements and appertanances against the claim of themselves and all and every other person or persons unto the said Cyrenius Wait and his heirs forever.

In Testimony where of the said John B. Curd for himself and as attorney in fact for Benjamen H. Perkins hath subscribed his name and affixed his seal the day and year aforesaid.

B. H. Perkins by his attorney in fact J. B. Curd
J. B. Curd
Helen M. Curd[10]

The Commonwealth of Kentucky, Pulaski County

I, William Fox, Clerk of County Court for the County aforesaid, do certify that this deed from Benjamen H. Perkins and John B. Curd and Helen M. Curd [blurred] Cyrenius Wait was this day produced at residence of the said Curd, by said Grantors and acknowledged by the said John B. Curd as Attorney in fact for Benjamen H. Perkins and also for himself to be his act and deed, and the said Helen M. Curd by an examination privately and apart from her husband, declared that she did freely and willingly [blurred] the said writing and wished not to retract it, and acknowledged the said writing again shown and explained to her, to be her act and deed, and consented that the same may be recorded. Where upon the said deed together with the foregoing Certificate hath been duly admitted to record in my office. Given under my hand this 1st day of March, A. D. 1832.

A copy attest   Will Fox, *Clerk*

Pulaski County, Kentucky
Deeds 18; 355[11]   28 February, 1859
Chrisley Tarter of Pulaski County, to Smith Cain of Russel County for $3175. $1500 in cash, balance secured by notes—all lands said Tarter owns on Pulaski County on waters of Wolf Creek beginning according to survey made by Samuel D. Combest on the 16th of this inst.—at old cemetery line etc., etc., to 25 acre survey patented to said Tarter—to George W. Garner's corner—Fisher's line—to White Oak above the spring—where the big road crosses the dry branch, being 1420½ A.

Signed: Chrisley Tarter
Elizabeth Tarter

---

[10]Deed in possession of Mrs. Harry Wait.
[11]This is near the present Caintown.

Recorded 11 April 1859
Deeds 20: 147   10, November 1863

An agreement between Daniel McDaniel of Russel County and Smith W. Cain of Pulaski County. Cain to bid off land purchased by Daniel McDaniel and Andrew Jasper and to be sold by order of court, and furnish the money etc.—land being on waters of Pointer and Wolf Creeks.

Deeds 33: 168   22 March 1883

I, E. L. Tarter of Cain's Store—land on waters of Wolf Creek, near the residence of said Tarter, beginning northeast of warehouse of Cain and Tarter, bck. of E. L. Tarter's yard—to stone on bank of the branch—to be used by Cain and Tarter for the purpose of distilling spirits from grain for term of five years, subject to all laws and regulations of the United States.

Examined and delivered to J. T. Tarter.

[This is indexed Tarter to Cain, but worded without the mention of Cain's full name]

FIRST MARRIAGE BOOK

Page 2—August 19, 1801—John Cooper by Rev. Thomas Hill, Polly McCowan

Page 2—August 19, 1801—Patsy Cooper by Rev. Thomas Hill, John McNish

Page 2—December 17, 1801—Rev. Thomas Hill, Polly Spencer, Abner Cooper

Page 14—(no month recorded)—John Milton Weddle, Polly McDaniel, daughter of Spencer McDaniel, Sr. Bond signed by Spencer McDaniel and Daniel Weddle

Page 53—November 23, 1817—Christian Tarter married Betsy Trimble, daughter of William Trimble by Rev. John Black

OLD RECORDS

Pulaski County, Kentucky
Court Records[12]
William Weddle married Elizabeth Spencer, February 2nd, 1830.
  (page 100) (son of Daniel Weddle, note.) (James Spencer, bondsman.)

---

[12]These records furnished by Bettie Tarter Shepard.

Sally Weddle married Jesse Tarter, November 1819. (page 84, also bond.) (returned December 20, 1820, by Rev. Thomas Whitley.)

Rebecca Weddle married Thomas Phipps, January 12, 1836. (1-129)

William Weddle married Celia Tarter, January 15, 1836. (page 129)

Solomon Weddle married Patsy Tarter, May 6, 1841. He is the son of John Weddle, who gave consent in note; daughter of Jacob Tarter, who gave consent. (1-159)

John M. Weddle married Polly McDaniel, August 29, 1803. (1-10) also bond. She is the daughter of Spencer McDaniel, who gave consent.

[This spelled Waddle, in register, but Weddle on bond, her father Spencer, Sr. gave consent, brother Spencer, Jr. gave consent, signed the bond, so did Daniel Weddle.]

Alfred Tarter married Eliza Todd, October 25, 1827. (John Porter, bondsman)

Peter Tarter married Polly Pearce, May 16, 1826. (Jesse Pearce, bondsman)

Jacob Tarter and wife Polly deed to Chrisley Tarter, 53 acres on Kings Creek. (4-619-620) about 1821.

Chrisley Tarter married Betsy Trimble, November 23, 1817. (page 53)

Peter Tarter to John Tarter, July 21, 1818. (3-349)

John Tarter, Jr. and wife Elizabeth T. deed to James Harry, Sr. tract of 200 acres where said Tarter lives, October 20, 1823.

John Tarter and wife Nancy deed to Enis Tarter, part of 200 acres patented to Peter Tarter, December 13, 1811. October 12, 1858. (18-251)

John and Nancy Tarter deed to Laban Tarter, October 10, 1840, part of 200 acres patented to Peter Tarter December 11, 1811. (11-99)

Chrisley Tarter, Jr. from Trustee Somerset Academy, 421 acres in White Oak Creek, also 145 acres. February 4, 1826. (6-123, and 125)

John Tarter and wife Nancy John Jr. deed to John Tarter, Sr. land off ice warrent No. 13638. (8-153)

Chrisley Tarter and wife Elizabeth October 5, 1831 deed. (7-526)

Chrisley Tarter and wife Elizabeth deed October 26, 1863, to

William Weddle land deeded to him by trustees of the Somerset Academy. (8-618)

Peter Tarter to John Tarter, July 21, 1811. (3-349)

MILITARY CLAIMS

The first military claim was to Thomas Hansford on April 22, 1800 and the second to Henry Waddle and Michael Stoner (Page 42, Order Book I). There followed those to Samuel Duncan, David McElmer, Thomas Banks, Henry Moore, Aaron Lawson, Edward Cooper, Isaac Ingram and Drury Lee. (Order Book I, page 39).

Andrew McDaniel gave power of attorney to Achilles Jasper to collect for troops commanded by Colonel Micah Taul, Seventh Regiment of Mounted Volunteers, he, (Andrew McDaniel) was entitled to pay as a private for two months and twenty-one days for services under Captain Samuel Tate, August 19, 1815. Spencer McDaniel had a son who served in the War of 1812, named Billy McDaniel.

MEMBERS OF THE LEGISLATURE FROM PULASKI COUNTY[13]

SENATE:

John Griffin, 1808, 1814-19, 1828-32
Thos. Dollerhide, 1819-21
John Cowan, 1821-24
Achilles Jasper, 1836-40
Tunstall Quarles, 1840
Fountain T. Fox, 1844-48
Cyrenius Wait, 1848-50, 1857-61
Berry Smith, 1850
Walker W. Haley, 1851-53

Thomas Z. Morrow, 1865-69 resigned 1866, succeeded by
John W. F. Parker, 1866-69
Wm. McKee Fox, 1869-73
From Pulaski and Wayne [counties]:
John McHenry, 1833-36
From Pulaski and Cumberland [counties]:
Jesse Richardson, 1800

HOUSE OF REPRESENTATIVES:

John James, Sen., 1800, 1802, 1807
Robert Maderil, 1806

Tunstall Quarles, 1811, 1812, 1828
Henry James, 1813

[13]From Collins, *History of Kentucky* (Covington, Ky.: Collins and Co., 1878) Vol. II, p. 683.

HOUSE OF REPRESENTATIVES — Continued

Thos. Dollerhide, 1814, 1815, 1816, 1817, 1818
Robert Gilmore, 1816
Jos. Porter, 1817
Gideon Prather, 1818, 1819
George B. Cooper, 1819, 1820, 1821
Chas. Cunningham, 1822
Bourne Goggin, 1824
Chas M. Cunningham, 1824, 1825, 1826
John Cowan, 1825
John Griffin, 1826, 1827, 1842, 1843
John Evans, 1827
John Hill, 1829, 1831
Berry Smith, 1830, 1840, 1841
Ephraim C. Faris, 1832
Thos. Jasper, 1833, 1834, 1835
Fountain T. Fox, 1836
Chas. Jasper, 1837, 1838
Micajah Sutton, 1839
John G. Lair, 1844
Milford Elliott, 1845, 1846
John T. Quarles, 1847, 1849
Silas D. Woods, 1848
Cyrenius W. Gilmore, 1850
Joel W. Sallee, 1851-53
John Griffin, Jr., 1853-55, 1859-61
Andrew J. James, 1855-57
Milton E. Jones, 1857-59
Thos. Z. Morrow, 1861-63
M. E. Ingram, 1863-65
J. C. Patten, 1865-67
Wm. N. Owens, 1867-69
Wm. H. Pettus, 1869-71
J. E. Cosson, 1871-73
Allen Jones, 1873-75

From Pulaski and Wayne [counties]:

―――― McKee, 1801
Archibald E. Mills, 1803

Chapter 4

... EARLY SETTLERS AND FAMILIES ...

COX

William Cox married Mary Hoff, and their son James Cox married Sallie Lester. To James and Sallie was born John Cox, their only son, on November 12, 1804. He married Catherine Hughes, daughter of John and Sabra Hardester Hughes.

Mrs. John Cox (Catherine Hughes) was a sister of Mariah Hughes (married William Love, 1832) and of Sabra Hughes (married Joshua Thurman). Sabra was born September 24, 1818. Joshua Thurman, a brother to Joseph Thurman, was the son of Benjamin and Lucy Richardson Thurman. Mrs. John Hughes (Sabra Hardester) was most likely a sister of Polly Hardester, daughter of Benjamin Hardester, as John Hughes was on the bond for the marriage of Polly to Thurston Clough on August 12, 1809.

To John and Catherine Hughes Cox were born four children: Cyrenius, dying when young; Jefferson Cox, born 1829, married Amanda Goggin Fitzpatrick; James Madison Cox, born 1831, married Elizabeth Hampton (Kempton?); Francis Marion Cox, born 1838, married Martha Ann Zachary, daughter of John Vaughan and Pamelia Porter Zachary.

To Jefferson Cox were born: Catherine, John William, George Washington, Mary Florinda, and Daniel Webster Cox. To John William and Leona Barnett Cox were born Amanda Jane Cox (Mrs. W. C. Owens); William Jefferson Cox; and Daniel Harrison Cox.

To James Madison Cox were born: Mariah (Mrs. James King Wesley); Kate Cox (Mrs. James Hines); Henry Cox; Sally Cox; and John Cox.

To Francis Marion Cox were born: Mary; Pamelia Catherine (Mrs. T. A. Hendricks); Joseph Porter; Bettie (Mrs. James Boling); Clay Hughes; Martha Frances (Mrs. L. C. Rice); Lula Neil; and James Zachary Cox. To Joseph Porter and Dora King Cox were born Ann Elizabeth Cox (Mrs. Richard Jenkins); and Josephine Cox (Mrs. Lloyd Crutchlow).[1]

CURD

Crawford, Keene, Gragg, Gibson Families

John B. Curd was born near Glasgow, Barren County, in 1802. He was a merchant and hotel keeper most of his life, but at the time of his death, August, 1850, he was cashier of the Farmer's Bank. He was the son of Daniel and Fannie Trigg Curd. Daniel's parents were John and Lucy Brent Curd, who immigrated to Kentucky before it was a state and settled on the Kentucky River at the mouth of Dick's River.

John B. Curd married Helen M., the daughter of William and Elizabeth Perkins Chaplin of Warren County. Mrs. Curd lived to a great age and died at her home on North Main Street.

Their children were: Elizabeth, married John Crawford; Sallie, married Major A. T. Keene; Mattie, married John B. Gragg; and William C., married Belle O. Saunders.

The children of Elizabeth and John Crawford were: Brent, married ——— Kendrick, lived in Wayne County; Mary Helen, married Henry Gibson, lived in Somerset; Elizabeth, married ——— Whinnery, lived in New Jersey; Flora, unmarried; and Andrew J., married Katherine Stokes of Louisville.

William Chaplin Curd, son of John B. and Helen Chaplin Curd, was born August 3, 1836. He received a good common school education. He was deputy county and circuit court clerk in 1851-52 in Danville and later a member of a business firm in Louisville. Returning to Somerset, he served as deputy circuit court clerk until 1862, when he enlisted in the Confederate Army, Company C, Sixth Kentucky Regiment under command of Colonel Grigsby and Captain M. B. Perkins of General John Hunt Morgan's Command.

[1]Information from L. C. Rice, Jr., son of Martha Frances Cox.

He served until the close of the Civil War, surrendering near Washington, Georgia, the day before the capture of President Jefferson Davis. He was one of the escorts of President Davis and General John C. Breckinridge from Charlotte, North Carolina, to Washington, Georgia.

At the close of the Civil War he returned to Somerset and read law with A. J. James and Colonel William Fox. He was admitted to the bar in 1867.

He served as county attorney and master commissioner for many years.

Mr. Curd married Belle O. Saunders, the daughter of G. W. and Jane Long Saunders, December 23, 1869.

DENTON

Dudley H. Denton came to Somerset from Garrard County, where he was born April 14, 1814. His wife was Nancy McKee, member of one of Garrard's pioneer families. He was elected county attorney for Pulaski three times and county judge of Pulaski in 1856. He organized a company in the Third Kentucky Federal Infantry of which he was captain.

His father was Henry Denton, son of John Denton, one of Daniel Boone's associates.

The children of Dudley H. Denton and Nancy McKee Denton were: Alec, married ———; Henry, married Sallie Elliot; James, married Anna Fox Goggin; Gertrude, unmarried; and Lincoln, married Emma Tate.

James was prominent politically in Pulaski for many years. He received his education in the common schools and the old Masonic College. He taught school at the age of sixteen, read law with his father, and was admitted to the bar in 1879. He was appointed a United States commissioner in 1885 and was elected to the legislature. He was a member of the Presbyterian Church where he served as teacher of the men's Bible class, superintendent of the Sunday school, deacon, and elder until his death, August, 1936.

ELLIOT

Samuel Elliot was born in 1745 on the eastern shore of Maryland and died in Kentucky, 1825. His father came to America from Ireland.

Samuel moved from Maryland to Virginia, and then to Kentucky when his son Robert was one year old (about 1802). He was twice married, first to a black-eyed English lassie, named Mary Oldham (born in 1750 and married in 1768). They lived near Culpeper Courthouse, Virginia. The Oldhams were noted for their large physiques and great strength.

Samuel Elliot served in the Revolution as private in Captain William Blackwell's Company, Eleventh Regiment, also designated as the Eleventh and Fifteenth Virginia Regiment, and the Seventh Virginia Regiment commanded by Colonel Daniel Morgan. He enlisted August 20, 1776, for three years; was transferred in June, 1778 to Lieutenant Colonel John Cropper's Company, same regiment; was transferred in December, 1778, to Captain John Marshall's Company, same regiment; and was discharged August 20, 1779. On January 4, 1806, he was allowed land bounty for his services as a private for three years in the Continental Line.

Children of Samuel and Mary Elliot were: John, Nathan, Asa, Josiah, George, Robert, and Betsy. John married Mary Barnes. George was married twice and his children's names were Dan, George, Amanda, Will, and Sam. Robert married Polly Kirkpatrick and had twelve children. After the Civil War, they moved to Texas and lived near Troy, Bell County, Texas, the rest of their lives. Betsy first married a Mr. Cummins and had two sons, Moses and John. Her second marriage was to a Mr. Jones and they had three daughters, Nancy, Louise, and Dorinda Ann.

The name of Samuel Elliot's second wife is not recorded but they had two sons, Cyrus and William. Cyrus married Dorinda Kirkpatrick, a sister of Polly Kirkpatrick, who married Robert Elliot (Cyrus' half-brother).

John and Mary Barnes Elliot had a daughter Nancye, born in 1793 (died, 1862). She married a first cousin Galen R. Elliot on January 12, 1810. Galen R. Elliot was born in 1786 and died October 30, 1837. Galen and Nancye Elliot had ――― children.

One of their sons was Tunstall Quarles Elliot, who was born April 20, 1820, and died July 30, 1889. On December 7, 1854, he married Maria Foster Porter, daughter of Joseph Porter. She was born June 20, 1836, and died July, 1923.

Joseph Porter was a surveyor (when he was fourteen years old), and he laid out the city of Somerset. One of his brothers went to Tennessee and was an ancestor of the Reverend J. W. Porter, Baptist minister at Lexington.

To Tunstall Quarles Elliot and Maria Foster Porter Elliot, the following children were born: Sallie, married Henry Denton; Robert Tunstall, married Jennie Colyer; Annie, married Owen Bilderbeck; George, married (first) Nancy Taylor, and (second) Hattie Cowan; Kate, married Will Pettus; and Rhoda, married Professor George Roberts.

To Robert Tunstall Elliot and Jennie Colyer Elliot were born: Nancy P., married Dr. L. B. Croley; Maria, married Ben L. Adkins; and Mattie Helen Elliot.[2]

WILLIAM FOX

William Fox, the first county court clerk and circuit court clerk of Pulaski County, served from June, 1799 to 1846. He was an excellent clerk, an outstanding citizen, and a large landowner. He owned twenty-one lots at the time of his death. According to a living descendant, he lived in a one-room log house on Columbia Street when Somerset was established. He afterward built a brick home on the site of the old Somerset General Hospital, opposite the present post office. Later he built where the J. M. Richardson home stands, back of the Presbyterian Church.

He had six children, Fountain Fox, William M. Fox, Amanda (Fox) Goggin, Jane Pickering (Fox) Caldwell, Elizabeth (Fox) Fitzpatrick, and Sophia Ann (Fox) Kendrick. His will, on file in the courthouse, is an interesting document dividing his enormous amount of property, slaves, and stock among his children. His remains rest in the City Cemetery, which, at the time he was buried there, was a family graveyard for the Fox family. Approximately two acres had been set aside for this purpose. On March 20, 1866, his children and grandchildren conveyed this graveyard to the Somerset Cemetery Company.

For his services as county clerk and circuit court clerk, William Fox was paid twelve dollars a year until 1808, when it was increased to forty dollars.

[2]Written by Maria Elliot Adkins.

On the simple shaft that marks his grave is the following tribute: "An impartial public officer, a faithful citizen, a kind friend, an affectionate husband and parent and an honest man."

His wife, Sophia, was born in 1779 and died in 1833.[3]

GASTINEAU

Matilda Jane Gastineau Isaacs was the daughter of an early Pulaskian, William Gastineau, who was born in November, 1809, and Matilda Godby Gastineau, who was born in December, 1809. According to Bible record, they were married January 1, 1829, and to them thirteen children were born, as follows: Sarah (Gastineau) Lee, born 1829; Wiston, born 1831; John, born 1832; James P. R., born 1834; William Harrison, born 1836; Job, born 1838; Elizabeth (Gastineau) Phelps, born 1840; Reuben Menifee, born 1842; Mary Frances, born 1843; Eliza Ann (Gastineau) Smith, born 1846; Josiah, born 1848; Thomas Jefferson, born 1850; and Matilda Jan (Gastineau) Isaacs, born September 24, 1854.

The above William Gastineau was the son of Job Gastineau, Jr. who was born approximately 1783 to 1786, in Virginia and died in 1867 in Pulaski County. He was married February 14, 1805, at Abington, Washington County, Virginia to Sarah Hays, who was born July 8, 1787 in Virginia, and died August 26, 1833 in Pulaski County. Sarah Hays was the daughter of James Hays and Elizabeth Lemon. William Gastineau and Sarah Hays had nine children, all born in Pulaski County as follows: Susie, born July, 1806, married James Price; William, born 1809, married Matilda Godby; Isaac, born 1811, married Polly Todd; George, born May 25, 1813, married Frances Ann Hubble; Christley, born 1815, married Elizabeth Todd; James, born March 24, 1817, married Susan McBee Barron; Betsy, born 1819, married Noah Lee; Rachel, born 1821, married William Newman; and Mary, born 1823, married William Dutton.

The above Job Gastineau, Jr., was a son of Job Gastineau, Sr., who was born about 1764 in France and died in 1856 or 1857 in Pulaski County. Job, Sr., was married about 1782 to

[3]Information, Mrs. E. B. Hill.

1785 to Elizabeth Mercer Brown, who was born approximately 1765-67 in Virginia. To this union seven children were born, namely: Job, married "Saryan" Hays in 1805; Charles, married Ann Douglas in 1812; Henry; Elizabeth, married John Douglas; William; Marion; and Jessie.

Job Gastineau, Sr., was of the Huguenot family that came with emigrants brought over from England and France by the Ohio Land Company of Virginia under George Mercer and George Washington. These people made settlements on a large tract of land granted them by the King of England prior to 1776.

Elizabeth Mercer Brown Gastineau was a daughter of Elizabeth Mercer who first married Daniel Smith, son of Daniel Smith of Smithfield, Salem County, New Jersey, and had children. She was married a second time to John Brown about 1763-64.

Elizabeth Mercer (mother of Elizabeth Mercer Brown Gastineau) was born September 22, 1732, and was a daughter of Robert Mercer II and Ann Mounce Mercer, who were married in 1727. Ann Mounce was a daughter of Christopher Mounce and his wife Martha Mounce, of Maryland. Christopher Mounce was connected with large companies under the King.

Robert Mercer II, son of Thomas Mercer and his wife Elizabeth, was born October 17, 1703. Robert Mercer II and Ann Mounce Mercer had ten children; Elizabeth, the above, was their third. Robert Mercer II had five sons from which distinguished descendants came through marriages into families of prominent landholders of the New England states in the early days—the Masons, the Fritchues, the Olivers, Davises, Wallers, Hayses, Pages, Taylors, Carters, Walls, etc. The Beesons and Lemons were connected with mining enterprises; a town was laid out by the Beesons in the Fayette County, Pennsylvania, coal district.

Thomas Mercer, above, owned 500 acres of land which embraced all the mineral rights (except one-fifth of any minerals discovered, as well as not discovered). These mineral rights are explicitly set forth in the deed to the land, which is on record in the land office at Harrisburg, Pennsylvania. Information discloses that a trust fund had accumulated from this ancestor's lands, drawing compound interest for more than a century. Thomas Mercer was a son of Jonathan Mercer. Jonathan Mercer was a son of John Mercer and Sarah Ann Moore Mercer.

JOHN GIBSON

John Gibson was born November 3, 1762, and was married to Phebe Hobbs (or Dobbs) who was born February 26, 1760.

Their children were: Martin, married Patience Burk; Sarah, married William Richardson; Thomas, married Elizabeth Cowan; Mary, married John Freeman; Elizabeth, married Thomas Smith; John, married Peggy Buster; Phebe, married Michael Buster; and Polly, married Joel Roberts.

Thomas Gibson was born May 28, 1788. He married Elizabeth Cowan February 16, 1815.

Their children were: Polly Ann; Andrew, married (1) Polly Zachary, (2) Nancy Hayden; John; Samuel, married Katherine Dysart; Nancy; Elizabeth, married —— Cowan; Jane, married John Frazure; Louisa, unmarried; and Zerelda, married Lee Nunnelly.

Andrew Gibson, born October 27, 1817, married Polly Zachary (his first wife), who was born on April 23, 1827. His second wife was Nancy Hayden.

His children were: Mary Jane, married Tom Frazure; Sarah Elizabeth, married Alvin Jones; Martha Ann, married Henry Bogle; John, married Mary Ham; Ben T., married Kate Wright; Samuel, married Effie Wright; Louisa, married William Cowan; Amanda, married Bourne Newell; and Thomas, married Fannie Wright.

Andrew Gibson was born and lived his entire life in Pulaski County on what is today the Jim Cowan place in the Pisgah community, where several of his children were born. He was president of the Somerset Banking Company at the time of his death.

He was a stanch Presbyterian and served as elder in both the Pisgah and Somerset churches. His strict observance of the Sabbath was proverbial — with his family the Sabbath started at noon, Saturday.

ROBERT GIBSON

Robert Gibson, born in Donegal, Ireland, October 8, 1827, was the son of Stephen and Ann Ramsey Gibson, both of Ireland. His parents came to the United States in 1837, landing at Philadelphia, Pennsylvania, where they remained for a short time. Traveling by boat, stagecoach, and on horseback, they came to Clay County, Kentucky. Stephen was the son of Edward Gibson, a native of Ireland, whose father was William, born in England. Ann Ramsey Gibson was a daughter of Robert Ramsey.

Robert Gibson received his education in the common schools. He farmed in Clay County until 1848, then moved to Laurel County and went into partnership with his brother Stephen. In 1856 he came to Somerset where he engaged in the mercantile business.

When the National Bank of Somerset was formed in 1871, Robert became a director serving until 1874, when he became cashier. He was married, January 9, 1855, to Pamelia Woodcock. Three daughters were born of that marriage; Anna, who married Charles Robinson, Meridian, Mississippi; Lucy, who was the wife of J. M. Richardson, Somerset; and Willie, who died just after graduating from Daughters College, Harrodsburg.[4]

Joe Gibson, the son of Mary Helen and Henry Gibson and a nephew of Robert, lived his entire life in Somerset. He was one of Somerset's progressive businessmen, a public-spirited citizen, officer in the Methodist Church, South, and assisted many young people in acquiring a college education. He was president of the First National Bank at the time of his death in 1939.

GIRDLER

Atticus Monroe Girdler and John Everette Girdler, who engaged in the hardware, furniture and undertaking business in Somerset, many, many years as Girdler Brothers, were sons of Joel Hayden and Viletha Floyd Girdler. They were loyal members of the First Methodist Church with J. E. Girdler

---

[4]Biographical information from Perrin Battle, and Kniffin, *Kentucky, A History of the State*, (8th ed.; Louisville, Ky., and Chicago, 1888: F. A. Battey & Co.), p. 828.

serving as trustee and steward fifty years. A. M. Girdler was a member of the first council of the city of Somerset.

J. E. Girdler married Sophia Gilmore in 1879, and their children were Mrs. Carl Norfleet, who passed away in 1921, and Maude Elizabeth Girdler.

A. M. Girdler married Lula Richardson in 1890, and their daughter is Mrs. Ralph Longsworth of Somerset.

Joel Hayden Girdler lived on a farm one mile from Somerset. He was the grandson of the James Girdler known as "Wee Jimmie," who served in the American Revolutionary War.

JASPER

Abe Jasper, one of the oldest settlers in West Pulaski County, came to Kentucky from Wythe County, Virginia. He settled at what is now known as the "Old Gid Gossett Knob," which was a land grant to him. He was the great-grandfather of John Abe Jasper, who was, for many years, in the revenue service, and served one term in the legislature. He was the father of Dr. Galen, Dr. Robert, and James Jasper of Somerset. Dr. Robert Jasper served a term as state senator.

MORROW

The Morrow family has been closely knit with Pulaski County for nearly one hundred years.

Thomas Z. Morrow was born in Fleming County, in 1835. He was the son of Alexander and Margaret Boyd Morrow, who were natives of Pennsylvania.

Thomas Z. was educated at Centre College, Danville, where his father was a merchant and hotel keeper. He was graduated in the famous class of 1855, of which future Governors Crittenden and Breckinridge, and others, who became prominent men, were members.

He then entered the law department of Transylvania College, Lexington, and was graduated in 1856. In 1857 he came to Somerset and took charge of a Democratic paper, which he edited for one year.

In 1858 he was elected county attorney and in 1861 was elected to the legislature. In 1862 he served for nine months as lieutenant colonel of the Thirty-Second Kentucky Infantry.

In 1865, he was elected state senator. He served in many official positions, both politically and fraternally, throughout his life, being elected circuit judge in 1886.

On December 24, 1858, he married Virginia Bradley of Garrard County, the daughter of Robert M. and Ellen Totten Bradley. Her brother, William O. Bradley, was a governor of Kentucky.

Of this marriage were born eight children: William, Mary, Thomas, Robert, Samuel, Boyd, Edwin P., and Charles. Boyd and Thomas are the only ones living in 1949.

Politically, Colonel Morrow was a Republican. He was a charter member of the First Presbyterian Church, of which he was an elder for many years.

SAMUEL NEWELL[5]

Samuel Newell I was the son of Samuel Newell and Elizabeth Colville Black Newell, a widow with six children. Samuel I had one sister, Elizabeth.[6]

According to documentary records, he was born November 4, 1754, on the voyage from Ireland to America. His first home was in Frederick County, Virginia, where his parents settled and he grew to manhood. He married Jean Montgomery (born October, 1764) who was the daughter of John and Esther Houston Montgomery, an aunt of Sam Houston of Texas fame.[7]

In 1780 at the age of twenty-six, Samuel took part in the expedition against the Tories on New River, and in the same year at the Battle of King's Mountain he was serving his country as a first lieutenant in Captain Colville's Company, Colonel Campbell's Regiment. Lieutenant Newell played a conspicuous part in that engagement. In spite of gunshot wounds[8] in the hip which crippled him for life, he fought through the action. Weakened by loss of blood, he was at last lifted from his horse.

---

[5] See footnote, page 47.
[6] Samuel Newell's Bible record, possession of Mrs. F. E. Tibbals, a great-granddaughter.
[7] Bible record and MSS in State Historical Society, Madison, Wisconsin.
[8] A tradition in the family is that when he received this gunshot wound (in the groin) he tore off a piece of his shirttail, put it on his ramrod, and pushed it into the wound to make sure the intestines were not punctured.

In December, 1780, he went on Colonel Arthur Campbell's Cherokee expedition, and was appointed a captain in 1781. Captain Newell had several skirmishes with the Indians while he was protecting the Kentucky Road and Powell's Valley. An unusual incident which occurred in 1782 during one of these encounters is "... he and his men surrounded an Indian camp, and his [Captain Newell's] gun alone went off, the others failed, from becoming wet; but his single fire killed one Indian and mortally wounded another."[9]

Draper, in his *King's Mountain and Its Heroes,* describes him thus:

> His appearance was rather imposing, tall and very straight, black hair, large clear eyes, prominent forehead. He was a man of superior powers of mind, unflinching integrity in honesty, very fearless and bold and was ready to sacrifice his life, his all, for his country's good, very stern and reserved in his intercourse with his fellows.

Later, in eastern Tennessee, he was one of those who helped in the unsuccessful attempt to establish the independent state of Franklin. He was secretary of state in the cabinet of the first Tennessee governor.

He early removed to the French Broad River, in Tennessee, where he figured among the promoters of the Franklin Government, was a representative, in 1785, of Sevier County in the Legislature, and also a member of the Convention that formed the Franklin Constitution at the close of that year; was subsequently a Justice and a Colonel of Militia.

In 1797 he removed to what is now Pulaski County, Kentucky, where he was a long presiding Justice of the County Court. About 1838, he removed to Montgomery County, Indiana, where he died September 21, 1841, at the age of nearly 87 years. He was six feet, one inch in height, of fine presence and superior abilities.

He left numerous descendants. In 1812, he was placed on the invalid pension list, drawing at first, ninety-six and subsequently increased to one hundred and eight dollars a year, and still later to two hundred and thirty-one dollars and ninety-three cents.[10]

---

[9]Lyman C. Draper, LL.D., *King's Mountain and Its Heroes* (Cincinnati: Peter G. Thompson, Publisher, 1881), p. 408.
[10]*Ibid.*, p. 408f.

In 1795-96, he moved, along with the Longs, Saunders, Owens, and other pioneer settlers—the blood of whose descendants has been intermingled these many decades—to this section of Kentucky. Here, he took up a thousand acres of land on both sides of the Cumberland River, and established a home on the south side overlooking that stream, near the site where the Clio Post Office was later built.

He was the first sheriff of Pulaski County and a justice of the peace.

He was opposed to slavery, although he owned slaves. Whether he gave them their freedom or left them to his children when he left Kentucky is not known—there is no record.

He was a Presbyterian elder, as were his father and two of his sons.

There were ten children in this family, several born after he came to Kentucky. All of them married and lived in Pulaski County, except one son and two daughters who went with their parents to Indiana in 1834. Samuel Newell I and his wife Jean are buried near Gosport, Indiana. Their graves are marked with U. S. government markers.

Children of Samuel and Jean Montgomery Newell were: Samuel, married Nancy Owens; Margaret, married William Owens; John Montgomery, married Margaret Beaty; Susannah, married Andrew Evans, moved to Indiana; Dorcas, died young; Elizabeth Colville, unmarried; Joseph Black, married Jane Kinkead; William T., married Pelina Fain, moved to Indiana; and Jean, married James Evans, moved to Indiana.

The following letter was found in "the little black box," a treasured possession in the G. W. Saunders' home:

Knoxville, Tenn. (10)
September the 9th, 1821

Dear Sir, I want you to see Mr. Dollarhide and tell him he can have that sorrel horse which I promised to him by paying fifty dollars; I could get more money for such a horse if I had him in Knoxville, but as Mr. Dollarhide is an old friend he may have the horse for the sum mentioned above. Tell George Saunders I was in Bedford County, Virginia two weeks ago and attended the burial of Julius, his father.

He was buried in the honors of war as he was in the capture of that old scoundrel Cornwallis at Little York, sixty-one years ago. Julius was a good soldier.

I was in the funeral escort, more than a thousand people were at his burial. Rev. James Shelburne, a Baptist preacher delivered a sermon at the grave.

He was four years younger than myself, I was born in 1754, he was born in New Kent 1758.

I will be at Somerset in October or first of November.

SAMUEL NEWELL

To—TUNSTALL QUARLES, Somerset.

OWENS[11]

William Owens came here from Virginia before Pulaski County was formed. He was of Welsh descent, the son of William Owens and his wife, Jude, whose maiden name is not known. William was born November 10, 1750, in Virginia and married Nancy Owens, his cousin, September 20 or 30, 1773, in the Shenandoah Valley. Nancy was the daughter of Vincent Owens, whose wife was Winifred Le Hue (Lehew), the daughter of Peter Le Hue and his wife, Frances Allen.

Peter Le Hue, a Huguenot, was born in 1692 in France. He came to America before 1707-12, settling at Front Royal, Virginia. "In 1760 Peter Le Hue was the leading citizen with the best house applied for, and was granted a license to keep an ordinary." A family legend, handed down from one generation to the next, says, "Peter Le Hue was shipped out of France at the time of the Reformation in a ventilated wine cask."

William Owens, the subject of this sketch, was a Revolutionary soldier who served as first sergeant in Captain James Newell's Company, Colonel Preston's Regiment. He and his wife, with several of their children, came here and settled on the bluff overlooking Pitman Creek, near the present town of Elihu. He built a one-room log cabin, which is now the living room of the house where Mrs. Lum Allen and her son Edwin are living. He died in the same house in 1836. He and his wife Nancy are buried in the old Baptist Cemetery in Somerset. They were the parents of six boys and six girls. Of their children who married into the family of Samuel Newell were

---

[11]William Owens and Samuel Newell I settled near each other; their children intermarried as did their descendants, even to the fourth generation.

William, who married Margaret Newell, and Nancy, who married Samuel Newell, the brother of Margaret.

The remaining children were: Judah; Reuben, married Sally Lockhart, moved to Clinton County; Jane, married Samuel Tate, lived in Pulaski County; Sarah, married Hansford Price, lived in Pulaski County; Rebecca, married Wesley Short, moved to Indiana; Avy, married John Short, moved to Indiana; Lavina, married Reuben Short, moved to Indiana; John, married Ann Chesney, lived in Pulaski County; and Martin, married Polly Chesney, moved to Rockcastle County.

Two of these sons, Samuel and Martin, were Baptist preachers, Martin being one of the early ministers of the Flat Lick Baptist Church.

The Shorts and Samuel Owens emigrated to Indiana. Their descendants are living near Bedford and Bloomington, Indiana, today.

There are many descendants of those who remained in Pulaski. One of them was Samuel Tate, a great-grandson who, at the age of eighty-four, wrote a history of the Owens family, from which the following quotation is taken:

> Grandfather Owens was quite wealthy when he died. He had fifteen Negro servants and several likely young men (Negroes) and women who were bought at his sale and taken south by traders. Grandfather lived with his daughter Jane and her husband [Samuel Tate] until her death. She kept one Negro man and woman to wait on her. When Grandfather went to housekeeping the family bedding was made of bearskins.

PETTUS

The old Pettus home in Norwich, England, still stands today, a choice example of the home of a prosperous citizen of our ancestors' times.

Five sons and one daughter came to Virginia about 1623. There, in Louisa County, Joseph Pettus, a farmer and school teacher, reared his family. One son, Richard Grover Pettus, came to Kentucky in 1806, and settled in Lincoln County, where he became a farmer and stock-raiser. He was a member of the Baptist church. He married Miss Nancy Adams and of this union were born three sons and one daughter.

William Henry Pettus, oldest son of Richard Grover Pettus and Nancy Adams Pettus, was born in 1827 in Garrard County. He received his early education in the Garrard County schools and subsequently attended Georgetown College. In February, 1850, he was united in marriage to Miss Elizabeth Hutchinson. They moved to Pulaski County in 1855, with their two small sons, Richard and Walter. Six other children were born to them in their farm home, located two miles east of Somerset. One child died in infancy.

In 1862 William H. Pettus was elected county judge and served one term. He was admitted to the bar in 1864. In 1869 he was elected representative from Pulaski County to the state legislature and while serving in that body was an advocate of the bill granting the charter for completion of the Cincinnati Southern Railway. He also took an active part in the reorganization of Kentucky's school system, and was a member of the insurance committee which reported the present insurance laws. In 1878-79 he served as a member of the first railroad commission in Kentucky. In 1889 he was unanimously elected an active member of the Filson Club, whose purpose was to gather from original sources historic matter relating to Kentucky or some section thereof. He was a Master Mason.

Elizabeth Hutchinson Pettus died in 1870 and six months later Judge Pettus married Miss Mary B. Milton. Of their two children only one, Eben Milton Pettus, lived to manhood.

Judge Pettus engaged in the practice of law with his son Walter B., as partner, until Walter moved with his family to Washington, where he was employed for forty years in the Pension Office of the United States.

Always an advocate of education, Judge Pettus provided his children the best opportunities for their advancement. He died at his home in Somerset in June, 1902. Until her death in 1911, Miss Nannie E. Pettus, a daughter, was known far and near as an outstanding member of the teaching profession, as were her sisters, Misses Sallie and Lillie Pettus. Old records that they have preserved show that many of the town's most prominent citizens as children attended the private schools taught by the Misses Pettus before the institution of Somerset public schools.

Two daughters of Judge Pettus, Misses Mary and Sallie, both octogenarians, lived in the old family home on North

Main Street, built seventy-five years ago. They were cared for by their niece, Mrs. Gilcin F. Meadors, of Greenwood, Mississippi, until their deaths in 1950 and 1951. Another niece, Miss Katherine Pettus, is the only other member of the family who is a resident of Somerset. Six grandchildren, five great-grandchildren, and five great-great-grandchildren of the judge live in various other states.[12]

PORCH

According to a historical paper on Somerset and Pulaski County prepared by the late Miss Martha Campbell, Ezekial Abbot Porch and his wife, Mary Bacheller, lived in Somerset when there were only ten houses.

Ezekial was the son of a Revolutionary soldier, Henry Porch, who was born in Abington, Virginia, and married to Rebecca P. Denton in Franklin County, North Carolina. The marriage record was dated December 12, 1786. Henry Porch was a messenger for General Greene. At the battle of Brice Creek, while carrying the money to pay General Greene's Army, he was pursued by the British. Being a very small man he was forced to stand in the stirrups and hold the money pouch above his head as his horse swam through the water. He and his wife settled in Whitley County, Kentucky.

Ezekial A. Porch was the first elected jailer of Pulaski County, being elected in 1838 and serving for twenty years. He refused to make the race again because of his age and the state of his health.

A visitor long remembered in Somerset was his mother, Rebecca Denton Porch. She rode from Williamsburg to Somerset when past ninety years of age, and was so little tired by the trip that she did some shopping in Somerset on the day of her arrival.

She made her second trip to Somerset by ox cart in September, 1862, to attend her son's funeral. Her age at this time was 112. The late Judge James Alcorn of Stanford, then a boy at Burnside, ferried her across the Cumberland River. He described her as the tiniest and oldest person he had ever seen. He borrowed a feather bed from his mother for Mrs. Porch

---

[12]Information by Elizabeth Pettus Meadors.

to rest upon, so that she might make the trip up the steep river hill in greater comfort.

Henry S. Porch, a son of Ezekial and Mary Porch, was a soldier of the Mexican War. He enlisted in Company H, Fourth Regiment, Kentucky, October 3, 1847, and was mustered out July 28, 1848, at Somerset. This company was organized by Captain John G. Lair at Somerset, September, 1847, and marched from Somerset to Louisville, arriving October 3, 1847.

A second son, Edwin D. Porch, was elected county court clerk, August, 1862, and he served in that capacity until his death March 15, 1874. He was succeeded by his son, Charles B. Porch, who filled out his father's unexpired term and was elected to a second term in 1880.[13]

JESSE RICHARDSON

Jesse Richardson (Richeson) was the son of Jonathan and Ann Richardson, born about 1760 though the exact date is not known. Of his several brothers and sisters, the following names are on record: Amos, Joseph, Mary, Nancy, Aimy, and Thomas. He was a native of Loudoun County, Virginia, but was living in Botetourt County, when he volunteered in 1778 for service in the Revolutionary War.

Jesse Richardson came to Kentucky about 1779; he served under Colonel Preston in the company of Captain James Newell. In 1780 he served in Colonel Benjamin Logan's regiment under Captain George Adams and Lieutenants William Moore and Joseph Kennedy. In 1782, he served under General George Rogers Clark in the Northwest Territory.

After the war he settled in Blazed Valley, where he and his numerous descendants lived through several generations. In fact, more than half that land is still owned by direct descendants. Having received several hundred acres by military grant and having acquired much more, he became one of the largest landowners in this section of the state. He owned practically all the land from what is now the Pump House to the post office of Ruth, or most of the territory bordering Pitman Creek, beginning at the old Kendrick farm, following the old

[13]Information by Lina Porch.

road to the crossing at Ruth. Each child was deeded several hundred acres. Rock Lick Church and burying grounds were a part of the old grant and were given to his daughter Lucy, who married Benjamin Thurman. This tract of land was in the Thurman family until sold by J. H. Thurman, the father of Mrs. V. D. Roberts.[14]

Doubtless the heart of this old pioneer would have quickened if he could have seen into the future; for today many worthy descendants are living in Somerset and Pulaski County. A tabulated record, which lack of space prohibits including, is kept by a descendant, Mrs. Mae Thurman Roberts.

SHEPPERD

The Shepperd family were among the early settlers of Pulaski County. They came from Wayne County in the early 1800's. Fount Shepperd, born in 1823, married Elizabeth Withers. For a time they lived on Fishing Creek in Pulaski County and later moved to Somerset, where they operated a hotel.

They had four sons and five daughters. One of their daughters, Margaret (who married Dill Moss), spent most of her life in Somerset and passed away March 7, 1945, at the age of ninety-three.

Will Shepperd, brother of Fount, was jailer in Somerset for twenty years. Thomas Hansford Shepperd, another brother who was born in 1840, married Elizabeth Porch of Somerset. He served with the Army of the Confederacy as a member of Company H, Sixth Regiment, Kentucky Cavalry under the famous General John Hunt Morgan. He was captured with several others by Union forces and spent two years as a war prisoner at Camp Douglas, Illinois.

STONER

Michael Stoner, intrepid hunter, prospector and Kentucky pioneer, was born George Michael Holstiener in 1748, near the present city of Philadelphia. His parents were John Leonhardt and Barbara Graff Holstiener, who were born in Rheinish Bavaria, Germany, and immigrated to America, via Eng-

---

[14]Information from Mrs. Mae Thurman Roberts.

land, in 1728, settling near Millbank, Lebanon County, Pennsylvania.

Prior to 1758 both his parents had died. By now the name had been shortened to Holstien.

He became apprenticed to a saddler but this life did not suit him, so he went down into Virginia where he met Daniel Boone. This was the beginning of a lifelong friendship. In Virginia his name took the permanent form of Stoner.

Early in their friendship he and Boone made a trip through Cumberland Gap into Kentucky, making headquarters at what later became Crab Orchard. It has been said they came down the Rockcastle River into Pulaski.

In 1785 or 1786 he married Frances Tribble, a daughter of Rev. Andrew and Sarah Ann Burris Tribble. After their marriage Stoner and his wife settled in what is now Clark County, near Winchester.

By 1797, Clark County was becoming too thickly settled to suit Stoner, who felt cramped and hemmed in if he could see the smoke from his neighbor's chimney. So, he moved down on the Cumberland River in Pulaski County. (Refer to Military Claims and First Tax List, 1799.) Here we find him acting as ferry man where a road, bearing his name, crossed the Cumberland River leading toward what is today Monticello.

It is said Stoner became a resident of Wayne in 1800. When he settled in Pulaski, 1799, Wayne County had not been formed. He probably lived on the same land after a part of Pulaski was taken to form Wayne, and it is likely he changed counties without changing his location.

Stoner died September 3, 1814, and is buried in Wayne County.[15]

TARTER

John Tarter came to Kentucky in 1788 or earlier from Wythe County, Virginia, and settled on the waters of White Oak Creek, about three miles from Nancy, near Gaines Precinct. He had four sons, Christian Logan, Jacob, Jesse, and William.

Christian Logan Tarter married Betsy Trimble, daughter of William Trimble, a Revolutionary soldier, November 23,

---

[15]Information from Bess Hawthorne, La Place, Illinois.

1817. The house to which he took his bride was on the waters of White Oak Creek, within a mile of the old "Duke Simpson" place. He lived there until 1844, when he moved to what is now known as Caintown, buying out Andrew Jasper, one of the first settlers in West Pulaski County. On February 28, 1859, he sold this land to Russell County, buying a farm on Goose Creek. He was a slave owner. He died at the age of eighty-four years and is buried at Coffey Chapel, Russell County.

Enoch L. Tarter, son of Christian Logan Tarter, married Lucinda Bernard. Their children were: Jerome Terrell, Christian Logan, and William. He was a farmer and served as deputy sheriff 1866-68.

Jerome Terrell Tarter was born at what is now known as Caintown, West Pulaski County. He was a descendant of Christian Tarter, who came from Germany and settled in Pennsylvania some time before the Revolutionary War. His mother, a Bernard, was of French descent. He attended Masonic College at Somerset, taught in private schools for a time, and studied law at night. In 1877-81 he served two terms in the Kentucky Legislature, and later was twice county judge of Pulaski County. He was a Baptist and Royal Arch Mason. He married Margaret Weddle, daughter of Solomon Weddle, son of John Milton Weddle, who established the village of Old Harrison, first settlement in West Pulaski County. While on a speaking tour with Hon. Frank Finley, candidate for Congress, he was drowned attempting to cross Pitman Creek at 4:00 P.M., October 26, 1888. The Somerset courthouse bell was tolled all that night.

The ford at Pitman Creek, where Honorable Frank Finley and Judge Jerome Tarter attempted to cross in a buggy, and where Judge Tarter was drowned, was very treacherous after heavy rains. It was located on the road between Somerset and Burnside. William Fox of Somerset was drowned trying to cross this creek at the same ford, and Mr. and Mrs. Edmund Chestnut, a young married couple, were also drowned there.

Mrs. Margaret Tarter was appointed postmistress at Somerset, Kentucky, July 18, 1889, serving until February 21, 1894. She was the widow of Jerome Tarter.

TATE

The Tate family in Pulaski County traces its ancestry back to the Revolutionary period when Major John Tate joined the Washington County (Virginia) Militia and Patriots, commanded by Colonel William Campbell who led them to victory against the Royal Forces at the Battle of Kings Mountain, South Carolina, on October 8, 1780.

In 1776, John Tate was a landowner in Washington County, Virginia, and a land treasury warrant (survey recorded May 1, 1781 for $9,059) added 100 acres to his lands. He was in the service of viewing roads from the Clinch River, Little Mockison Gap, Big Moccasin Gap, down Mockoson Creek to the Kentucky Road (the road made by Daniel Boone). He was also active in political life and the formation of the county of Russell (in Virginia) where he was located in 1786. He was in the commission of the peace for that county in 1797, was an officer in the militia from 1786, and in 1802 was appointed a colonel.

His tombstone, located about fifteen miles southwest of Lebanon, Russell County, Virginia, indicates he died September 15, 1825, at the age of eighty-five years, and that Mary Bracken Tate, his wife whom he married about 1766, died March 13, 1817, age seventy-five years. Their children were: Robert, Hannah, Samuel Bracken, Isaac, Jane, Martha, Lydia, and John.

About 1803 Samuel Bracken Tate left the well-established background of his father's home in Russell County, Virginia. Tradition says that he followed the Daniel Boone Trail to Kentucky, passed through Cumberland Gap, and settled in Pulaski County. He acquired (according to Jilson's records) a large area of land on the Cumberland River and Indian Creek at the present site of Tateville—the first survey recorded February 12, 1805.

The meritorious military zeal of Colonel John Tate was handed down to his son Samuel, who formed and led a company from Pulaski (read chapter on wars) in the spectacular victory at the Battle of the Thames under General Shelby. Captain Tate subsequently held the rank of major in the state militia and served as justice of the peace and magistrate.

Samuel Bracken Tate was born in Fincastle County, Virginia, on November 11, 1775; married Jane Owens, August 14, 1798, in Russell County; and died November 24, 1861. Both are buried in the Tateville Cemetery.

There were eight children. One son, Bowan Goggin Tate, served in the Civil War.

Perhaps the most widely known descendant who lived his entire life in Pulaski was Samuel Tate, born December 19, 1825, and died June 22, 1914. He married (first) Minerva Martin, on June 2, 1846, and (second) Mrs. Eliza Jones.

He was a respected and loved citizen of the county, often referred to as "the grand old man." He contributed much to the up-building and development of Pulaski County. In public life he served as constable, magistrate, appointed deputy sheriff, and elected sheriff (for more than one term). He was a devout member of the Christian Church, serving on the official board for a number of years.[16]

When the old Tate home at Tateville was torn down, the old stone chimney was removed and used in the construction of a log cabin which Mr. and Mrs. Harry Wait built in the yard of their Burnside home.

CYRENIUS WAIT

According to records still in existence, Cyrenius Wait (1794-1868) came from Chester, Massachusetts, in 1818, taking nearly two years to make the leisurely journey. He was accompanied by his brother William, who wrote a diary of the trip. (This diary is now in possession of Ruth Wait Tuttle, Somerset.) They traveled with team and wagon, evidently peddling and trading on the way. Soon after his arrival here, according to records now available, Cyrenius began to appease his land hunger by securing grants from the state and by purchases at low cost.

In the year 1843 he was state school commissioner for Pulaski and Casey counties. This was at the beginning of the common schools. It was he who was largely responsible for the

---

[16]This information is from a history of the Tate family, written by Mrs. Pearl Catron DeRake of Baltimore, Maryland. She recounts many interesting family "get-togethers" at Grandfather Tate's home out the Rush Branch Road.

common people's opportunity to learn the "Three R's." He also delved into politics, for we see from old records that in 1850 he was a senator in the Kentucky Legislature.

One of the businesses of Cyrenius Wait was that of salt-making. Salt wells were drilled and the water boiled down to make the finished product. A farm on Fishing Creek has long been known as "Salt Well Farm." This venture, like many others of his, was not very profitable. At one time he was probably owner of more acres of land (a great deal of it barren, mountain land) than any man in the county. An old assessment list showed he was paying taxes on over 40,000 acres. He was engaged in various mercantile ventures in the county, the largest being the business at Waitsboro on the Cumberland River, eight miles south of Somerset. He was in partnership at different times with various well-known men of the day. At one time he engaged in the silk industry at Somerset at what is known as the Shadoan home on Mt. Vernon Street (known today as "The Pines"). At this home, which he built, he grew rare imported mulberry trees on which the silk worms fed.

At the time of the War Between the States a pass was issued him by the Union Army permitting him to go through the lines on business trips. He was not a true abolitionist, as he was the owner of several slaves.

In 1848 he was justice of the peace. He ran several farms and operated coal mines on the upper Cumberland near the mouth of Buck Creek. This coal was boated down the river on barges to Nashville, Tennessee.

Cyrenius Wait was the son of Jonathan and Margaret Smith Wait. His first wife was Eliza Beaty and his second was Mary Jane Newell. His last home was at the top of Wait's Hill in Somerset.[17]

From the aforesaid we learn that Cyrenius Wait was associated with the chief business interests in the county, in addition to which the *Somerset Democrat* of 1855 shows he was president of the Somerset Branch of the Farmer's Bank. He was also agent for the Mutual Life Insurance Company. Old business letters and papers prove he was a painstaking and careful, as well as a very able man.

---

[17]Written by Harry Wait, a grandson.

His various enterprises prove him to have been Pulaski's foremost businessman and the most public-spirited citizen of his time.

He left a large estate to his family, which consisted of his wife and six children. These children were named for famous men of that day. They were: George Washington, John Quincy, Millard Fillmore, Benjamin Franklin, Henry Clay, and Margaret. By his first marriage he had a son who is remembered as Webb—perhaps short for Daniel Webster.

JOHN MILTON WEDDLE

John Milton Weddle was born in Wythe County, Virginia, September 3, 1776. He came to Kentucky from there about 1797. He formed a settlement which he called "Old Harrison," located about one and one-half miles from Faubush and three miles from Nancy. (There are no buildings now standing on the site of this village.)

He married Polly McDaniel, daughter of Spencer McDaniel, August 29, 1803. He was the father of Solomon Weddle, who was magistrate at Waterloo for twenty-five years.

John Milton Weddle was the maternal grandfather of Roscoe, Jerome, and Chris L. Tarter; the great-grandfather of Dr. A. A. Weddle, Claude Weddle, and John Sherman Cooper.

ZACHARY [18]

Betty, Sallie, Benjamin, and John Zachary were known to have been brothers and sisters, and it is thought that they were children of William Zachary.

Matilda Zachary, daughter of William Zachary, married Will Fitzpatrick on June 25, 1832. Margaret Fitzpatrick, daughter of a Will Fitzpatrick, married Henry Neikirk on August 29, 1850.

Since both Sallie and John Zachary had a child named Willis, the Willis Zachary, born March 10, 1796, died January 29, 1857, may have been their brother.

Betty Zachary married ——— Cundiff.

---

[18] A History of Casey County gives the Zachary family in that county as having descended from a John Zachary of Dutch descent, but no connection between the families can be found.

Sallie Zachary married Stephen Woodcock on January 26, 1819, and her children were Willis, William, Robert, Green, and Mary Woodcock.

On March 6, 1810, John Zachary married Frances Vaughan, daughter of Samuel and Mourning Hope Vaughan. His children were: Willis Fields; Jane (Mrs. John Arthur); Elizabeth (Mrs. Allen Jones); Louisa (Mrs. Dave Cundiff); Permelia (Mrs. Dickey F. Cundiff); Harriett; and John Vaughan Zachary, who married Pamelia Q. Porter, daughter of Joseph and Ann Campbell Porter.

John Vaughan Zachary's children were: Mary Frances (Mrs. James Knox Polk Collins); Martha Ann (Mrs. Francis Marion Cox); Bettie (Mrs. Will Jones); and James Brent Zachary.

James Brent Zachary's children were Eva and Everett Zachary. Everett's children were James and Etta Zachary.

Among Benjamin Zachary's children were: Polly, who married Andrew Gibson, December 14, 1839; Amanda, who married James Richardson; Charles, who married Louise Moore; and Addie Eliza, who married Mit Ingram.[19]

[19]Information by L. C. Rice, Jr., son of Martha Frances Cox.

Chapter 5

..EARLY SETTLEMENTS AND VILLAGES..

INCORPORATIONS

These Pulaski County incorporated villages, in addition to Somerset, are listed in Collins' *History of Kentucky*[1] as existing in 1874. Of those listed, Grundy, Waitsboro, and Woodstock are the only ones in existence in 1951.

Waitsboro (originally spelled Waitsborough), on a stream (Cumberland River) navigable for small steamboats several months during the year, was incorporated March 2, 1844.

Harrison, in the western part of the county, was incorporated 1842.

Grundy, five miles east of Somerset, was incorporated February 13, 1858. Its population was about one hundred; it had a church, two hotels, store, grocery, carding factory, shoe shop, and schoolhouse.

Mt. Gilead, with a hotel and store, was incorporated February 26, 1850. The population was about fifty.

Stylesville, off the Crab Orchard Road, north, was incorporated 1852.

Sublimity, northeast of Somerset on Rockcastle River, was incorporated 1860.

Woodstock, Crab Orchard Road, was incorporated 1866.

Jugernot, an early community on Buck Creek, exists today.

WOODSTOCK

The following was written about 1890 by W. H. Bently, M.D., for Lizzie Reynolds Burgin, whose teacher asked her to write an essay on Woodstock. Dr. Bently helped her out of her difficulties. This is the way the story goes:

[1]Vol. II, p. 682.

Woodstock is a post office hamlet of Pulaski County, in the northern part of the county, on the Somerset and Crab Orchard Road, halfway between the two towns. The first settlement was made about 1820, by a man named Griffin. About the year 1829 Griffin sold his possessions at Woodstock to a man, by the name of Freancy, from Lexington. He soon erected a comfortable dwelling, and a store house, and was the first merchant of that place. The name Woodstock was not conferred until 1832 when the post office was erected which went into operation in July, 1832.

About the year 1845, Mr. Freancy sold out to Mr. Elkins, who continued to sell goods and added to that business, agriculture and tavern keeping. He had the address to have a stage line along the Somerset and Crab Orchard road and his wayside inn was a dinner station.

The first physician to locate at Woodstock was a Dr. Barnard. He was a young man and had just graduated from Transylvania Medical School, at Lexington. He came to Woodstock through the influence of a Mr. Elkin. He did not remain long as he soon felt he had chosen the wrong profession.

Concerning the post office, there is a discrepancy in this date. This is probably an error in the manuscript, as a letter from the Assistant Postmaster General states:

The Woodstock post office was established September 25, 1853 and discontinued December 19, 1855, and reestablished on June 25, 1875.

W. W. HOWES, *first Assistant Post Master General.*

The holder of the letter further states it was permanently discontinued in 1940, when Rural Route 3 took its place.

Dr. Bently was born at Carthage, Tennessee, and married Mrs. Emma Bell Hudson of Monticello, Kentucky. They located at Woodstock and Dr. Bently is remembered by many people of Pulaski, Rockcastle and Lincoln counties where he practiced for a number of years. He died in 1902.

BURNSIDE

One hundred and fifty years ago the high and rugged point of land lying between the Cumberland and the South Fork rivers was just another point along the Cumberland. The Indians roamed and hunted at will over those hills, and the river held absolute sway—sometimes overflowing, and again winding peacefully between the green fields and wooded bluffs.

This place did not possess a name. In later years the people, who settled there first, called it Point Isabel. There was a legend that a maiden (by that name), disappointed in love, threw herself over the bluff to her death, hence the place always carried her name.

Time moved slowly for this small community. It was not until the Civil War that this place, because of its natural position as a military objective, received any mention. Even the stagecoach route was via Waitsboro into Wayne County, bypassing Burnside.

During the Civil War a detachment of General Burnside's army was stationed there. He had lookouts on all the high points, thus controlling the entire countryside as well as the river. At this time the name was changed from Point Isabel to Burnside in honor of the General. But the people changed slowly. Some of the older ones called it "The Point," and others called it "Point Burnside."

In later years after the Civil War, the federal government made some improvements on the river, building dams to throw the current to the deeper side. This made a deeper channel for the steamboats, affording navigation the entire year.

There was a great amount of lumber floated down the river to Burnside. Since the advent of the railroad, Burnside has done a thriving business in the making of railway ties. The Burnside Veneer Mill has been the leading industry for many years, and is still in operation.

Burnside's situation at the end of navigation on the Cumberland served to make it an important shipping point. There was a great deal of traffic with such towns as Burkesville and Jamestown, and even ones as far away as Nashville. Some of the old steamboats were called the "Rowena," "Selina," and "The City of Burnside."

During these years the business houses were located in lower Burnside, along the river, while the promoters with their families lived on the hilltop, overlooking the beautiful Cumberland River Valley.

More years passed, the mills furnished lumber for two wars. During that time Burnside flourished. But a change took place in transportation. Highways were built, and trucks took over much of the shipping. The trade on the river declined, and the boat business went into liquidation. The old boats fell into disuse and were sold for junk.

Burnside suffered financially at this time.

In 1950 the mammoth Wolf Creek Dam in Russell County was nearing completion, which meant the waters of the Cumberland River would be impounded 101 miles upstream. The entire lower part of Burnside would be covered. The federal government bought and relocated all the homes, as well as the business places, on the hill above in what we call Upper Burnside. By April, 1951, "Old Burnside" was no more and "New Burnside" promised to be a beautiful resort town.

The house where General Burnside had his headquarters, with the cannon in the yard, grim reminders of the Civil War; the quaint house with the outside stairway; the Seven Gables Hotel; and the little Presbyterian Church were all torn down and their sites lie on the bottom of new Lake Cumberland.

Four new bridges have been built near this town. One crosses the old Pitman Creek; another long one spans the Cumberland on Highway 90 to Monticello; yet another, over the Cumberland on Highway 27, leads directly into Burnside; the last is a railroad bridge on the Southern Railway System.

March 24, 1951, these bridges were dedicated by Governor Lawrence Wetherby of Kentucky. He was graciously received by the people of Burnside and Pulaski County. At this time he laid the cornerstone for the Girl Scout House. Into this stone were sealed the history of Burnside's first Girl Scout Troop, and the names of its members.

A modern water system, new streets, a telephone building, and many new buildings housing old businesses, spell a new town called Burnside. The residents are constructing hotels, tourist resorts, and restaurants for the benefit of the vacationists who are expected to enjoy the new lake.

ELIHU

The village, Elihu, came into being after the Cincinnati Southern Railroad was completed. A prosperous young farmer (the father of Miss Eva Taylor, who now lives on a part of the original farm) realized the need of a country store and started a small general store on a corner of this land which belonged to his wife's father, Owens Price. Later, a post office was established in this store. Two or three names were sent to the Post Office Department for approval but each time these names were refused because there were other towns of the same name in the state. Finally, a letter came from the Department selecting the name Elihu, in honor of the first postmaster, Elihu Taylor.

But, the pronunciation of the name caused much controversy. Some approved El'-i-hu. Perhaps they thought E-li'-hu was too plain a name for a new post office along the newly completed railroad.

It was settled at last by Mr. Taylor who said, "My name is E-li'-hu," and by this name it has always been known.

WEST PULASKI COUNTY

The first settlers in the western part of the county were William Trimble, Seton Lee, John Tarter, Daniel Weddle, Andrew Jasper, Abe Jasper, Jack Hammonds, and John Cooper.

William Trimble settled near Nancy; Seton Lee, at what is now known as the "Old Lee Graveyard," near Nancy; John Tarter, on the waters of White Oak Creek, about three miles from Nancy and near Gaines Precinct. Daniel Weddle had a 500 acre tract and land grant at what is known as the "Brack Seivers Place" near Waterloo. Andrew Jasper, at what is now known as Caintown, claimed a 500 acre land grant. Abe Jasper settled at what is now known as "The Gid Gossett Knob," a land grant to him. Jack Hammonds located on House Fork Creek near the Russell County line. John Cooper located not far from Waterloo and near Hopeful. These settlers, according to tradition, came to West Pulaski County in 1788 or earlier. Some of them came by way of Lexington, Fayette County.

Other settlers coming to the western part of the county as early as 1797 or before were: John Milton Weddle, Spencer McDaniel, Sol McDaniel, and Peter Tarter.

Peter Tarter was a Revolutionary soldier, who came from Wythe County, Virginia, and settled near Faubush.

> Peter Tarter, Revolutionary soldier, deed to John Tarter and wife Nancy, deed to Enis Tarter part of 200 acres patented to

Peter Tarter, December 13, 1811.
October 12, 1858 (18-251).

The following are names of other settlers in West Pulaski County, some of them found in marriage records, etc., of Pulaski County, as far back as 1826:

Baker	Davidson	Kizzee	Porter
Bray	Eastham	Marsee	Rainwater
Brown	Emerson	Molen	Simpson
Burton	Gadberry	Muse	Taylor
Combest	Henderson	Norfleet	Warner
Compton	Hudson	Pearce	Wilson

OLD HARRISON

John Milton Weddle, who came to Kentucky from Wythe County, Virginia, formed a settlement about one and one-half miles from Faubush and three miles from Nancy, which he called "Old Harrison." There is not a house left where this village of over three hundred inhabitants once stood. At the time Somerset was made the county seat of Pulaski, there was some talk of making Old Harrison the county seat.

Among those who owned stores in Old Harrison in later years, around the time of the Civil War, were: Jack Weddle; Jim Weddle, grandfather of Dr. Brent Weddle; Bill Logan, grandfather of Dr. Vola Trimble; Christian Sievers, grandfather of Dr. Robert Sievers; Hugh Frank McBeath; and Josh Taylor.

There was a Baptist church called Mt. Pisgah, of which John O. Southerland was pastor for many years, and a temperance society. There was a saloon—hence the need for a temperance society. There were a blacksmith shop and a tan yard, owned by Jim Holder and Jake Warner.

EARLY CHURCHES IN WEST PULASKI COUNTY

The oldest churches in West Pulaski County are Mt. Pisgah and Hopeful. John O. Southerland was pastor of Mt. Pisgah Church about the time of the Civil War. He was considered a great preacher for his time. The first pastor of Hopeful Church was Levi Cooper. James Cooper was one of the early pastors of Oil Center or Fishing Creek Church.

The Reverend Thomas Whitley, the Reverend Thomas Hill, and the Reverend John Black settled in West Pulaski County as early as 1800, as shown by records.

Daniel Weddle performed many of the early marriages in West Pulaski County. He was the great-great-grandfather of Dr. A. A. Weddle and Claude Weddle and of Judge Roscoe, Chris L., and Jerome Tarter.

William Porter of Porter's Ridge was a Baptist preacher of the Civil War era. He was said to be an exhorter. His sons, John, James, and Thomas, were also Baptist preachers. William Porter was the grandfather of Mrs. Wilmoth Cain and Mrs. Bannie Bolin of Somerset.

John Porter was a noted evangelist and was pastor of the Baptist Church at Winchester, Clark County, for many years. He was the father of Paul Porter, OPA head during World War II.

SOUTH OF THE CUMBERLAND

(This article was written by Miss Amelia Saunders, *aged ninety-two, from her own personal recollections.)*

The earliest settlers of this section owned large farms, and most of them, before the Civil War, owned slaves who tilled the soil.

John Beaty, whose wife was Polly Forgey, owned the first farm below the river. He built a substantial two-story log house (this was later weather-boarded) with a large cellar kitchen which stands today. It has been occupied by his descendants all through the years, and is now the home of W. O. Newell II, a great-grandson. Near the river, a spring gushes out of the bluff (the house stands on the bluff overlooking the river). This spring furnished water and power for a gristmill, and another spring makes a waterfall of fifty feet and is called the Cascades. Adjoining the Beaty farm on the South Fork of the Cumberland was the John Long estate. Mr. Long, with the help of thirty slaves, ran a carding machine, a gristmill, a tannery, and a distillery. He reared a large family. But since he was an elder in the Presbyterian Church, his conscience condemned him, and eventually he stopped distilling.

Adjoining these estates were farms owned mostly by members of the Methodist Church: the Emersons, Pierces, Govers,

Stigalls, and others. They had the only church building in that section. It was known as Alexander's Chapel. They had a Sunday school where all denominations were welcomed. It was one of the first Sunday schools in the county. The large farm on which this church stood was the original pioneer home of a Revolutionary soldier, named Samuel Newell I, later the home of Joseph B. Newell, and still later the home of Joseph's son William O. Newell I. There was a general merchandise store and a post office, known as Clio, but this did not exist after stagecoach days.

It was at this store that the first barrel of coal oil was brought into the county.

Of the children of Joseph B. Newell, four sons and one daughter grew to maturity. Two of the sons were graduates of Centre College, the only college graduates in the vicinity at that time. One of the sons, "Big" Sam Newell III, was a lawyer, a surveyor, a farmer, a bank president, and a popular teacher. His influence was felt throughout the county, always helpful and encouraging. Joe Newell's youngest son, "Clio Bill" (W. O. Newell I), remained on his father's farm, and ran the store and post office. After his marriage he built a red brick residence that remains there today and is known as the Bob Mercer place.

The first schoolhouse that was built in that section was known as the Beaty Schoolhouse. It was built of logs, large and substantial. It was burned during the Civil War but later rebuilt on the same site. This building became the Community Center—school, Sunday school, music classes, classes in penmanhip, debating societies, lectures, preaching by all denominations were held in this schoolhouse.

About the close of the Civil War Miss Ellen Brown taught a private school, in a house on her brother Nix Brown's farm, now owned by Sam B. and John M. Newell. When a store and post office were located here and it was necessary to choose a name for the spot, it was called Bronston, a contraction of Brown Town.

The first superintendent of the Sunday school that met at Beaty's schoolhouse was G. W. Saunders. Each year he was re-elected, and if health permitted he was always there. In 18— a Baptist Church was organized which met at Beaty's schoolhouse one Sunday each month, till a church building was built in Bronston. This church served the religious interests of the neighborhood. G. W. Saunders was superintendent of that Sunday school until too old to serve. Then his son James was elected and held the office until his death, in 1932.

The church building was used until 1947, when it burned. The citizens began immediately soliciting funds to rebuild. The result was a beautiful church building with Sunday school rooms.

Chapter 6

.... DEVELOPMENT ....

MILLS

Perhaps if Pulaski County were to pay tribute to a single natural resource which enabled the county to be settled, this tribute would be to the numerous springs which furnished fresh water, and to the creeks which furnished power for gristmills.

Water gristmills were erected by early settlers as soon as suitable locations were found, and they must have been numerous as the records show so many of them being established.

At the second court, which met in August, 1799, five permits were asked to erect water gristmills: Charles Collier on Brush Fork of Buck Creek; John James on Flat Lick; George McWhorter on Cold Water Creek; Isaac Meadows on Bond Creek; Andrew Turner on Sinking Creek. These were reported favorably in later courts.

In order to establish a mill a person had to appear in court and state just where he desired to erect his mill. The court then issued a writ of *ad quod damnum* to the sheriff, commanding him to summons a legal jury of twelve. This jury met at the site of the mill to see what damage would be caused by its erection, and to make a report at the next meeting of court.

The person desiring to erect the mill must own the land on both sides of the stream, and the report must read that no damage would be occasioned to adjoining property or to the health of the neighborhood. There were fifty-five permits at this court.

Some of these mills were: the John Long Mill on the South Fork; the Mose Lewis Mill on upper South Fork, which was built in a cave, with a large undershot wheel; Parker's Mill on Pitman Creek; Cundiff's Mill on Owens Branch (now

69

Allen's Branch); Wait Mill, which was in the bottom, west of the present railway station; and Mill's Mill.

There was also the old Cameron Mill on South Main Street, which was run by Cameron and Klinginsmith during the 1880's. At one time Dr. George Perkins owned an interest in this mill, which furnished Pulaski County's first bolted flour. An attachment was added which made rolls for spinning. This furnished a home market for wool.

PARKER'S MILL

The best known of the previously named mills was built in 1849 by Lewis Parker, who came to Pulaski County from Wayne at the request of the citizens. As an inducement to get him to come, they offered him the land for the site. He located on top of the hill, three and one-half miles south of Somerset, overlooking a natural basin on Pitman Creek. Here he built a sawmill and a gristmill about 200 feet apart—the gristmill on the north side of the creek and the sawmill on the south side.

In the memoirs of Mr. Joe Parker, a grandson who lived to be ninety years of age, he says:

> Prior to 1850 there probably were no sawmills in the county. When people wanted lumber for building purposes they sawed lumber by man power; made a scaffold and rolled a log upon it and sawed the log with a whip saw operated by two men—a man on top to pull the saw up and a man on the ground to pull it back. Most of the houses built were of hewn logs and the lumber for floors, etc., was sawed and stacked outside to season for sometime, then dressed with hand planes. The floors were dressed by hand or just seasoned and laid without dressing.
>
> When the railroad came the circular saws run by steam power replaced the whip saw; then came roller mills for dressing and making all kinds of lumber needed in building.

The setting of this mill, at the base of a perpendicular cliff which was shingled with mountain laurel with a stream of cold water pouring over it, was one of Nature's rare spots.

The sparkling water of the creek poured over the dam, furnishing power for the undershot water wheel, then tumbled over rocks to a natural swimming pool below. Through the years this charming rustic scene was a popular picnic spot.

The sawmill was discontinued in the early eighties. The corn mill passed into the hands of a son, Elisha Parker, who continued to operate it for many years.

It was here that the kindly, white-haired, dusty miller made famous "water ground" meal for all the surrounding country.

About the turn of the century, Mr. Parker, realizing the need for a recreation ground and this being an ideal place, made extensive improvements—a rustic bridge for horse drawn carriages, a dancing pavilion, dining hall, dressing rooms, running water, canoes, and boats on the mill pond—all for the pleasure of the outdoor lover.

Parker's Mill was synonymous with pleasure. Many picnics, fish fries, and watermelon feasts were enjoyed here, many dances were held under the starlit sky. Parker's Mill was to Pulaski citizens, in those years, what Cumberland Falls is to Kentucky today.

In the years following 1910 Mr. Parker passed away, the mill was not used, and was finally destroyed by fire. The mill dam and the bridge rotted away and fell to pieces, but to borrow a quotation, "You may break, you may shatter the vase, if you will; but the scent of the roses will linger there still." So it is with the memories of Parker's Mill.

DEVELOPMENT OF NATURAL RESOURCES

Coal

The first industry was mining coal up the Cumberland and South Fork rivers; this provided the chief source of income for the inhabitants until the railroads came. Many of Pulaski's citizens were owners of large areas of coal-producing lands and became quite wealthy for that day.

When the coal was mined it was thrown over the bluffs, loaded into boats or barges, and shipped to Nashville, where it was exchanged for necessary commodities such as sugar, coffee, salt, etc.

In an old letter to Cyrenius Wait from a Nashville firm, mention is made of the shipment of one large iron kettle from the Red River Iron Works. Probably this kettle was to be used in making salt as Wait produced the first salt in Pulaski County. This letter also urges Wait to ship a barge of coal by the first coal boat tide.

The coal boats or barges were about seventy-five feet long and made of very heavy hand-hewn timbers. They held approximately fifteen thousand bushels of coal. They were piloted by experienced river men as it was a hazardous job to steer these bulky barges during a "tide" through channels, over shoals, and around treacherous bends. The pilots, two of them, were assisted by several men at each end of the boat; by the expert handling of two oars, forty feet long, they steered the craft. It was not always successfully done, and many boats went down. When the barges went through to their destination, they were never brought back. The men who piloted them made the return trip on foot.

A story goes that twenty-four barges were sunk in one day. I remember that for several years the coal from these barges would be washed up on the river bottoms, during a bottom sweeper, and the people who lived nearby would take wagons to the spot to pick up their winter's supply of coal.

The shoals north of Burnside were very rough for the coal barges. At an early date there was extensive work done on these shallow, rough places in the river. On Smith's Shoals a series of seven steps were built entirely across the river. At other places walls were built along the sides. These were sometimes ten or fifteen feet high and as much as two or three hundred feet long. They were designed to throw the current to one side of the river and make it deeper. Tradition says the method was not successful and that the barges piled up on the rough banks and were sunk. It was a financial disaster for the builders of the walls.

Today, shipment of coal by trucks to points north has become a lucrative business.

TIMBER

From the 1850's until 1930 lumber production ranked as Pulaski County's chief industry; even now it rates high. The timber, largely hardwood and among the finest of its kind, was abundant.

In the early days timber was cut in the forests, rolled by chutes over bluffs to streams where it was tied into "booms," and rafted down the Cumberland River. After the railroad was built every place along the road became a shipping point; Burnside, Sloans Valley, Tateville, and Greenwood (now in

McCreary County) were the largest. Today there are many sawmills from which the lumber is trucked north.

During the first Chicago World's Fair, 1893, Dr. J. W. F. Parker shipped one piece of poplar timber which received the premium in that exhibit. My informant does not remember the diameter but says that it took three flat cars to ship it. This poplar tree had grown to great height without any limbs, as they often do. It came from "Pumpkin Hollow," east of Elihu and five miles southeast of Somerset.

Giant trees, perhaps hundreds of years old, recently have been cut from the river and creek bluffs to make ready for the lake formed by Wolf Creek Dam.

IRON

Iron ore was found on the bluff of Buck Creek, near the present site of Hail post office. The deposit was small and never worked to any extent. According to Senator George Shadoan[1] and Robert Hail, there was evidence of some type of a furnace there.

There has been some conjecture concerning a tall stone chimney which stands in the river bottom below Waitsboro. There is no one living who knows when, or for what, it was built. The crumbling stones are seemingly held together by the vine growth of years.

The late G. Harry Wait, whose opinions were respected, held that it was an iron furnace. The following letter seems to confirm his belief. In June, 1950, his son, in searching for an old black suit of clothes to wear in a home talent play in Burnside, dug into an old trunk and pulled out a suit of his grandfather's, from which fell a yellowed slip of paper on which was written:

July the 27th, 1852

M. C. WAIT

Dear Sir, please send me a hundred and 50 lbs. of Bacon as I think that will do me while building the 2 boats. Danill Rese.

Sir, our Smelter will be a residence of your town [supposedly Waitsboro] in the last of next week, if no axcedent, he intends worken our ore.

Yours truly,
DANIL RESE

[1]Frequently spelled Shadoin in record books.

Yet, there are others who discredit this for these reasons: first, it was too great a distance from where the iron was found (Buck Creek) to barge it down the Cumberland River to this point; second, iron furnaces were built at the base of a hill or bluff and were said to be about fifteen feet high, while this one was approximately thirty feet and in a flat field in the river bottom.

It may be that this structure was built to be used as an iron furnace, which was soon abandoned and quickly forgotten because the deposit of iron ore was too scant to make a furnace a practical venture.

CLAY AND LIMESTONE

Bricks were made from a clay suitable for this purpose which was found in Pulaski County.

Quarrying of enormous quantities of limestone, used to make roads and buildings, is a revenue-producing occupation today.

TRAVEL AND TRANSPORTATION

Transportation has always been an important factor in the development of the county. Due to existing conditions in the early settlement of the county—no roads and only a little trade, which was by barter—progress for the first fifty years was slow. Trade was dependent on transportation up and down the Cumberland River, and by mule freight-wagons overland to Louisville. During this period there was traffic in mules and hogs which were driven on foot overland to the cotton planters in the South.

ROADS

The first record of a road is found in Pulaski County Court Records, Order Book I, page 8, and reads thus:

> September 24, 1799 Joshua Jones, Michael Stoner and Samuel Forbush were sworn to view the nearest and best way for a road from Stoner's Ferry, one mile across Beaver Creek.

Because this ferry, and the road leading to it, changed hands several times the name was changed and the road forgotten, but research has proved without doubt the exact location, and that Michael Stoner was here. The following is from a historical paper written several years ago by Mrs. Jennie Newell Hail to which she gave time and research:

The landmark that helps best to locate us is the Cumberland River, and Collins' *History of Kentucky* tells us that the first map of the Cumberland was made in March, 1780. It is spoken of as a fine river, navigable at least 700 miles from its mouth. Most transportation in and out of the county was by way of the river, until 1876, when the present railroad was built.

The Tellico Indians had a trail across the country by way of Lexington, Crab Orchard and Somerset, crossing the river at Smith's Shoals above Burnside through Tateville, on into Jacksboro, Tennessee, and into the Carolinas. When the white man came and the Jacksboro Iron Works desired a way to market cattle, and horseshoes, rakes and other manufactured articles, they built a road following this Indian trail, and freighted their articles to Lexington by wagon. They named this road the Jacksboro Road. There is still a part of this road through Somerset and the southern part of the county. A road leaving this road near Tateville, crossing the South Fork at the Long Spring and going to the salt wells in Wayne County was often called the Jacksboro Road.

We find in that section of the county near Quinton, an Indian trail leading through Double Head Gap. The citizens of that section claim a lone grave in the gap is that of Chief Double Head.

Another interesting road is the Stoner Ferry Road[2] that leaves Somerset at the south city limits, goes through Oak Hill neighborhood to the Cumberland River. We find a number of land grants for that section of the county, and it was through this section that Samuel Newell I passed and crossed the river to the south side, settling on top of the hill at Clio. Clio is a beautiful name for this place. (Clio is one of the nine sister goddesses of song and poetry.) The view from the hill is certainly song inspiring. Clio is on the Monticello Highway No. 90. Samuel Newell I owned the first toll ferry in the county, the permit being granted in 1799.[3]

C. Stewart Boertman, in his *Document on Michael Stoner*, located a road (1799) toward Monticello in this manner:

---

[2]A deed in the possession of Dr. F. E. Tibbals, calls for corners on this road—the Stoner Ferry Road, but now the Oak Hill Road.
[3]Quotation by Mrs. Jennie Newell Hail.

"from Stoner's Ferry to Isaac West's, to Joseph Hind's, to William Beard's and then to John Francis'." Isaac West's place was about one mile south of Mill Springs and is the present Metcalf farm.

This road order is in Pulaski County Court Order Book I, page 14, and, comparing information, it must have crossed the Cumberland at Mill Springs.

During the Civil War stretches of roads were paved with cedar logs placed side by side, making it possible to get the artillery over the impassable spots in bad weather. These were called "corduroy roads." One stretch, reaching along the bank of the river and the base of the bluff west of Burnside, was still there when the present road was built in 1916. Mrs. Hugh Crozier of Harrodsburg, says: "During the Civil War my husband's father, Captain William Crozier, had that road laid to get the artillery over to the Army at Burnside." She says further, that "in 1916 when my husband, an engineer working for the Kentucky Highway Department, was building that road, he dug up the cedar logs that his father laid many years before, and after more than fifty years found them in good condition."

From the earliest days the main road of travel was north-south, the same as the present U. S. Highway 27, and was always spoken of by the old inhabitants as the "big road."

During Judge Robert F. Jasper's administration, 1914-18, a bond issue of $300,000 was voted for road construction. A macadam road was made which reached ten miles north of Somerset and south to Burnside. This was completed to the Lincoln County line during Governor Morrow's administration as governor in 1922-24. It was improved with black top in the years following.

Agitation by the Chattanooga Automobile Club for the construction of a road, connecting Cincinnati and Chattanooga, had extended over several years.

The road south, at this time, was no more than a rough road used for hauling logs. The route was suggested and discussed for more than two years before any meeting was held. The second meeting was held in Somerset in 1921. A year or more after this conference a motorcade, organized and participated in by practically all of the towns in Tennessee along the route, came to Somerset. Despite many meetings held in different places between Cincinnati and Chattanooga, U. S. 27 was not completed until 1930.

The county's second important highway, Highway 80, was completed in 1939, and runs east-west, connecting Somerset with counties in both directions. This highway opened up a large territory of coal and timber. During the WPA program of Franklin D. Roosevelt's administration, this area was dotted with CCC camps which housed boys, in the employ of the government, who built miles and miles of auxiliary hard-surfaced roads. With the state aid and gasoline tax the road extension continues.

Because of the lake created by Wolf Creek Dam many concrete bridges are being inundated. For this reason four tremendous highway bridges, the railroad bridge, and several miles of new road were completed in 1951.

Stagecoach Days

Even though the ox cart, pack saddle, and covered wagon were the most used means of transportation in the early days, people rode horseback to some extent. With the manufacture of better saddles, this became the principal means of transportation. People took great pride in, and placed great value on, a good saddle and horse. Evidence of this was shown in a will where a husband made a special bequest for "my dear wife to have Bluebird, my favorite horse, and the best side saddle and bridle."

The stagecoach was the first public vehicle in and out of the county. It served a dual purpose: to carry the mail[4] and passengers. The first stagecoaches were crude, handmade affairs, but later became more comfortable. The body was swung on heavy leather straps that gave a swinging motion to the coach, especially over rough places if driven fast.

The driver's seat was on the outside, well to the top, and on the top was a seat for sight-seeing passengers. The roads were dusty and as a protection both ladies and gentlemen wore long linen dusters. Their luggage consisted of the carpet satchel and valise. (In 1845, my mother, carrying all her clothes in a carpet bag, rode by horseback to Richmond, Kentucky, where she attended school.)

---

[4]Refer to Postal Service for date of mail route, supposedly the first stagecoach run in the county.

The heyday of the stagecoach was from 1850 to 1878, when such dignified lawyers as John Bridges, John Boyle, William Logan, William Owsley, Solomon Brent, Thomas Montgomery, and Archibald Mills came to circuit court from upper counties and stopped at the Harris House and the National Hotel. These were the days when Somerset's professional men and army officers proudly introduced their young wives to their visitors.

Kentucky had been settled only a few years; there were few settlements in this part of the state. The men were adventurous and daring—they had to be for travel was hazardous. The roads were long and sparsely settled—sometimes robbers concealed themselves in isolated places. The drivers, necessarily daring and doubtless reckless, were jolly, devil-may-care fellows, resourceful, and equal to any emergency. They were in their glory and the envy of the young boys, when, at five in the morning, seated on their high seats, with the reins of four fresh horses in one hand, the long whip in the other, they would drive up in front of the hotel where men and boys gathered to see the start—ready for the thirty mile trip to Stanford, where they would arrive at 3 P.M. A schedule in a *Somerset Gazette*, 1853, showed that only two trips were made in a week. John Hall had a contract for this line, and Larkin Edge and Dick Hall were two of the drivers.

Quoting J. Winston Coleman, Edge said: "A man can't drive from Stanford to Somerset and be a Christian. The mud is so deep and the road is so long, that a Christian would lose all patience with himself and his horses before he got to Waynesburg. After that, Job himself would get out of heart."

Although Larkin Edge derided the long drive and the muddy roads, the varied experiences must have appealed to his unique character, as his death-bed request was that he "be buried under the road where the stagecoach will roll over my grave."

Late in the sixties and seventies railroads were laid in Pulaski County. The Cincinnati Southern ran from Cincinnati to Chattanooga. The year 1878 saw the first passenger train go through Pulaski County. At this time the stagecoach route to Somerset from the north was discontinued, but the service from Burnside to Monticello in Wayne County continued for many years. During the early 1900's, the line was operated by Charlie Burton and later by his son, John Burton, of Wayne County.

These coaches met the trains in Burnside. Out of Burnside there were only five miles of route in Pulaski, but this was a hazardous part of the trip. After the driver received the mail bag and the passengers were comfortable, he climbed to his seat, picked up his reins, and flourished that prized possession, his long whip, cracking it over the horses' backs—the signal for the start over the steep hill to the river. Here they crossed on a ferry. On the other side was the steep hill leading to the level stretch to Monticello. It would be hard to say which was the more exciting, the ride up the steep hill with the horses straining at their traces, or down the hill when the driver let his horses loose. They rounded the hairpin curves with the coach careening from side to side and lurching in the ruts—the occupants wondering if the coach would hold together. The driver was never disconcerted; he knew his horses and his ability to bring them to their destination safely.

However, the river at flood stage was dangerous. Many times the riders wondered if the ferry would make the opposite bank. There were times when the river was frozen, and occasionally frozen solid. One such time Miss Costello (Mrs. H. C. Kennedy) was a passenger bound for Somerset, where she was teaching school. Since the mail must go at any hazard, the test was made, and driver and passengers made the crossing on the ice.

After the advent of the automobile the stagecoach line went out of business. In 1911, the last stagecoach run in Kentucky was made on this Monticello and Burnside route. The coach is in the possession of John Burton, of Monticello, who keeps it rubbed and polished and exhibits it with honest pride.

STEAMBOATS

It was not until 1833 that steamboats made their appearance on the Cumberland, which was navigable for small boats as far as Waitsboro and Stigall's Landing during several months in the year. Early bills of lading dated 1846, found among old papers of Cyrenius Wait, consigned cargo for landing at Waitsboro, the first river port on the Cumberland in this locality. Some of the early boats were: "Rose of Sharon," January, 1846, and "Clarksville," 1846. Outward-bound boats for

New Orleans were: "James Dick" and "Pride of the West." Nashville boats were: "Alpha," "Edmund," "George Collier," 1850; the steamer "Republic" and steamer "Monticello," 1855.

Quoting Mrs. Amanda Hicks, of Midway: "The first steamboat to run on the Cumberland was the 'Mayflower' on February 2, 1833." The "Burnside," "Celina," and "Rowena" were the last boats on the river. They were sold and taken away in 1933, ending one hundred years of steamboating on the Cumberland.

Mention of steamboating on the Cumberland brings to mind such names as Captain Tom Ryan, Dave Heath, Clate Heath, Logan Ramsey, "Boomer" Thurston, Hiram Irvine, "Preacher" Gann, and above them all "Commodore" Massey.

The middle period of steamboat days was a colorful time to the people who lived along the Cumberland; the hoarse whistle of the stern-wheeler could be heard for a distance of four or five miles. This warning brought old and young, white and black alike, to the river's edge. The music of the calliope, which most boats had, was seemingly from another world. There were, sometimes, passengers from as far away as New Orleans who landed at Waitsboro or Stigall's Ferry. Some sickened and died from the long trip, others took the stagecoach for points north, while some remained in Pulaski.

Conveyances

During the late 1860's private conveyances made their first appearances. Old inhabitants say the first buggy was owned by James Newell, a prosperous young man who held large estates and interests in coal mines up the Cumberland. These buggies were high and inconvenient to get into. About the same time there was a more luxurious equipage, the rockaway, which had a square top and door on both sides, with a small seat in front for the driver, a colored boy. The low and more comfortable phaeton followed this. Then came a double seated carriage, with a span of horses to pull it. Next came the undercut surrey with its flat, fringed top, and this was used during the gay nineties. The fly net—some were made of netted cord and some of narrow strips of leather—gave a prosperous look to the horse, whether it scared the flies away or not. The whalebone whip, often decorated with a bow of ribbon, lent an air to these "turnouts." One of the joys of buggy driving was its slowness; the passengers had time to enjoy what they saw, and bystanders could enjoy the elegance of the turnout.

About 1890, Joe Gibson had the first bicycle; it was a tall, ungainly affair with a high wheel above which the rider sat and a small wheel which trailed behind. Later the modern bicycle with two wheels of even size was ridden. Some of the girls who rode these early bicycles were: Sue Brinkley (Mrs. Cabel Owens, Sr.), Mae Pinnell (Mrs. Morris, Florida), and Lizzie Calvert (Mrs. Ellis Ogden).

There was the old horse-drawn bus which did double service. It met all trains and often carried the girls and their escorts to parties and dances. John Hall and his son Dick, who had operated the stagecoach line, operated this bus service.

The "Black Maria" or "All Out," a covered spring wagon affair drawn by two thin, spiritless black horses, was owned and driven by H. C. Gann. When ready to leave the Public Square for downtown or South Somerset, he could be heard above the noise calling, "All Out"—thus the conveyance was called the "All Out."

In 1904, T. V. Ferrell brought the first automobile, a Cadillac, to Somerset. It caused a great sensation. Reuben Jones had the second car.

Railroads

When the Civil War came, all of Kentucky was affected. While the state endeavored to remain neutral, it was finally swept into the conflict. The fact that Kentucky was the dividing line between the North and the South, was responsible for both armies sweeping across her lands. The progress Pulaski County had made was retarded, two battles being fought on her soil.

As always in time of war, everything gave way to accomplish the task of winning the war. Farms were neglected, property suffered, and roads, already poor, were rendered worse. It took several years for a semblance of recovery to take form.

The beginning of Pulaski County's greatest development came in 1877, when the railroad from Cincinnati to Chattanooga via Somerset was completed. For many years the railroad was a single track; it has just been completely double-tracked within the last year. The first station was built on land, donated by Dr. J. W. F. Parker, three-fourths of a mile from the courthouse. One man did most of the work. In addition to being ticket agent, he was freight agent, baggage master and yardmaster. The first to hold the job was Charles Denham, a very efficient young man who came here from Cincinnati. He remained until 1882, when he was transferred to Atlanta, Georgia, after the road was extended and connected with the Southern.

The first little depot burned in 1888 and was replaced with a larger one, which burned in 1909. The third and present one, constructed of brick, was built about a half-mile farther down in the railroad yard, in the curve of South Main Street and Jacksboro Street, on the site of the old roundhouse. This roundhouse was torn down and rebuilt as a part of the Ferguson shops.

Ferguson, a town south of Somerset, came into being when the shops for the Southern Railroad were built and put into use. It grew out of the need for homes for the workers. When the roundhouse was moved to the new location in 1907, Dennis Brown was the man chosen to do the job. He transferred and installed every piece of machinery. He was liked by the men who worked for him, was an exceptional mechanic, and the men respected his ability.

Before 1905 the road was divided into four divisions with the shops and terminal being in Somerset. In 1905 it was changed to three divisions, and the freight terminal moved to Danville. The passenger terminal was never moved from Somerset. Transportation continued to increase and the demand came for more trains, more crews, more office men, and better equipment in all departments. World War I and World War II tried the road to its capacity.

For several years talk of the Diesel engine was current, and on September 19, 1941, the first Diesel electric road freight locomotive, Number 6100, crossed the Cumberland River at Burnside. The fireman on the engine was Charles Denny, seen waving his hand from the window of the cab. Mr. Denny was a young man of Somerset, who joined the U.S. Marines May 26, 1944, and gave his life in action on Okinawa, June 13, 1945.

Mr. L. L. Waters, division superintendent of the Southern Railway System, says of the railroad:

The railroad was owned by the City of Cincinnati and was completed and opened to traffic from Cincinnati to Somerset in July 1877. The first two freight trains enroute to Chattanooga, left Cincinnati March 8, 1880.

This road has been designated at different times as the Queen and Crescent, the C. N. O. and T. P. (Cincinnati, New Orleans and Texas Pacific). It was leased by the Southern Railway System of which it became a branch road.

On May 29, 1941, the Southern placed in service its Number 6100, the world's first Diesel road freight locomotive. Although the 6100 is the first Diesel road freight locomotive ever built anywhere, it is not the first Diesel freight to go into regular railroad service. It was built late in 1939, as an experimental model, by the Electro-Motive Division of General Motors, and was demonstrated on the nation's railroads throughout most of the year 1940.

The Southern's decision to buy the "6100" was made during its demonstration tour. On May 24, 1941, the world's first Diesel road freight was added to the Southern's locomotive roster.[5]

POSTAL SERVICE

In the early days of Pulaski County mail was carried overland by messenger. There were no envelopes and no stamps. In possession of the Harry Wait family, descendants of Julius Saunders, is a letter written by Samuel Newell (see page 46) on a sheet of paper, folded and sealed with a dab of wax, addressed to Tunstall Quarles and postmarked, Knoxville, (10) September 9, 1821. The "10" is supposedly the price of delivery.

This service existed until the stagecoach came, which had a government contract for carrying the mail. According to records from the National Archives, Washington, D.C., a contract for a star mail route—No. 4862 from Stanford (via Waynesburg), Lincoln County; Adam's Mill, Somerset, Waitsboro, Pulaski County; Clio, Mill Springs, and Oak Forest, to Monticello, Wayne County, sixty miles and back, twice a week in stages, for $1200 per annum—was let on April 27, 1842 to F. Frederici and C. C. Carson.

[5]This information was given by office of Assistant to the President, Southern R. R. System, Washington, D. C.

According to the records of the Post Office Department for the period 1789-1930, a post office was established at Somerset shortly before January 1, 1803. Names of postmasters and dates[6] of their appointment were:

Archibald M. Sublitte	January 1, 1803
Phillip A. Sublette	April 1, 1807
William J. Sallee	January 1, 1810
Henry L. Mills	June 25, 1813
John Gumelson	August 22, 1815
Micajah Haie	December 20, 1816
John Tummelson	November 22, 1817

(name changed to John Tomlinson by legislature)

Joseph H. McBeath	October 24, 1854
Frank J. White	December 7, 1854
John E. Cosson	July 9, 1861
John R. Richardson	October 3, 1861
William A. Sallee	January 26, 1863
Solomon Turpin	February 7, 1868
Wiley Turpin	March 24, 1869
William C. Murphy	March 14, 1871
John Inman	June 6, 1883
Cyrenius W. Richardson	April 12, 1888
Maggie Tarter	July 18, 1889
Joseph C. Claunch	February 21, 1894
Henry G. Trimble	June 22, 1898
William M. Catron	January 16, 1903
Thomas M. Scott	June 15, 1911
Robert L. Brown	April 24, 1914
Robert L. Waddle	December 14, 1922
Chris L. Tarter	May 5, 1927
M. E. Burton	August, 1933

[6]Date of first return or account from the Deputy Postmaster to the Postmaster General.

Post Offices in Pulaski County, from the National Archives

Post Office	Established	Postmaster	Discontinued	Re-established
Adams Mill	1828	Alexander Adams		
Somerset	1832	Charles Tomlinson		1836—Thomas Hansford
Somerset	1835	Joseph McBeath		1837—Edwil Kelly
Flat Lick	1837	Thomas J. Smith	1838	
Waterloo	1839	Josiah Duck	1839	
Somerset (continued)	1845	Joel Sallee		1850—William Farris ...... 1851—Hiram Gragg
Dallas	1846	John Bobbitt		
Waitsboro	1846	William Wait		1860—Jno Barnett ...... 1863—Sam'l Renfro ...... 1866—Hampton Brinkley, etc.
Grundy	1847	Robert Graves	1847	
Line Creek	1848	Charles Warner		late in Rockcastle Robert Cooper—1899
Woodstock	1853	Reuben Elkin		1875—Howard Garner
Dabney	1853	Joel Hubble		1875—James Doolin
Dobbsville	1853	Rufus M. Dutton		
Cuba	1855	Armstrong Adams	1857	
Telico	1855	William Hyden		
Thompsonville	1857	James Moddrell		
Wightsville	1857	James P. Colyer		
Cartersville	1858	John W. Eubanks		
Cato	1858	John V. Higgins		
Sublimity	1860	Josephus Campbell	1863	
Hargisville	1862	George Hargis	1863	
Cains Store	1863	Christopher Gossett	1863	1865
Clio	1864	Joseph B. Newell	1878	William O. Newell—1855
Stigalls Ferry	1864	William L. Anderson	1865	Henry Clay Newell—1866
Shopville	1865	William Hargis		J. W. Hansford—1871
Shopville	1870	Greenup Claunch		
Lincolnsville	1865	William H. Logan		

Post Office	Established	Postmaster	Discontinued	Re-established
Valley Oak	1866	James L. Bobbitt		
Plato	1866	David O. Gibson		
White Oak Gap	1867	John McHargue		William Hail—1867
Garden Cottage (late Stigalls Ferry)	1867	Samuel R. Owens	1878	
Durham	1874	Linville W. Edwards		
Cumberland	1874	Oliver Coffey		1874
Tates Store (Tatesville)	1874	H. G. Smith		Jerimiah Goodwin .... William T. Goodwin —1880
Science Hill	1874	William B. Gragg		Napoleon Barnett—1877 ... William Tomlinson—1890
Dallas	1868	Hampton H. Brinkley		William A. Anderson—1877
Greenwood	1876	Henry C. Farris		
Point Isabel (Burnside)	1877	Henry Beaty	1878	
Eubank Station	1877	Wilson Gooch		Josephus Campbell—1880
Rockcastle Springs	1878	Eleanor Goodin		
Sloans Valley	1879	George Lester		
Pulaski Station (late Adams Mill)	1879	Mack Newell		
Faubush	1879	Hugh McBeath		Jesse Norfleet—1883
Burnside	1880	Frederick Wallace		George P. Taylor—1881
Norwood	1880	James M. Clark		David Hubble—1880
Coolidge	1880	Middleton B. Holloway		James Nelson—1889
Gover	1880	William Hubble		Gideon Prather—1882 .... Wesley Gover—1883
Bronston	1882	Thomas C. Brown		James Weaver—1883 .... Robert McKechnie—1884 .... John McKechnie—1888
Trimble	1882	John C. Ford		
Lankford	1883	Francis Linville		

Post Office	Established	Postmaster	Discontinued	Re-established
Elihu	1883	Elihu Taylor		Edward Chilton—1884 ...... Wesley Bruce Gover—1886 .. Andrew J. Ford, Jr., 1887
Newell	1888	J. W. Floyd		
Nancy	1884	Nancy S. Logan		Volantis K. Logan—1884
Estesburg	1886	William S. Warren		
Burnetta	1886	James S. Weddle		
Happy Hollow	1888	Irvine Williams—changed to Alpine		Winfield Weatherford—1892
Dykes	1888	James L. Sears		
Juno	1888	Mathew Warren		
Glades	1888	John Riddle—changed to Walnut Grove	1889	
Hail	1890	George G. Gregory		
Addlemus	1890	B. P. Addlemus	1890	
Retta	1890	Marshall Dick		
Le Roy	1890	Christopher McQueary		
Ansel	1886	Ansel L. Wood		
Tolena	1891	James L. Jones		
Hillside	1891	John Hitchcock		
Woodline	1891	Jackson Price		
Lincoln	1891	Eli Farmer		
Small	1891	Josephus Reynolds		
Oil Center	1891	Quarles M. Cooper		
Pointer	1891	Thomas D. Dick		
Skip	1891	Amos Chaney		
Sawyer	1891	Thomas W. Sawyer		

Chapter 7

.... *CHURCHES* ....

The early churches were a result of the work of pioneer missionary preachers, who came from Virginia and the Carolinas into Kentucky, and more especially Pulaski County, pressing right on the heels of the first settlers. They had inherited from their forebears courage and determination, with a desire to carry to the new land the church and education without which no country has ever prospered.

These preachers were predominantly of Scotch-Irish descent. The first were Baptist, with a sprinkling of Presbyterians and Methodist circuit riders. Proof of the religious fervor of these early preachers and settlers is shown in the inventory of Samuel Newell's estate (father of the Samuel Newell who came to Pulaski County in 1795; found in Estate Book I, Knox County Records, Knoxville, Tennessee, 1794). The inventory lists one large Bible, one hymnbook, Dodridge's *Rise and Progress of Religion in the Soul,* and Doctor Bowen's *Unity of the Trinity.*

The names of the churches are legendary. Some are Biblical, as the following: Mt. Zion, Mt. Olive, Mt. Gilead, Mt. Victory, Eden, Pisgah, Antioch, Bethany, Bethel, Soul's Chapel, Fellowship, Freedom, and Hopeful. Others are derived from local place names.

There is a legend regarding the churches built on a hill: The builders were preparing to erect a church in a low place when a woman said, "Who ever heard of going down to worship the Lord?" She picked up a stone, labored to the top of the hill, and laid the cornerstone.

Rules regarding discipline and decorum were different in former times. Men were expelled from church membership if they were known tipplers, although those who sat in judgment on the guilty might be running a "still" or keeping a jug in the corner cupboard. Dancing was not permitted. It was improper for a female member to speak or pray in public. Indeed, the early churches were puritanical in their standards. In many of these churches, not too long ago, the men sat on one side of the church and the women on the other side.

For three-quarters of a century none of the churches had an organ; the psalms were "lined out" by a male member who possessed a strong voice, and the congregation followed him.

The Christian Church in Somerset did not approve an organ or any kind of instrument in the church for many long years. It is a matter of record that the Somerset Christian Church nearly split apart in the eighties, when the question of instrumental music came before the members.

THE FLAT LICK BAPTIST CHURCH[1]

Located nine miles east of Somerset a short distance off Highway 80, is the Flat Lick Baptist Church. It was organized January 4, 1799, with nine members. Early organizers were Thomas Hansford, Elijah Barnes, John James, and Charles Westerman. James Fears is said to have been the first pastor. Other early pastors were Joe Martin James, Robert McAllister, John James (the son of Joe Martin James), and Martin Owens (who was remembered for his long sermons).

In 1801, this church had 106 members; but as the result of sending out some of its members to form other churches in the surrounding country, its membership was reduced to 47 by the year 1812. The first building, made of logs, was some distance from the present church. The church now standing was built between the years 1830 and 1840 and was constructed of stone. The walls are still in a state of good preservation after a hundred and fifteen years. The interior was burned on the night of February 26, 1866. It was repaired and re-dedicated in 1899.

This church has become a landmark in the community, and it is recognized throughout the county as a builder of Christian citizens.

---

[1]Information gleaned from W. A. Moore, Mrs. James Roberts, Miss Sue Bobbitt, George Elliot, and Church records.

FIRST (SINKING CREEK) BAPTIST CHURCH[2]

The First Baptist Church (originally called Sinking Creek) was organized June 8, 1799, and was located on a knoll some few hundred yards west of "the old town spring." It was built of logs, but later the log structure was replaced by a brick building, the brick having been made of native red clay by the slaves. This church was often spoken of as the "Red Brick Church." The building had a gallery for the colored members.

Those organizing the church were Isaac Newland, Peter Woods, Henry Brooks, John Turner, and others. The membership at that time was twenty-one. Thomas Hansford was its first pastor, and under his guidance and ministry it enjoyed peace and prosperity. In 1812 it numbered 109 members, and in 1823, 164.

An old church record shows that a contract was made with John O. Southerland to serve the church as a pastor for five years, for which he was to receive the sum of $600.00. The records, however, leave some doubt as to whether this amount was ever paid in full.

This old pioneer preacher, in relating some of his experiences, tells how he labored in the cornfields day by day to support his family, and on Saturday rode sixteen miles to preach at the little church. "And sometimes, they gave me a pair of socks to take back with me."

This church entered into a constitution of the Cumberland River Association in 1809, and it remained a member of that body till after the formation of the South Kentucky Association of the United Baptists. About 1850 it divided on the subject of benevolent societies. Those opposing such organizations formed the Pitman Creek Baptist Church. This church is known today as the Cabin Hollow Church and is near Elihu. The affair finally got into the Cumberland River Association and divided that old fraternity. From this breach resulted the Cumberland River Association Number 2, in 1861.

In the early seventies, a claim was filed with the government for damages incurred during the Civil War, the church having been used as a hospital for the sick and wounded. So swiftly are government adjustments made that, in the year 1912, the present congregation received $1,200.00 damages.

[2]Source of information, George L. Elliot and William Ramsey, Somerset, Kentucky.

The colored Baptist Church grew out of this church. The following motion is found in one of the old record books dated July 1867: "On motion and second our colored brothers and sisters in good and regular standing will be granted letters for constitution upon application."

The only reminder of this old Sinking Creek Church, after one hundred years, is a neglected cemetery on the slope west of the town spring, where the ashes of many of Pulaski's early people lie in unmarked graves. The stones are crumbling; some are defaced by weather; some are broken and almost covered with dirt; others have been carried away. The following names were copied in 1940, but are not to be found today (1949):

Nancy Owens	born 3/15/1754	died 10/2/1840
William Owens	born 1750	died 8/9/1836
Joseph Porter	born 11/17/1781	died 8/—/1856
Ann Porter	born 4/16/1795	died 12/29/1869
Francis Lea	born 10/15/1781	died 1/12/1865
John B. Lea	born 12/17/1780	died 1/12/1865
Thomas Hansford	born 1/28/1797	died ———
Martha Hansford	born 11/25/1800	died 12/25/1871
John Owens	born 3/25/1792	died 4/18/1875
Ann Chesney Owens	born 1/30/1800	died 9/3/1856
Captain John Lair	born 2/13/1816	died 1/7/1862
Lewis Patterson	born 4/—/1804	died 6/8/1904
Keziah Owens	born 5/30/1817	died 1/12/1861

During the following years, the town grew and changed. The main part of Somerset was around the Public Square and up and down Main Street. In 1878, after a battle of words and many hard feelings, it was decided to move the Sinking Creek Church to a better location. Accordingly, the old church was torn down in the year 1878; the brick was sold, and a new brick church was erected on North Main Street.

The church had twenty-eight pastors in the one hundred and fifty years of its history. These pastors have been men of unshakable faith in the inspiration of the word of God and have believed and taught the doctrines held by Baptists. The church membership has been faithful and loyal to her pastors, giving cooperation and service, sympathy and financial aid.

The union has always been one of devoted fellowship and Christian forbearance.

In 1910, the church having outgrown the building then in use, the members voted to remove it and build a much larger church in order to accommodate their numbers. They erected a church auditorium that seated some six hundred people and a Sunday school annex that would accommodate more than three hundred. In 1917, the church was visited by a disastrous fire, and again, it was necessary to build. The lines of the burned church were retained, and the Sunday school annex was enlarged to care for more than six hundred pupils.

In 1950, First Church again felt the need of additional rooms for its Sunday school work, and a new three-story educational building was voted by the church. By April of 1951 the building was almost ready for use. This building was planned to accommodate a Sunday school enrollment of twelve hundred and fifty.

This church in its many years of service to the Lord has had the pleasure of starting several missions and has watched them grow from missions to fully developed Baptist churches, serving their communities faithfully and well. The names of these churches are: High Street Baptist Church, Somerset; Ferguson Baptist Church, Ferguson; Science Hill Baptist Church, Science Hill; and Calvary Baptist Church, Highway 80, East Somerset.

The original pastor of First Church was Thomas Hansford. Stephen Collier, Joseph Martin, James and Martin Owens all served as pastors prior to 1838. From 1838 to the present time the following have been pastors:

Daniel Buckner	1838-53	Ballinger E. Wright	1876-78
Josiah Leake	1854-55	No pastor	1878-80
John James	1855-56	Green Clay Smith	1880-83
John O. Southerland	1856-64	T. O. Probert	1883-85
Thomas H. Coleman	1864-68	John R. James	1885-87
No pastor	1868-69	Virgil Maxey	1887-88
William S. Taylor	1869-70	H. C. Roseman	1888-89
John M. Sallee	1870-72	A. C. Caperton	1889-90
William S. Taylor	1872-73	A. J. Ward	1890-94
John O. Southerland	1873-74	Allyn K. Foster	1894-95
W. M. Harris	1874-76	W. O. Millican	1895-97

W. O. Borum..............1897-1903 W. E. Hunter..................1912-39
J. W. Rawles..................1903-05 D. L. Hill........................1939-45
O. M. Huey....................1905-12 Preston L. Ramsey..........1945-—

THE FISHING CREEK BAPTIST CHURCH

The Fishing Creek Baptist Church was an early church, having been organized before 1813—the date is not definite, as the first pages of the record book are gone. The first minutes, on page 7 in this well-kept record, were written April 24, 1813. There is no mention of a preacher's name until 1821, when Elder James Cooper was ordained. Because the male members were always spoken of as brother, it is impossible to distinguish between the preacher and deacons. The first mention of a meetinghouse was on November 26, 1814, when "Brother E. Cooper and A. Sargent were appointed to employ a workman to make a pulpit, lay a floor and make a door."

According to the minutes, there was much discord in the church, not because of the doctrine, but because of personal feeling, which finally caused a split. The different groups became known as the Majority and the Minority, and they were at last excluded from the association. Meanwhile, the Majority attended to business in the ordinary way, and about 1828 this group was again received into the association.

All this time Elder James Cooper served the church as preacher. Under his pastorate, a great revival increased the membership from sixteen or seventeen to about seventy.

The names on this church roll include the Coopers, Dyes, Weddles, Wares, Roys, and many others who were prominent in the building of Pulaski County, and whose descendants are distinguished citizens in the county and nation today.[3]

THE HOPEFUL CHURCH

On the first page of the records of the Hopeful Church is found:
> Articles of Faith of the United Brethren.
> Church Discipline or Decorum.

[3]Information from Church records, courtesy of Claude Weddle.

This church was constituted October 23, 1849, at Hopeful, and consisted of the following elders: James Cooper, Abraham Weaver and William D. C. Haney.

The above Presbytery proceeds to constitute the same under the above, later name according to the rules and regulations of the Cumberland River Association.[4]

THE BAPTIST CHURCH, COLORED

The Colored Baptist Church of Somerset was once a part of the white Baptist Church. It was pastored by the Reverend John O. Southerland, who baptized a number of the colored people. The colored people held membership in that church until sometime in the year of Our Lord, 1867. At that time they organized a church separate from the white church and named it "The First Baptist Church, Colored, Somerset, Kentucky." It is reported that the Reverend John Southerland and the Reverend Henry Curd, first pastor of the new church, were the organizers.

The order in which the pastors served cannot be accurately established, but, as well as can be remembered, those who have served this church are the Reverends Henry Curd, ——— Shears, John Goggin, A. W. Puller, J. W. Lackey, P. H. Clark, ——— Knox, W. H. Williams, A. F. Martin, R. L. Childs, E. B. Johnson, and W. B. Wood.

If all reports are true, this church was organized and the first services were held in an old cow shed on Elm Street between North Main and Maple Streets. After a few months, the church members bought a lot fronting on Maple Street—sixty feet, running north from Elm, and back to Main Street. Here they built a house of worship which they soon outgrew. They remodeled it and worshiped in it until a storm wrecked their building, in March, 1913, and they were forced to build a new house of worship.

They bought a lot on the east side of Maple Street, almost fronting the old church on the west. On this lot, in about fifteen months, they erected the present house of worship, after much struggling and prayer. In August, 1914, the church was

---

[4]Church records, courtesy of Claude Weddle.

dedicated with great rejoicing and thanksgiving to God, and for thirty-five years the members have been able to serve God in this house according to the dictates of their own conscience.

Among the first deacons were: Brothers Jim Woods, Edd Wood, Daniel Gibson, Thomas Richardson, Peter Hurse, James Smith, followed by Mat Cambel, Cary Meadors, Brit Watkins, Clark Coffee, and others.

The Reverend W. B. Wood was called to the pastorate of this church in the year 1910, in April, and pastored for about fourteen years. He resigned in 1924 to take up the work of foreign missions. After three years, he again entered the pastorate, and was called to come back home in 1938. He returned, and has been laboring since in this old historic church. All told, he is now in his twenty-fifth year as pastor, and the church seems to be doing well. Most of the members now living are those that were baptized by the Reverend W. B. Wood.[5]

THE HIGH STREET BAPTIST CHURCH

The High Street Baptist Church was organized on November 25, 1915, with fifty members. The first building was a small frame structure. In 1923 a brick edifice was erected at a cost of $52,650.00. The Reverend T. C. Duke was the first pastor and organizer.

Mr. Duke says, concerning the building of the church, "We asked no one for help, but Dr. Hunter, one of God's choicest men, proposed to the First Church, of which he was pastor, that they give us $10,000.00, which they did.

"We dedicated it to the Lord, October 3, 1943, free of debt."

Mr. Duke retired February, 1949. He was a devoted pastor, a consecrated man and beloved by his congregation and the community.

The new pastor, the Reverend Gerald K. Ford, took up his work in February, 1949. At this time he is completing his work for his D.D. degree at the Southern Baptist Theological Seminary, Louisville. He was a chaplain in World War II.[6]

---

[5]Written by the Reverend W. B. Wood.
[6]Written by the Reverend T. C. Duke.

THE CATHOLIC CHURCH

The Catholic Church in Somerset had its beginning in the year 1878; about this time the Cincinnati Southern Railroad was built. There were many Irish Catholics who came to Somerset in connection with this work. For a time, they were attended by missionary priests from the Catholic Church in Danville. Until 1888, the Holy Sacrifice was offered periodically in the homes of the parishioners. The old McCabe Hotel was conveniently located, and Mass was offered there many times.

After a few years, more Catholic families came to Somerset, and a small chapel was secured in Johnston's Hall, where Mass was celebrated every Sunday. In 1885, a campaign was started by Rev. ——— Volk to raise funds for building a church. He was later called to missionary work in South America, and the task was turned over to Rev. A. J. Brady.

In 1887, a lot on High Street was purchased from R. A. Johnson for $150.00, and on this lot a small frame structure was erected as the first Catholic Church in Somerset, and dedicated in honor of St. Mildred. St. Mildred's was a missionary church until 1901. In that year, a rectory having been erected, Father B. J. Wight became the first resident pastor.

In January, the Reverend B. J. Boland was appointed pastor, and he remained nearly eighteen years. During his stay, he raised funds for and in 1908 built a three-story brick school building with living quarters for the Sisters. After Father Boland came the Reverend Ignatius. During his pastorate, on January 29, 1928, the church, school, and rectory were destroyed by fire. Until another building was erected in 1929, Mass was offered in different places adjacent to the former church.

For a number of years, the basement of the new school building was used as a church, and the upper stories served as the school. In 1942, the Rev. J. A. O'Bryan came as pastor. It was he who launched "A Begging Campaign" to secure funds to rebuild St. Mildred's. Letters, asking for voluntary contributions, were sent over the entire eastern area of the United States. People were generous; and on October 20, 1949, the new church, school, newly bought rectory, and Sisters' home, with a total value of $270,000, were dedicated by Archbishop Floersh in solemn ceremonies.[7]

THE CHRISTIAN CHURCH

The Christian Church in Somerset was the result of a general movement in the vicinity surrounding the town. Before 1840 church members met at different times in groves, apple orchards, and homes. Among the early preachers was the well-known John Smith, familiarly known as "Raccoon" John Smith. In 1840-41 the first house of worship was built on the spot where now stands the Methodist parsonage, formerly the home of Mr. and Mrs. Rucker. (This is the same Mr. Joseph B. Rucker who was at one time editor of the *Somerset Reporter*.) Mrs. Rucker's father, Thomas Smith, held a meeting in this church when he was quite an old man.

In 1842, the noted evangelist, John T. Johnson, effected the first real organization, with five charter members: Elder Jenkins Vickery and wife, Elder Jonathan Dutton and wife, and Lucy A. Hail.

The church remained in this home until about 1848, when, for some reason, the house was sold, and the church in town seemed to have closed. On June 18, 1840, Green McAllister, himself a preacher, deeded to John Cundiff, Willis Eastham, and George Gastineau, as trustees, a lot on which was built the Caney Fork Church, this being the first real church home. This church was finally absorbed by the church in Somerset. In 1865, a lot was purchased from Eben Milton and conveyed to Robert Chesney and Jonathan Dutton, as trustees, for the consideration of $125.00. This was the church on Vine Street which stood just north of the present residence of Judge William Catron. It was a frame building, the modest cupola of which was, until recently, on the back of the Catron lot. The building was dedicated by Green Lee Surber in 1868. At length, this church home was vacated for the brick building on South Main Street. The lot for the new building was donated by Mrs. Pamelia Woodcock Gibson, the mother of Mrs. Lucy Richardson, who was a bulwark for liberality and charitableness in the church as long as she lived. The new

---

[7]The early history was published by the Catholic Church at the dedication.

church was built in 1892 and dedicated by John S. Sweeney on January, 1893.

In 1912, a lot farther down on Main Street was purchased, and a larger church was erected. It was destroyed by fire, and another very commodious and modern building was erected on the site of the building that burned. The present pastor, the Reverend Lee Davis Fisher, has ministered to these people for fifteen years.[8]

The following is copied from the diary of an early Christian preacher, the Reverend James Davis.

> My father was a Virginian, coming to Kentucky in 1847 with Benjamin Fortune, and settled in Madison County. I was educated by a learned Presbyterian preacher. I preached in Madison, Rockcastle, Estill, Laurel, Knox, Lincoln and in 1852 came to Pulaski County, locating on Buck Creek. I first preached at the following places: Salem, Union, Freedom, Caney Fork, Antioch, and in the Reformed Church in Somerset in 1863 . . . The early Christian Church or Reformed Church met with opposition and like all the early churches had their internal discords. Dissolution would take place, and for several years we find they would be without services.

Mr. Davis mentions a letter of recommendation from the brethren of Madison County to be delivered to the elders in the Somerset Church, namely, William Ward and Thomas Hansford.

AN EARLY METHODIST CHURCH

Nancy Kelly, the wife of Samuel Kelly, had strong religious tendencies and inclined to the Presbyterian faith. "Hearing of some meetings held in the vicinity by a Methodist circuit rider, she asked her pastor's advice as to whether she should attend—the Methodists being considered a set of fanatics."

He replied, "If they are all like John Wesley, they are not bad people." She became powerfully converted, and as result of her earnestness, her eldest son was an ardent Christian, becoming a preacher at eighteen years of age.

This son was Clinton Kelly, born June 17, 1808, who was remarkably converted and his preaching drew so many hearers that his room would not take care of them.

---

[8]Information from a published booklet in the possession of Mr. Edgar Murrell.

With his yoke of white steers, he drew the logs and stones and built a schoolhouse where he taught school. He and his brothers, with some outside help, in 1826 or 1827, built a church.

The name of this site was Mt. Gilead.[9]

THE METHODIST CHURCH

The Methodist Episcopal Church, of Somerset, was organized about the year 1830, at which time a circuit was formed called the Somerset Circuit, embracing ten or twelve preaching places. Some years later, a small building was erected on South Main Street and was called the Main Street Methodist Church. This building was completed in 1849. It was on a lot donated by John Curd, the grandfather of W. B. Gragg, and stood on the site now occupied by the Pinnell Apartments. In fact, the apartment building includes the entire church structure.

Near this building, directly to the south, stood the parsonage. It was built of logs, such as housed early settlers in this section of the country. Though consisting of only three rooms, it served the pastor quite well, and was as comfortable as any of the homes of the time. It was not removed until 1915, though it had long since ceased to be used as a parsonage by the Methodist Episcopal Church, South. It had been occupied for years by the caretaker of the church and grounds. Later, the Young Men's Bible Class, in search of a meeting place, used it as a classroom and a recreation center.

When the old log cabin was taken over by the caretaker, a new site for a parsonage was purchased on the southwest corner of East Oak and College Streets. (Incidentally, the parsonage of the Methodist Episcopal Church was directly across Oak Street on the northwest corner.) This College Street parsonage was the church home until the present property on Mt. Vernon Street was acquired. On the new property was a residence (formerly the home of the Rucker family), which was used for a few years, but the house, old and very undesirable, was replaced as soon as it was practicable by the modern structure, now occupied by the pastor's family.

[9]From a booklet in possession of Miss Viola Gragg.

In 1860, not long after the completion of the church building, came the great War Between the States. Somerset, being almost in the center of the great struggle, was used as a base for the wounded soldiers of the Federal Army. During this period the Methodist Church gave its home to be used as a hospital, and for that time the Methodists worshipped with the Presbyterians. When the building was no longer needed as a hospital, the Methodist congregation returned to their own house of worship.

It is a well-known fact that the Methodist Episcopal Church in America was divided by an act of the General Conference in 1844. The various local churches throughout the country, as a natural result, were affected by the division, but for several years following 1844, the Methodist people remained united and continued to worship in the old church on Main Street. The pastors who served the church before the division were: Mr. Emerson, Mr. Robinson, Mr. Smith, Mr. Hudson, and Mr. Zimmerman. Mr. Zimmerman was followed by Mr. Joshua Taylor.

Mr. Taylor, for some reason, thought it wise to effect a division of the local church, and the Methodist Episcopal Church (northern conference) in Somerset was organized about the year 1866. The first church building was erected on a lot donated by Robert Woodcock and occupied the site where the Virginia Theater now stands. It was a beautiful little church, set far back on a shaded lawn, and was a great force for good in the town and county. This property was disposed of about 1918, and the church disbanded.

The first pastor of the Methodist Episcopal Church, South, was the Reverend Morris Evans. Succeeding him were the Reverends John Peoples, W. H. Snively, ——— Emerson, J. N. Current, Clarence Read, and C. C. Newton.

Dr. Newton left this charge and went into the mission fields of China and Japan, where he served for more than forty years as a missionary from this church. At stated intervals, he returned to this country and imparted valuable information on the advancement of the kingdom of God in those fields. He was a great source of inspiration to the home church in carrying on its missionary program. The church feels justly proud that one of her pastors accomplished so much in the mission fields and gained recognition throughout the church and in the nations of the earth as a great missionary. With his passing, the church lost a great spirit, and the mission fields, a sympathizer and friend.

The Reverend ——— Hays succeeded Dr. Newton, and was in turn followed by the Reverends J. R. Savage, in 1885; E. P. Gifford, in 1887; J. H. Williams, in 1888; S. W. Peoples, in 1890; J. P. Strother, in 1891; C. P. Oney, in 1892; and C. H. Pierce, in 1894.

Since 1894 the following have served the church as pastors:

Rev. W. E. Arnold	1895-97	Dr. G. W. Banks	1924-26
Rev. F. M. Hill	1897-1901	Dr. W. P. Fryman	1926-29
Rev. J. M. Simpson	1901-03	Rev. B. C. Gamble	1929-30
Rev. F. T. McIntire	1903-07	Dr. R. J. Yoak	1930-35
Rev. W. F. Vaughan	1907-11	Dr. A. R. Perkins	1935-40
Rev. C. F. Dickey	1911-15	Dr. O. B. Crockett	1940-42
Rev. W. L. Clark	1915-21	Dr. F. D. Rose	1942-47
Dr. J. L. Clark	1921-24	Dr. J. W. Weldon	1947-—

In 1917, under the leadership of the Reverend W. L. Clark, the present church building was begun. The laying of the cornerstone took place on June 24, 1917, and the building was dedicated on Easter Sunday in 1918. The lot on which the building stands was donated by Joe H. Gibson, the great-grandson of the Mr. John Curd who gave the lot for the first Methodist Church in Somerset. The remainder of the church property was bought from the Gibson estate. The beautiful and imposing parsonage, one of the finest in the state, was built during the pastorate of Dr. A. R. Perkins, and makes a perfect home for the pastor in charge. Many of the furnishings are permanent, relieving the pastor of much work when changing charges.

In the earlier years of the church, the principal organization doing local or home missionary work was the Ladies' Aid Society. This society was very active, and practically all the church women were members. It was organized about 1890, during the pastorate of the Reverend J. H. Williams, and included among its charter members Mrs. Bettie Crawford, Mrs. Mattie Gragg, Mrs. H. H. Gragg, Mrs. John Richardson, Mrs. Lucy Bash, Mrs. M. H. Gibson, and Mrs. Elizabeth Whinnery. Succeeding generations carried on very well in this church until the Uniting Conference in 1937, when the three branches of Methodism (the Methodist Episcopal Church, the Methodist Episcopal Church, South, and the Protestant Methodist Church) were united to form the Methodist Church, and the local or home work was included in the larger scope of the Woman's Society of Christian Service of the church.

The general superintendents of the church school have been: James DeHuff, 1863-94; J. E. Girdler, 1894-1918; V. D. Roberts, 1918-22; W. C. Wilson, 1922-23; and E. T. Wesley, 1923-1924.

A. G. Jones was made general superintendent in 1924 and served for several years. He asked to be relieved, and Neil Waddle, the assistant superintendent, became superintendent. After a few years he resigned, and Mr. Jones was again made superintendent. He held the office until September, 1948, when Starling Gregory was elected.

The Methodist Church, born, as it were, in Oxford University, has held its requirements high and has always made great demands of its clergy. Some of the bishops who have served the local church are: Bishop Warren A. Candler, Bishop Henry C. Morrison, Bishop J. C. Kilgo, Bishop W. F. McMurry, Bishop Collins Denny, Bishop U. V. W. Darlington, and the present Bishop W. T. Watkins. All these men have been great educators, as well as great churchmen.[10]

DAVIS CHAPEL A. M. E. CHURCH (COLORED)

Davis Chapel A. M. E. Church (colored) was organized in the late sixties, and a schoolhouse near Allen's Branch[11] served as a meeting place. In 1868, Galen Gibson, a schoolteacher, leased the old Masonic Hall, located on the north side of the Fountain Square, and it was used until June 22, 1875. On that date, Major Nelson, John Gaines, and Galen Gibson purchased the site on which the church now stands, at the foot of Harvey Hill, Main Street. This lot was purchased from Jane Stephenson for the sum of $300.00.

[10]Written by Mrs. V. D. Roberts.
[11]One of the pastors of the Allen's Branch church was Rev. Lewis Fitzpatrick. He was of that age of humble Negroes, but he was physically, morally, intellectually and spiritually superior, and was assuredly the leader of his race in the community. This is by the writer, Mrs. F. E. Tibbals, who knew him personally.

The first known minister was Major Nelson, who was followed by the Reverend David Armstrong. The Reverend Robert Davis was the next pastor, and under his supervision was erected the present church, which still bears his name.

On April 5, 1919, the trustees of the church, Sam Cowan, Sam Fitzpatrick, W. H. Wellington, R. O. Cooper, Dr. E. R. Alexander, Wesley West, and Lee McBeath bought a lot from Mrs. Minnie Stigall for the sum of $30.00 to build the annex.

Some of the pioneer officers, who struggled for the church's survival, were Alex Scott, Wesley West, Sr., Campbell Cowan, Adam Newell, Sam Fitzpatrick, and A. J. Crawford.

Pioneer women workers included Jane West, Frankie Crawford, Grethe (or Geretta) Gibson, Nancy Bogle, Lettie Smith, Harriet Coffee, Nellie Barker, Amanda Williams, Serelda Peters, Amelia Wood, Lizzie Fitzpatrick, Elvin Adams, Catherine Scott, Mary Scott, and Kitty Beaty.

About 1919, under the pastorate of the Reverend E. Kelly, the Mite Society was organized, with Mrs. Munford as the president, Josie Fitzpatrick as secretary, and Sallie Wellington as treasurer.

The first individual communion service was purchased. At the same time, pulpit chairs were purchased. The First Methodist Church (white) donated the bell, the stained glass windows, and the altar rail.

Space forbids mention of all the splendid accomplishments of this church. Among these was the organization of the Home Department Sunday school in 1944 by Mrs. Willie Gover, a granddaughter of Galen Gibson, one of the founders of the present church. The first organist was Mrs. Jennie Morrow, the mother of Governor Edwin Morrow. The Reverend W. H. Mundy has been pastor since 1935. He and his faithful wife, who has modestly, but efficiently, helped him, are shepherding the flock which includes the Deaconess Board, Stewardess Board, and six progressive clubs.[12]

PISGAH CHURCH

A community five miles south of Somerset, on Highway 27, is known by the name of Pisgah. Most of the land of this com-

---

[12]Written by the Reverend W. H. Mundy.

munity was a land grant to one of the early settlers named Quarles. Others who came at an early date and bought from him were John Beaty, Richard Goggin, Charles Hays, John Fitzpatrick, Charles Owsley, and William Stigall. These tracts of land were settled in 1800, but have been divided and subdivided, until today (1950) many of them are only building lots or small plots of ground, from seven to fifteen acres. Interest in this land has been stimulated by the lake created by Wolf Creek Dam. Each day more and more of this land is being taken for airports, parks, boat docks, camp sites, etc.

Pisgah community was built around a small brick church, which had been founded by settlers of Presbyterian faith, and largely of Scotch-Irish descent. According to original church records, the Reverend Joseph Witherspoon came to Wayne County in 1806 and, finding a few Presbyterians, organized them into a church, called the Monticello Church. He became their pastor, but, as is often true, the new church had a struggle to survive: dissentions arose; and, after a few years, Mr. Witherspoon became discouraged and moved to Tennessee. After his departure the Reverends Jeremiah Able, Samuel Robertson, and Thomas Clelland occasionally visited the church, but many members grew discouraged, some died, others went to other churches, and in 1815 this church was dissolved by Transylvania Presbytery.

The Reverend William Scott and the Reverend William Henderson, missionaries sent out by the general assembly, preached for some months in Wayne and Pulaski counties. This situation continued until the autumn of the year 1828, when the remnant of the Monticello Church and fifteen other members who had been received on profession of faith, were constituted into a church by the Reverend William Dickson.

On March 26, 1828, the church was regularly organized, and was given the temporary name of Pulaski County Church. On the same date, two elders were ordained: Will G. Cowan and George B. Cooper.

On July 24, 1828, it was resolved to build a place of worship on the farm of Mr. Richard Goggin, who gave the ground for that purpose. This church was built of brick burned on Mr. Goggin's farm. George B. Cooper, W. G. Cowan, and John Beaty were the trustees of the church to manage and direct its fiscal concerns.

At a meeting in July, 1830, under the preaching of James T. Smith, Brothers Stephen Scott and A. Fitzpatrick were elected ruling elders, and it was decided that this church should be known as the Pisgah Presbyterian Church. Why the name? The mountain from which Moses viewed the Promised Land may have come to the minds of these weary first settlers as they stood on the hill overlooking a beautiful land that was at one time owned mostly by Presbyterians.

At this early date there were (to the writer's knowledge) only three other churches in this section of the county, and this was the only Presbyterian Church. It drew its membership from an area of twenty or thirty miles, a great distance at that time.

An interesting and true fact handed down from that time to living descendants today shows the strict observance of the Sabbath. Often members who lived in Wayne County would have to spend the night with friends. There was no cooking done after the sun went down on Saturday, and if the corn light bread, called "Presbyterian bread," gave out, Irish potatoes were boiled, this simpler cooking being considered a lesser desecration of the Sabbath than making bread. The traditional hospitality was never allowed to intrude on the peace and serenity of the Sabbath.

The following names appearing on the first record of the Pisgah Church are interesting because these people were among the founders of Pulaski County, and many living residents of the county today can trace their ancestry back to them.

Samuel Newell	Mary F. Beaty (Polly Forgey)
Jean Newell	Francis Aldridge
Archibald Woods	Margaret Bain
Mary Woods	Margaret Fisher
Margaret Cooper	Margaret Owens
George B. Cooper	Elizabeth Prather
Jane Fitzpatrick	Stephen Scott
John Long	Margaret Woods
Nancy Long	William Cowan
Robert Modrell	Margaret Newell
Polly Hunter	Tobias Brown
John Beaty	Sarah Brown

Sarah Kennedy	James Gilmore
Anderson Fitzpatrick	Martha Gilmore
Robert Gilmore	George Cooper
Mercy Tomlinson	Elizabeth Newell
Jane Newell	Malinda Fitzpatrick
Zerelda Cowan	Polly Ann Cowan
William Fitzpatrick	Isaac Cowan
Joseph Daugherty	Sophia Norfleet
Richard Goggin	Jane Cowan
Nancy Goggin	Elizabeth Daugherty

Robert Rankin and wife (from Free Presbyterian Church, Scotland)

In October, 1834, the Reverend William Dickson returned to Pisgah as pastor. He was assisted by the Reverend James C. Barnes in a thirteen-day revival, during which fifty-three members were added to the church. Mr. Barnes must have been well liked, for he was urged to become pastor, but it was not until 1852 that the Presbytery released him from his charge at Hanging Fork (Lincoln County) Church.

In June, 1853, he became pastor of the Pisgah Church, and a manse was built for him in the garden of Bourne Goggin, son of Richard Goggin who gave the land to the church. The pastor called this home Garden Cottage. During stagecoach days this became a post office called Garden Cottage. Dr. S. R. Owens was the postmaster.

Pisgah Church was used as a hospital during the Civil War. Pastors who served this church were the Reverends:

Joseph Witherspoon	1806-8	Robert W. Sandy	1860
James T. Smith	1830	A. A. Hogue	1861
William Dickson	1834-36	J. T. Lapslay	1862
T. Root	1837	J. H. Byers	1862-64
———— Stonestreet	1838	H. M. Painter	1866
William Thompson	1839	Charles Hill	1868-78
Joseph Platt	1840	William T. McElroy	1878-82
———— Montgomery	1841	H. B. Zernow	1882-84
A. Wiley	1842	W. E. Williamson	1884-85
———— Williams	1843	J. K. Hitner	1885-88
Henry Thompson	1843-50	Harvey Glass	1888-94
William Pawling	1851	J. R. Cook	1894-98
James C. Barnes	1853-60	William Crow, Sr.	1898-1900

J. Rockwell Smith	1906	C. R. Blain	
Harry Moffett	1906	H. B. Boyd	
W. H. Hopper			

These last five were students from the Presbyterian Theological Seminary in Louisville. They served during the years 1906-10. In 1911 W. H. Hopper, having completed his studies, became a regularly ordained minister, and was called as pastor to Pisgah.

It was during the pastorate of the Reverend William Hopper that the old brick church, built almost eighty-five years before, was razed to its foundations by a cyclone in 1913. The brick fell in such a way that the pulpit, with the open Bible, was left standing while everything else was practically demolished.

After much concern and prayer, the church was rebuilt, on the original foundation, and dedicated in May, 1914, free of debt, by Mr. Hopper.

In 1915 the Reverend W. T. Overstreet was called to the pastorate. He was followed by the Reverends --- McLaughlin, Barclay Watthall, C. F. Newland, Thomas B. Talbot, Sanford Logan, W. W. Astel, A. Erickson, and D. T. Brandenberg. From 1938 until 1942, clergymen from other denominations visited the Pisgah Church, each in turn preaching for a few Sundays.

Then in 1942, the Reverends Joseph B. Ledford, Dan Rhodes, and J. H. Harper filled the pulpit. During Mr. Rhode's pastorate (1942-43), the building of a community center, designated as memorial to the veterans of World War II from this community, was planned. It was carried to completion during the pastorate of the Reverend J. H. Harper, who gave untiringly and unstintingly of his time to this building. This serves the church as a Sunday school classroom, kitchen, and dining room, and it is used for both church and community social gatherings.

D. H. Stigall holds the honor of being the only elder Pisgah ever sent to the Transylvania General Assembly.

The annual home-coming, held the first Sunday in June of each year, with a worship service in the morning, a freewill offering, and a basket dinner served by the women of the church, takes care financially of the cemetery, which is adjacent to the church and where many of the founders of the church are buried.[13]

THE FIRST PRESBYTERIAN CHURCH

The First Presbyterian Church had its origin in the Pisgah Church, which was organized March 26, 1828. The Pisgah Church was the first Presbyterian church in the county. Presbyterians living in Somerset were a part of the Pisgah organization. It was not until 1860 that they had a house of worship in Somerset. In that year a lot was purchased on the corner of Water (now Vine) and Columbia Streets from Mrs. Jane Fox Caldwell for the sum of $100.00. The deed was made the nineteenth day of April, 1860, by Mrs. Caldwell to William McKee Fox and Andrew Gibson, trustees of the Somerset church, and acknowledged before E. D. Porch, clerk. The building was not completed until 1861. The first recorded minutes were dated 3:00 P.M., September 14, 1861. At this meeting of the session, the Reverend A. A. Hogue was chosen as moderator, and four elders were chosen: W. M. Newell, Andrew Gibson, William Harvey, and Samuel Owens. At a congregational meeting following, they were elected and ordained. Four deacons, Samuel A. Newell, S. Owens, T. Milton, and D. Cowan, were elected to serve the Somerset and Pisgah churches, two with Pisgah and two with Somerset, for the Somerset church was still a part of the Pisgah organization with the same pastor serving both churches. The Reverend J. H. Byers was the pastor. Members were:

C. W. Adams	Samuel Newell
Mrs. M. J. Byers	Mrs. Mary Newell
William Harvey	Mrs. Kate Kendrick
Mrs. Barthenia Harvey	Samuel Owens
Thomas Z. Morrow	Andrew Gibson
Mrs. Jennie Morrow	Thomas Gibson
Eben Milton	Mrs. Lou Ingram
Caroline Milton	Mrs. Emma Klingman
Sallie Milton	Thomas Frazure

[13]Written by Mrs. Jennie Newell Hail.

Fountain Fitzpatrick
Sarah Roth
William McKee Fox
Mrs. Mary Richardson
S. Newell
Margery Fitzpatrick

The Somerset Presbyterian Church was a frame building, weather-boarded and painted white. A letter in the church history, written by Ben Zachary Ingram shortly before his death, describes the interior "... with the walnut pulpit and pedestals, on which were tall red lamps, the marble-top communion table, and the walnut-paneled gallery in the back, where the colored members sat."

The Civil War came on, and for the duration of the war no services were held in the church. As were all the other churches, it was used as a hospital for both the Federal and the Confederate armies.

After this lapse of time, a protracted meeting was held by the Reverend J. H. Byers and the Reverend J. T. Lapslay from July 4 till August 10, 1866, first at Somerset and then at Pisgah. At the entreaties of a young lady, Miss Mary Helen Crawford, who was deeply interested, the meeting was taken back to Somerset. The records say: "Rarely has such a revival as this been seen; the people of God were aroused from their coldness and united with the ministers in the great work."

It was in 1888 that the Reverend Harvey Glass came as pastor to the churches of both Somerset and Pisgah. Realizing the need for a full-time pastor, the church members in Somerset petitioned Transylvania Presbytery to organize a congregation to be called the Somerset Presbyterian Church. (The congregation at this time was in regular communion with the Pisgah church.) This petition was granted, and Dr. Glass remained as pastor for twenty years. He was followed by the Reverend J. B. Parke who, in turn, was succeeded by the Reverend James Venable Logan. In 1914, the Reverend Charles H. Talbot was called, and he remained for twenty-seven years. On April 19, 1942, the Reverend Joseph B. Ledford became pastor. He was succeeded by the Reverend J. Harrell Harper, who resigned April 24, 1949, to accept a call to the Presbyterian Church at Georgetown.

During Mr. Talbot's pastorate, in the year 1927, the church was extensively remodeled; the building was brick-veneered; memorial windows were installed; and a kitchen, dining room, parlor, and classrooms were built.

On January 29, 1943, the church was badly damaged by fire. World War II was in progress, and war priorities made it impossible to repair the damage until 1946. The result was a beautiful sanctuary and many additional improvements. The re-dedication was held on August 10, 1947. This is the only church in Somerset which stands on its original foundation.[14]

Ministers who served through the years were the Reverends J. H. Byers, Charles Hill, William Crow, Sr., William T. McElroy, H. B. Zernow, W. E. Williamson, John K. Hitner, Harvey Glass, James Venable Logan, J. B. Parke, Charles Talbot, Joseph B. Ledford, J. Harrell Harper, and John Parks.

[14]Information from the Church records.

Chapter **8**

. . . . *EDUCATION* . . . .

EARLY EDUCATION

Acquiring an education one hundred and fifty years ago was not easy. Conditions were in a chaotic state; the people were necessarily concerned with establishing homes and making a livelihood. However, letters in existence today that were written by some who received their schooling in that period are models in penmanship, spelling, and grammar. Well-kept early records are proof that education was not neglected.

Tradition tells of the one-room log schoolhouse, poorly lighted and heated and badly ventilated, with wooden benches and few books; the children walking through rain and snow; beginners learning the alphabet from letters stamped on wooden paddles.

It took ambition with determination behind it to get an education under such difficulties. Character molded under such conditions was the foundation for the advancement and improvement of the people who fathered prominent lawyers, doctors, preachers, senators, governors, and successful businessmen.

The earliest record of a school was the Somerset Academy. According to Mr. George Shadoan, this academy was located where the colored school is today.

> William Fox, James Hardgrove, Robert Modrell and Jesse Richardson shall be and are hereby constituted a body incorporate and shall be known by the name of the Trustees of the Somerset Academy and permanent seat of said Academy shall be established in or near the limits of the town of Somerset, December 18, 1802.[1]

[1]From *Littrell's Laws* by permission of Mrs. Amanda Hicks.

In 1822 the county was divided into fourteen school districts. According to the first education report in Frankfort in 1829, there were twenty schools in the county and 2,438 children between five and fifteen years of age with only 589 attending school. The average size of a school was twenty-five pupils, the average tuition, $6.74. The average income of each teacher was $75.00 per year.

In 1838, the state legislature enacted a law creating the common school system, with five commissioners to each county. (The only one whose name we have found any record of was Mr. Cyrenius Wait who served until 1852.) Under this school system, schools were taught three months a year and open to children from six to eighteen years of age.

Many of these schools were taught by preachers, who found it helpful to supplement the small stipends of the church with the similarly meager salary paid for teaching.

From various sources we have gleaned the following information about a few of the early teachers.

Mr. J. Newton Davis, who had been educated by a Presbyterian minister but was himself a minister of the Christian Church, preached and taught school in 1849 in the eastern part of the county, at Freedom, Caney Fork, Pisgah, and other places. (Mr. Davis' father had come from Virginia and settled in Madison County.) The Reverend Charles Hill, a Presbyterian minister, and Mr. Samuel Newell III, a graduate of Centre College, also taught school in Pulaski County.

EARLY SCHOOLS IN SOMERSET

An early school was taught in the First Baptist Church by a Mr. Drummond. Another teacher was Mr. Joseph Porter, a Baptist minister, considered to be a man of marked ability and a wonderful teacher.

The following reminiscences are quoted from a paper by the late Mrs. George Sallee.

> I remember hearing my mother talk about a Presbyterian Scotchman, a Mr. Henry Anderson, that taught a very early school which she attended. He was true to his Scotch heritage, a thorough and a fine disciplinarian.
>
> The first school I remember was taught in the old Baptist Church on the hill west of the town spring, by Mr. and Mrs. Dick Grey.

Mrs. Grey was a sister of Mrs. Mary Woodcock and Mrs. W. O. Newell. Several years later a Miss Bishop, a little homely woman with big feet, came from Massachusetts—I guess through the influence of Cyrenius Wait, for he came from that state and was interested in the education of his children. Miss Bishop was an efficient teacher and after her first year she brought a Miss Andrews, who taught the beginners.

We all loved her and tried to be like her. She was quite pretty, and captivated and married our young Presbyterian minister, Reverend J. H. Byers, the pastor of the First Presbyterian Church, 1860. This school was taught in the First Baptist Church. We took our lunches, played under the forest trees, and sailed boats on the little creek that ran just below the hill.

When the War Between the States came, Miss Bishop went home, and all our churches were used as hospitals for the soldiers.

During the war Miss Mollie Milton, who later married Judge W. H. Pettus, taught what we would now call a kindergarten, in a building back of where the Hotel Beecher stands. Later Miss Fromia Vickery (Mrs. George Perkins) taught the primaries in a building in the yard of her beautiful home on the hill, where the Greyhound bus station now stands. This home was called the "St. Charles," from a famous hotel in New Orleans. In her reminiscences she mentions the names of some of those who attended the old Masonic College. George Shadoan, who later became a senator, was our orator. Among the girls were Elizabeth Porch (Shepperd), Mag Shepperd (Moss), Anna Harvey (Mourning), Elizabeth Crawford (Whinnery), Nannie Perkins (Thatcher), Amanda Gibson (Newell), Dora Lair (Thomas), Jennie Sandifer (White), Sallie Sandifer (Parsons), and myself, Mrs. George Sallee.

THE MASONIC COLLEGE

The following excerpt, from the minutes of the Presbyterian Church, is evidence that the Masonic College had its beginning in that church.

June 10th, 1865: On this day the church took into consideration the enterprise of rearing and establishing a high school under the care of our church, in the town of Somerset. Many eloquent speeches were made in support of the enterprise, and all seemed deeply interested in its setup. Committees were appointed to solicit subscriptions for the same.

WILLIAM HARVEY, C. S.

The above date and the date of the purchase of the lot by the Masonic Lodge from William Harvey, himself a Mason, seem to show that he was interested in education and that, through his interest, he influenced the Masons to erect a building which would serve them for a lodge room and also for a school.

Without a doubt this was the beginning of the present school system; its location was the same as the first public school building and was the highest seat of learning until the public school system was established.

We find on the Pisgah Church roll of membership the following names of professors and teachers, who are remembered by old inhabitants: Professor Benjamin Borden (not Presbyterian); Professor Tom Mourning; Professor Frank Reppert; Mrs. Anna Harvey Mourning (wife); Professor Samuel Newell III; Mrs. Mary Bradley Newell (wife); Professor Noel; Miss Emma Borden (daughter), history, disciplinarian; Professor John Montgomery, D.D.; and Mrs. Montgomery (wife), history, English.

SOMERSET PUBLIC SCHOOLS

From its beginning Somerset had some type of educational facilities, which have been modified to meet the changing needs that have come with the growth of the community. At first there were private or subscription schools. Later there was the small district school, supplemented by the private academy; then followed the founding of the state school system in 1838, which served the people of Somerset for half a century.

On April 26, 1886, a petition drawn up by Senator Shadoan for the establishment of the Somerset Graded School was approved by the general assembly. On June 11, 1888, W. J. Davidson, superintendent of Pulaski County schools and later state superintendent of Public Instruction, administered the oath of office to the members of the first Board of Education of the Somerset Public School.

This Board of Education, on March 30, 1889, after very careful consideration purchased for public school use the Masonic building and lot on College Street for $3,500.00. This lot, the site of the present Central Elementary Building, had been bought by the Masonic Lodge from William Harvey, October 22, 1866, for $400.00. On this lot had been erected the Masonic College, a large three-story brick T-shaped building which was the pride of the city. Dedicated in 1867 with a banquet and a dance that lasted for two nights, this building had been used both for private school purposes and as headquarters of the Masonic Lodge. Here in the fall of 1889 the Somerset Public School opened with J. M. N. Downes as superintendent and J. W. Asbury, Miss Lida De Frees, Miss T. A. Parker, Miss Lena Long, and Miss Martha Campbell as the first corps of teachers.

The physical plant of the Somerset school system—the buildings and grounds—has grown consistently with the growth of the city. From one building it has grown to many buildings through the sixty years of its history.

On the site of the Masonic College the present Central Elementary Building was erected in 1891-92. This burned in 1902 and was rebuilt at once. The Carnegie library in 1907 and the high school building in 1912 were added to this structure. The capacity of the high school was doubled by the addition of eight classrooms, a library reading room, and the largest high school gymnasium in Kentucky. This addition, an extension southward, completed and occupied in January, 1937, was erected by the city of Somerset for the Board of Education as a project of the Public Works Administration of the federal government.

In 1891, the present Fourth Ward Building was erected and its capacity was doubled in 1923. In 1903, the present Parker School Building was erected and its capacity was increased by adding four rooms and an auditorium in 1923. This building was named for Dr. J. W. F. Parker who donated the land on which it stands.

In 1926, the Columbia School Building, a four-room brick structure, was erected on a two-acre plot on Columbia Road, donated to the Board of Education by the citizens of West Somerset.

Independent of the white school district the Dunbar Elementary and High School Building on South Maple Street was erected in 1909 by a colored Board of Trustees. It was transferred to the jurisdiction of the Somerset Board of Education in 1920. The old building was replaced in 1941-42 by the present building which was erected by the city of Somerset for the Board of Education as a project of the federal Works Progress Administration.

The Somerset Vocational School, one of Kentucky's twelve trade schools, was added to the Somerset school system in 1942-43 and housed in the former Morrow residence on College Street, which was acquired by the Board of Education in 1941-42. The shop-type buildings were added in 1943-44 and 1947-48. Beginning as a training center for war workers, this school has grown into an institution that serves not only Somerset in training high school pupils but also a wide area of fifteen or more counties in the training of World War II veterans. The Somerset Board of Education operates this school with its corps of ten teachers and 250 students.

The citizens of Somerset have always been justly proud of their school system which is recognized as one of the best in Kentucky. Many things have contributed to its success: the interest and loyal support of its patrons, the untiring efforts of its capable Board of Education, the broad vision and efficiency of its superintendents, and the loyalty and devotion of its trained teachers.

In former years some of the citizens of the community who served as board members were: O. H. Waddle, James Denton, J. C. Ogden, George Wait, and I. B. Powell (who constituted the first Board of Education); William Catron, George M. Reddish, Schuyler Hail, A. J. McCarty, A. W. Cain, George Sallee, Virgil P. Smith, Ben V. Smith, George Elliot, and T. E. Jasper. In more recent years M. H. Barnett, C. B. Hall, W. B. Gragg, H. F. Jeffrey, and R. C. Sievers have served. These men and many more with shorter terms of service have made worthy contributions to the progress of Somerset schools.

In the sixty years of its history the Somerset school system has been under the direction of only eight superintendents: J. M. N. Downes, 1888-93; William S. Maxson, 1893-94; George S. Ellis, 1894-95; A. Livingston, 1895-1902; D. N. Boynton, 1902-4; J. P. W. Brouse, 1904-20; R. E. Hill, 1920-27; and P. H. Hopkins since 1927.

Of the many teachers in the Somerset schools who have served long and faithfully, Miss Amelia Saunders' tenure of fifty-seven years was the longest. Among those who have taught in city schools are: Miss T. A. Parker, Miss Martha Campbell, Miss Elizabeth Harvey, Miss Catherine Keife, Miss Lillie Pettus, Miss Sallie Pettus, Miss Ora Enoch, Miss Adele Dorsey, Miss Viola Gragg, M. A. Tustison, Clay Miller, Mrs. Adella Ramsey, Miss Mae Hail, Mrs. Grace Ragon, Miss Cecil Gooch, Miss Cloda Ashurst, Miss Lina Porch, Mrs. Adele Keeney, Miss Clara Guffey, Miss Margaret Claunch, Mrs. Mary Richardson, Mrs. Lillian Nelson, Edwin Allen, Mrs. Helen Cooper, Miss Freda Baugh, Maurice Christopher, John (John Bunny) Phillips, and Miss Mildred Ellis.

Among the principals of the elementary and high schools who have contributed to the development of this school system are: Miss T. A. Parker, Miss Agnes Scott, Miss Emma Taylor, Miss Sallie Pettus, Mrs. Adele Keeney, Miss Margaret Claunch, Miss Evelyn Sandusky, J. W. Barnett, Mrs. Ralph Hill, C. W. Purdom, and W. B. Jones.

The growth of the Somerset school system during the sixty years of its existence may not have been equaled by any other city of its size in Kentucky. From a faculty of five and an enrollment of 150 it has grown into an institution with a faculty of seventy-nine and an enrollment of 2,000. Beginning in 1894 with a high school graduating class of only one, Mrs. Sam Morrow, nee Miss Fox Curd, there have been hundreds of graduates who have found their places in the life of the community, state, and nation. There were 100 high school graduates in the class of 1948-49, one of the largest in the history of the school.

When Somerset's public schools were first organized the program of studies was traditional and narrow as was that of all such schools in the 1880's. (Only those who looked to college and the learned professions were concerned with high schools.) However, with the turn of the century Somerset began to meet the growing educational needs by broadening and enriching the school program along both cultural and vocational lines. Music and speech were added. The Carnegie library was erected by the Board of Education and became a part of the permanent school plant.

Early in the century, industrial arts courses were added to high school curriculum. Somerset pioneered in this field, probably the first of the smaller cities in Kentucky. First, there was woodwork, carpentry and cabinet making, the printshop, the forge and foundry, and special courses in science and vocational economics. Now the Somerset Vocational School has become a permanent part of the school system with its broad program of trades training. Early in the school system's development, physical education and competitive sports found their place in the program. Now, in the post World War II period, no school system in Kentucky or elsewhere offers a broader program than Somerset.

Sources of information for this article written by Mrs. P. H. Hopkins are:

Early records of the Somerset Board of Education, Minute Books.
Bulletins (courses of study, reports, etc.) published by the Board of Education.
"Pulaski County," A sketch by Miss Martha Campbell published in the *Somerset Journal* in 1934.
"Progress of Education in Pulaski County," A paper by Mrs. Sarah Harvey Sallee, prepared in 1935.
"History of Pulaski County" by Clarice Payne Ramey, 1935. University of Kentucky library.
Many of the older citizens of Somerset.

Chapter 9

NEWSPAPERS, BANKS, HOTELS, OLD HOUSES

NEWSPAPERS

Information concerning early newspapers has been gleaned from different sources and is sometimes contradictory.

Collins' *History of Kentucky,* copies of the *Gazette* and the *Somerset Democrat,* published in 1855 and in existence today, agree that the first newspapers were published between 1850 and 1860. These were four-page six-column sheets and, after nearly one hundred years, are in a good state of preservation.[1]

The *Gazette* was published by John G. Bruce; the *Democrat,* by White, Barron and Company. Oddly, these papers carried news of national importance and very little local news.

The *Democrat* was devoted to politics, news, science, literature, agriculture, amusement, and the markets. One item of interest is "... the second session of the Thirty-second Congress regarding an appropriation for Texas..." [in which Sam Houston took a prominent part]. A London dispatch reveals the following: "At a conference of the Nations at Vienna, overtures of peace from Russia were given little confidence in her proposal war is inevitable." It is interesting to note that the same situation and feelings toward Russia exist today.

The *Gazette* showed an interest in the welfare of the state. It carried articles on the "Progress of Infidelity and Temperance." The editor was recognized as a strong and unflinching friend of temperance, and took an active stand, through his paper, in favor of the "Great Temperance Reform" of that day in Kentucky.

Resolutions were adopted by the order, "Sons of Temperance," recognizing John Bruce's advocacy of temperance, and

[1] Possession of Everett Dagley, Somerset.

bore the signatures of T. Hansford, L. Parker, J. Vickery, J. G. Lair, E. D. Porch, and J. S. Dutton as the committee.

Advertisements were the index of business and citizens. Most of these advertisements were those of Nashville firms, while some were of firms in New Orleans, bearing witness to the fact that the Cumberland River was the artery of commerce. Louisville and Lexington, although nearer, did not have so many advertisements because these towns could be reached only by wagon and ox teams and bad weather frequently made transportation impossible.

The following advertisement is of interest: "M. L. Locke, Marshall Key, Louisville, Importers of China and Queensware from potteries in England." [An appropriate firm name for valuable china.]

Steamboat schedules were given of the "Steamers 'Monticello' and the 'Republic,' from Nashville and Point Isabel."

Stagecoach schedules were listed as "U. S. Mail Line, by stagecoach; Somerset and Stanford, three days a week... leave Somerset five o'clock A.M., arrive Stanford same day at three P.M. Return trips scheduled the same."

Local advertisements were:

James D. Mayhern—Robert Woodcock, Boot and Shoe Manufactory, Vickery Corner.

Walder's Daguerrean Gallery, now open at Stewarts Building, South Side of Public Square.

Robert M. Bradley—O. B. Bachellor, Attorneys at Law.

J. W. and S. M. Hail and Co., dress goods, bonnets and trimmings, hardware, groceries, feathers, ginseng, beeswax, wool and socks.

D. H. Denton, Attorney at Law, opposite the Farmers Bank, Main Street.

Paperhanging, James A. Dunn.

There were numerous rewards for runaway slaves. The following advertisement for reward for a slave was found in the *Somerset Democrat,* dated February 21, 1855. The advertisement was striking and attracted one's attention with a picture of a slave bent forward, walking rapidly, with his belongings swinging from a stick across his shoulder.

$300.00 Reward—ran away from my residence near Clio, Pulaski County, Kentucky, sometime in February last, a negro man named Moses, aged about 35 years, rather heavy built, black color, about five feet, five inches high, voice coarse and rather slow in communication. Said boy has been concealed in the neighborhood by some person or persons until within a few days. There is no doubt but he has been promised a trip to a free state and is now on his way to the South with the thief who is running him for the purpose of selling. I will give the above reward for the apprehension and delivery of said negro and thief in any jail where I can obtain them, or one hundred and fifty dollars for either—if taken in Pulaski or Wayne or the adjoining counties.

JOSEPH B. NEWELL
Clio, Wayne County, Kentucky
November 15, 1854

There seemed to be little local news, however, as most of the items were similar to these examples:

Reverend Josiah Leak will preach in the Baptist Church, in this place, on the fourth Saturday, and the Lord's Day in March.

Married at Mt. Gilead on the 23rd ult., by W. F. Hansford, Esq., Mr. M. L. McClure to Miss Mahale, daughter of Isaac Surber, all of this county.

The *Reporter*, a Democratic paper, was edited by Robert Barron during the Civil War. In 1870 it was sold to W. C. "Red Bill" Owens, who transferred it to Joseph B. Rucker. Mr. Rucker edited and published this widely-read paper until his death in 1892.[2] Mr. Rucker was an advocate of law and order, and at the time of his death he was engaged in a movement to reform and improve conditions in the town and county. He was fearless and outspoken in his editorials. As a result, he was the victim of an assassin's bullet on September 19, 1892, en route from his home to his office. His home stood where the present parsonage of the Methodist Church stands. The assassin was never apprehended. Mr. Rucker's murder was followed by a wave of indignation. Funds were subscribed by the citizens of the town and county, and a monument was erected to his memory in the Somerset Cemetery.[3]

The *Somerset Paragon* was published by William Hansford and his son Essie H. Hansford, during the 1890's.[4]

---

[2]Paper in possession of the Pettus Family, Somerset.
[3]Personal knowledge of Mrs. F. E. Tibbals, Somerset.
[4]Paper in possession of Spurgeon Rainwater, Faubush, dated September 9, 1897.

A copy of the *Reporter* dated July 5, 1894, shows that John S. Van Winkle, who came to Somerset from Danville, was editor and publisher.[5]

In 1899, Flavius Josephus Campbell (called "Seph" by his associates) came to Somerset from Rockcastle Springs (where he had operated a resort) and took over the *Reporter,* changing its name to the *Somerset Journal.*[6] At that time, it was the only Democratic paper in the Eleventh Congressional District. Mr. Campbell edited the paper; his wife, B. B. Campbell, was associate editor; and O. L. Moore was business manager. The publication of May 24, 1907, contained these items of interest: "... trolley lines completed from Woods Crossing to College Street... the organization of a Commercial Club in Burnside, Kentucky, by Mayor Hail... an ordinance passed, naming streets and changing the names of some of the old ones... T. R. Griffin, mayor; E. H. Hansford, city clerk."

After Mr. Campbell's death, his son-in-law edited the paper and later sold it to Woodson May and Robert Brown.

About 1908, Cecil Williams acquired the paper and was sole owner and publisher until his death in 1942. Since then, his wife, Mrs. Mae Berry Williams, has continued its publication.[7]

The first Republican paper after the Civil War was the *Somerset Republican,* started in 1877 and edited by J. M. Hansford. In this paper are found the following advertisements: "G. H. Ensel, dry goods; J. W. Hail and Co.; Beaty and Wait, dry goods; Harvey and Newell, hardware."

A copy of the *Somerset Republican,* dated May 23, 1907, shows Will B. Hansford to be editor and publisher.

Another newspaper, *The Republican,* was started by Jim Hamilton in the 1880's; but he soon gave it up for the more lucrative profession of piano tuning. In 1899 *The Progressive Home Journal*[8] was published by L. E. Hunt in Hunt's Machine Shop, across Monticello Street from Railroad Drive. The staff was: Will C. Owens, foreman, and J. K. Sewell, W. F. Mason, and Fred Hunt. In September of that year, Mr.

[5]Paper in possession of Mrs. F. E. Tibbals.
[6]O. L. Moore, Winnetka, Illinois.
[7]Mrs. Mae Williams, Somerset.
[8]Fred Hunt, Somerset, Kentucky.

Hunt sold it to F. J. Campbell, who merged it with the *Somerset Journal*.

During the 1890's a sheet, *The Hornet*, was published by Kirk Boone. It merited its name.

The *Commonwealth* was launched by William Schooler about 1916 and was later sold to R. M. Feese. Mr. Feese sold it to George A. Joplin, Jr., of Danville, in 1925. In 1934 it was awarded the prize for being the best all-around weekly newspaper in the state.

The following excerpt is from the editorial column of the *Somerset Gazette*, published February 21, 1855.

WHAT UNCLE SAM HAS DONE IN 70 YEARS

Uncle Sam was born a nation seventy years ago—since then he has whipped his mother and one of his brothers; thrashed the Barbary cousins, threatened France and made her pay up, and cleared docks for battle with Austria. He set an example of liberty and popular power, that has thoroughly frightened the despots of the earth and periled their ancient thrones. He has grasped a continent and is covering it with a free, educated, and thriving people. He has built more ships than any other nation in the same time, and his flag is now seen on every sea and ocean, and in every harbor and river.

He has built more steamboats, more railways, more telegraph lines, more schoolhouses, more churches, more cities, bigger babies in that seventy years, than any other nation in five hundred years. And has printed more speeches, and done more bragging than any other nation has done in a thousand years.

BANKS

The first bank was organized January 26, 1818, with Tunstall Quarles as president, and was known as the Farmer's Bank. This was an independent bank. Its charter was repealed February 10, 1820, along with other independent banks of the state.[9]

On November 29, 1820, a branch of the Bank of the Commonwealth was chartered in Somerset and was called the Somerset Branch of Farmer's Bank, and continued to func-

---

[9]Collins' *History of Kentucky*, Vol. I, p. 29.

tion until after the Civil War.[10] It was situated on Main Street near the Public Square. Cyrenius Wait was president (1853-55); early cashiers were John B. Curd, John Lair, and William Goggin (clerk). The directors were William Owens, B. Goggin, A. J. James, S. M. Hail, William Ward, and J. Vickery.

The third bank was the Deposit Bank of Somerset, approved by a committee named in the Act of the Legislature, entitled "an act to incorporate the Deposit Bank of Somerset, Kentucky, on February 12, 1866."

A meeting was called, and met at the Farmer's Bank in Somerset; the stockholders met at ten o'clock P.M. to elect directors. The following stockholders, by proxy or person, were present [figures indicate amounts each subscribed]:

William Owens II	$20,000	Carrie Milton	$100
Walter Owsley	5,000	John Hail	100
Milford Elliot	2,000	J. R. Richardson	100
J. B. Girdler	2,000	C. W. Richardson	100
William F. Scott	2,000	W. McKee	100
Nancy Pettus	1,000	J. E. Cosson	100
J. M. Perkins	500	Charles Adams	100
W. Woodcock	500	William Harvey	100
Samuel Tomlinson	1,000	Eben Milton	100
Sallie Milton	100	W. H. Pettus	100

W. M. Owsley was appointed chairman of the meeting. William Woodcock was elected President, and Eben Milton, Cashier. A proposition from the Farmer's Bank of Kentucky for the banking vault, safe, and furniture was accepted for the sum of one thousand, five hundred dollars. The directors elected were Robert Gibson, William Scott, J. M. Perkins, and Milford Elliot.

May 8, 1871, S. A. Newell as committee of William Owens, who is owner of more than one-third of the stock in the Deposit Bank, the cashier is requested to open a called meeting of the stockholders on Saturday, the 27th day of the present month. On motion of S. A. Newell, committee of William Owens, it is ordered that the affairs of this Bank shall be closed on the first day of October next and the indebtedness of the bank be paid. On the 27th day of May, 1871, the resignation of William Woodcock as President of the

---

[10]Biographical sketch of John Curd, Advertisement, *Somerset Democrat,* 1855.

bank was accepted and recorded. W. H. Pettus was unanimously elected President in the place of Woodcock.

September 30, 1871: Due to much damage to the bank caused by the fire of this year, the cashier offered the bank for sale. A bid of $850.00 was made by S. A. Owens, but Samuel A. Newell being present offered $1,295.00, which was accepted.[11]

In December, 1870, The First National Bank was organized with Samuel Newell III as president. Deposits for the first day were $21,978.68. First stockholders were: Robert Gibson (cashier), William Woodcock, Samuel Newell III, W. H. Pettus, Frank Crawford, John McGinty, J. M. Perkins, William Gibson, Owens Price, J. P. Burke, Smith Cain, G. W. Ingram, W. J. Buster, W. H. Pettus, D. W. Butte, U. P. Moore, William Hubble, M. Elliot, J. R. Ingram, W. A. Colyer, S. H. Tate, J. H. Dye, J. H. Woodcock, M. P. Sallee, Samuel Ingram and R. H. Pettus. The bank went into voluntary liquidation in 1888. A new charter was granted. Samuel Newell III remained as president, and the directors were: O. H. Waddle, G. P. Sallee, W. J. Goodwin, John M. Richardson, George Perkins (Dr.), James A. McGee. Robert Gibson was director and cashier. From 1890 to 1937, J. M. Richardson was president of this bank, James McGee, cashier. From 1937 to 1939 Joe Gibson was president. After the death of Mr. Gibson, Richard Williams was elected president and continues to the present.[12]

The Somerset Banking Company was organized in 1885 with George Wait as president and Robert Hail, cashier. It functioned until 1901, when it petitioned for a federal charter, which was not granted, so it closed its doors. (For further details, see the radio program quoted below.)

The Citizens National Bank was organized February 14, 1920 with Dudley Denton as president. After his death, Judge B. J. Bethurum was elected to that office. He served until his death in 1949, when Colonel J. B. Williams became the president.[13]

---

[11]Minute book of said bank in courthouse.
[12]Records of First National Bank.
[13]Lewis Waddle, cashier, Citizens National Bank.

A Radio Program Given by Harold (Bucky) Cain January 1948 over WSFC, Somerset, Kentucky

Howdy Neighbor: Yes, it's your old friend from the Farmer's National Bank. You know, before coming over here, I was sitting by the radio listening to Somerset's new radio station WSFC. Just happened to tune in on 1240 and heard the strains of that swell old song, and it put me to thinking of years long ago . . . I was a young'n then around 1900 . . .Somerset and Pulaski County were not what they are today. Back then we didn't have the radio . . . we didn't have this and we didn't have that, like we have today . . . you know, where the Farmer's National Bank is located now, back 47 years ago was a modest old brick building, a remodeled old produce house; it was called the Somerset Banking Company. This company, serving the needs of the small community, saw the need for expansion and, holding a state banking charter at that time, petitioned the national banking authorities for a federal charter. The charter was not granted, so the bank closed its doors. Well, realizing the need for another bank in Somerset to serve Pulaski County, John C. Ogden in partnership with John Inman, in the grocery business then, contacted a few other business men and started organization proceedings for the present Farmer's Bank. I believe the records will show that the first meeting of the stockholders was held on May 27, 1901. Yes, I remember talking with some of the men that attended that meeting. They adopted articles of incorporation. These were signed by Judge Sherman Cooper and Dr. A. W. Cain. Well, as I remember, the bank was capitalized at fifty thousand dollars . . . but due to some minor difficulties, the money was not raised on that day, and three men turned to some friends in Boyle County to help subscribe the stock, with the understanding that they would resell later to interested Pulaski County parties. For this help and assistance, the bank was named the Farmer's Bank, for the same name in Danville. Well, they finally got the stock adjusted and stockholders elected H. S. Robinson, James A. Warriner, A. W. Cain, and J. Sherman Cooper directors.

The board of directors then elected J. S. Cooper, president; Dr. A. W. Cain, vice-president; John Ogden, cashier. John Inman (father of Mrs. Maggie Ingram) was elected assistant cashier. At that time, the banks did not have adding or posting machines by which the customers' accounts were kept. They used giant and now obsolete books. All were by hand and in ink. The bank opened its doors for business in the old Somerset Banking Company's quarters, July 9, 1901.

At the close of business this first day, the statement showed that a total of $49.97 in checks was handled and $4,609.82 was deposited. Bank accounts were opened in Louisville, Danville and Burnside.

The bank made its first loan the next day. It was a loan of $50.00. It is interesting to know that the bank's building was carried on the books at $3,581.45, and the furniture and fixtures were carried at $1,622.95 . . . now just one posting machine costs more than all the fixtures this early institution had.

Well, a little later a young fellow just then sixteen years of age, by the name of George Orwin, came to work for the bank. George had on short trousers and was given the job of handling the savings books that had been purchased by the depositors. He also acted as runner and I remember seeing him scurrying over the town to present drafts and collections to bank's customers . . . yes, George grew with the bank and at his death a little over a year ago, had become president of the bank.

Let's see . . . it was in March, 1904, when Edgar Murrell came to Somerset to work in the bank. He came here direct from a business college in Bowling Green. Edgar was given the job of bookkeeper. Like George, he too was to become president of the bank. Well, there were Boyd Morrow, E. T. Wesley, Floyd Wilson, and the ones mentioned that composed the board of directors back then. Say, let's just sit back and listen to a good old song and kindly play it for those old friends of mine that organized and ran the Farmer's National Bank.

These old friends laid a swell foundation for the present Farmer's National Bank. The other day I heard a couple of fellows talking, and they were discussing the bank statement put out by this good bank. Total resources now are $4,622,689.54. The surplus $85,081.27 in the undivided profits account . . . The deposits total $4,344,608. The present board is composed of Claude M. Barker, Harold Cain, Frank Crawford, Judge W. B. Morrow, W. A. Perkins, J. F. Prather, Jr., Finley Tarter, Colonel William Solander Taylor, Miss Eva Warriner, Gladstone Wesley, and Truesdale Wilson.

Instead of the old and obsolete books the bank has the latest and most modern equipment. Just this year a new oil-burning furnace was installed . . . new lighting fixtures add much to the appearance of the lobby and to the efficiency of the bank's personnel. The latest methods of accounting are practiced under the guidance of Will Curtis, cashier, and Kathleen Hill, assistant cashier ... Denton Russel, the note clerk, and Willard Hall, general bookkeeper, practice the teachings of the best authorities on accounting. The customer's accounts are kept by Ula Hail Meece and Virginia Claunch. Nancy Adams handles the savings accounts and her duties as teller in the most business-like manner. Eva Warriner acts as secretary of the board of directors and custodian of the safe-keeping facilities. She also handles the new Christmas Club.

Well, this institution has come a long way since it started back there in 1901, but it is not by itself ... Somerset has grown ... new business has come to town. New neighbors have moved in. I just hope and believe that will continue.

TAVERNS, ORDINARIES, AND HOTELS

On September 24, 1799, one of the first court orders was to "Henry Francis to keep a tavern at his dwelling house in the County of Pulaski with Samuel Newell as his security."

On February 25, 1800, the county seat not yet having been established, we find another, the second tavern license, in an order which follows: "On motion of James Boyle [or Bogle] he is permitted to keep a tavern in his dwelling house in the county of Pulaski, who entered into and acknowledged bond with James Gilmore as security."

Neither of these seem to have been in the town of Somerset. An early tavern in Somerset was run by William Fox.

It seems that the sale of liquor was common—even at that early day when necessary commodities were hard to get—as on this same day a license was granted showing liquor rated as follows:

To whiskey, per gallon	12 shillings
To rum, per gallon	1 pound and four shillings
To wine, per gallon	1 pound and four shillings
To beer, per gallon	3 shillings
To dinner	1 shilling and 6 pense
To supper	1 shilling and 3 pense
To breakfast	1 shilling and 3 pense
To lodging	6 pense

In April, 1801, William George was permitted to keep ordinary at his dwelling. Whether this was the first tavern in Somerset we do not know, as there is nothing to show whether Mr. George lived in Somerset or not.

"Tavern" is defined by Webster as "a house where liquors are sold . . . a house where transient guests are accommodated." An "ordinary" is defined as "a tavern or eating place." We infer that both food and drink could be obtained at either place.

Sometime before the Civil War, the most noted hostelry, the Harris House, stood on the ground now occupied by the Newtonian Hotel, Somerset. Here, with its well-remembered bar, it entertained the travelers and the officers of the court in the days before we had a railroad, when Somerset was reached by the stagecoach and the "kivered" wagon. Many of Kentucky's lawyers were entertained here at that time.

After some years this hotel came into the hands of Benjamin Zachary, then to his son, Judge Charles Zachary; and the name was changed to Zachary House. Then it was operated by the judge's son-in-law, M. E. Ingram, and was known for some time as the Ingram House.

Judge Sim Hicks was the next to run it. He later built a two-story brick hotel—the Hicks House—on the corner of Main and Columbia Streets, opposite the post office. The Hicks House was sold to Mr. Frank Barker in the nineties, and it was operated under the name of the Barker House until it was sold to the Somerset Hospital.

After this time, the Ingram House fell into the hands of Mr. Hampton Brinkley, a prosperous farmer of the Dallas section. He moved into town and built rather a pretentious three-story frame hotel on these grounds and ran it himself for a number of years. After Mr. Brinkley, it went into the hands of a Mr. Hart of Cynthiana, who ran it for several years.

Next, the property was acquired by the Newton brothers, who came here from Campbellsville and built a three-story brick. They conducted it for several years. One of the brothers, Abe Newton, died, and Sylvester Newton became owner; in 1950, Mr. Newton was still owner, although advanced in years. His son Robert was the manager.

This hotel has had the misfortune of being badly burned three times.

On the southeast corner of the square was a hotel, called by some the Cumberland Hotel, and run by Misses Nellie and Elizabeth Griffin. Few facts are obtainable concerning them. Some think it was at one time known as the Zachary House. This seems probable, as the narrow street at that place is called Zachary Way.

Another hotel stood on the northwest corner of the square, where the Masonic Building stands today. A rambling, two-story frame building with porches on three sides upstairs and down, it extended from Main Street on the west to the present site of the Denny Murrel Ramsey Funeral Home. The upstairs was reached by an outside stairway. On the front, in large black lettering, was the name of this really pretentious hotel—The National Hotel. By the time it was torn down in 1884, however, it had become a rat-infested rooming house. It must have been over one hundred years old, judging from the picture taken in 1884 just before it was razed.

The Popplewell House was located farther south on Main Street, across the narrow street from where the Beecher Hotel now stands. It was run by a goodly couple, Uncle Jeff and Aunt Ellen Popplewell, who came here in the eighties from Russell County. After the death of the Popplewells, it was sold to T. J. Candler. It had its flourishing days, but was finally destroyed by fire in 1912.

After the railroad was built, the south end enjoyed prosperous days. A neat hotel was built on the opposite side of the street from the first railroad station. It was built by Mrs. Kate McCabe and run by her. After her death, that building was destroyed by fire in 1888, when the depot and all surrounding buildings were burned. Her daughter, Mrs. Robert Kolker, erected on the same site a three-story brick hotel, which had a long period of splendid patronage. It was known as the Cumberland Hotel. After it was abandoned as a hotel, it was used as railroad offices until the new station was built.

About 1915, J. J. Adams purchased the old buildings at the sharp corner in Main Street at the top of Wait's Hill. He and his daughter erected the three-story brick building that stands there today. It has been known as the Adams House, the Alexander House, and now is called the Kenwick Hotel. It has been used consistently by traveling men in this territory.

There have been smaller places which have been known for their hospitality and splendid service through the years. Among these were The Huskinson House, Mrs. Hatch's (in the south end), The Colyer House, The Candler House, and The Little Inn.

A result of the completion of U.S. Highway 27, from Cincinnati to Chattanooga, was the erection in 1930 of the Hotel Beecher, as a community interest. The cost was more than $250,000.00, with the added amount of $75,000.00 for furnishings—a large sum for that time. A lot on South Main Street was purchased from the Methodist Episcopal Church. The Methodists had begun a building on this site, intended for a church and community center; this structure was used as a part of the new building and is now the spacious dining room of the handsome modern hotel.

This hotel was promoted by a stock company of which Mr. Beecher Smith held the controlling stock. For this reason, the building was given his name, and a life-size portrait of him hangs in the lobby. The progress of over a century separates this modern four-story hotel from the Bob Harris, the National, and the Zachary.

Just south of the Beecher, in the same block, is the Stout Hotel, built in 1946.

OLD HOUSES AND ANTIQUE FURNITURE

The oldest house left standing in Pulaski County is the Vickery house. This house is located on Spring Street, adjoining the Hotel Beecher in Somerset. The land on which this house stands was deeded to Mr. Vickery by Mr. Fountain Fox on March 23, 1839. The house was built in 1839.

What is known as the Andy Crawford home stands on East Mount Vernon Street. This was converted into apartments and covered with stucco. This stucco shell covers the original log house which was built by Mr. Wort, who sold it to Mr. John Crawford in 1855. The original stone chimney and fireplace, which was a part of the slave quarters belonging to this place, stands in the yard and is used for an outdoor fireplace.

Mr. William Fox built the large brick house, known as the Richardson place, on the north side of West Columbia Street.

This house has been converted into apartments and the land which surrounded the original home has become a subdivision known as Richardson Division.

In the Oak Hill section stands a very old house which was built by Mr. Charles Kelly before 1809. Mr. John Montgomery Newell bought this place in 1817 for his home, and it will be remembered as the home of Mrs. Lizzie Sallee Newell.

On the farm of Mrs. J. D. Koger, on Highway 27 south, stands an old brick house which was built for a Mr. Prather. This house was evidently built by a brick mason named Haney, for a brick in the wall near the door has the inscription "Haney 1806" cut into it. The bricks in this are hand molded and were made on the farm. For some years this house was the home of Judge and Mrs. H. C. Kennedy.

The home of Mr. and Mrs. Sam Allen on Highway 27 south, was built by the Owsley family in 1803. This house is also built of handmade brick. A part of the slave quarters is still standing and is used as a garage.

On the east side of Highway 27, on the brow of the hill opposite the Pisgah Road, stands the home built by Mr. William Hays in 1803. Originally built of logs, with stone chimneys and fireplaces, the outside has been covered with clapboards and the inside walls plastered. Mr. Hays sold the place to Mr. Christopher Goggin, and in 1852 Mr. William Newell and his wife, Jane Goggin Newell, bought it. The farm remained the property of the Newell family until 1907, when it was sold to Tom and James Rankin, who later sold it to Mr. Bourne Goggin. This farm is now owned and occupied by Mr. and Mrs. William Tuggle, whose hobby is restoring the house to its original simple beauty and furnishing it with Early American furniture, all of Pulaski Couty origin.

At the top of the Cumberland River Hill on the old Waitsboro Road stands the Newell home. This house was built in 1836 by Mr. George W. Saunders, who sold the place to Mr. William Newell in 1858. The house is built of logs, but through the years has been plastered inside and covered outside with clapboards painted white. Members of the Newell family have lived in this house continuously since 1858, and it has been kept in its original beautiful condition, with modern heating, lighting, and plumbing added. The enormous old stone fireplaces in the original stone chimneys are kept open, and the original handsome old mantels reach almost to the ceilings. The simple stairway remains in the wide central hall, and the original wide ash floor boards gleam with the patina of age. Much of the old furniture is still in use in this home—handsome four-posters (one with a trundle bed), a corner cupboard, Jackson presses, small tables, a beautiful pedestal table, a six-legged, drop-leaf table (banquet) with end tables to match, Hitchcock chairs, and many other pieces that were brought up the Cumberland River from Nashville. This place is now the home of Mr. and Mrs. Henry S. Hail. Mrs. Hail was Miss Jennie Newell.

South of the Cumberland River, at Bronston, stands a house built by John Beaty before 1799 which was used as a lookout post by General Burnside during the Civil War.

The Saunders home, located at Bronston, was built in 1840 by Mr. John Long.

At Elihu, overlooking Pitman Creek, stands the old house built by Mr. William Owens in late 1804 or early 1805. Mr. Owens bought the site from Mr. Edward Mobley, June 4, 1804, and it was part of a land grant issued October 6, 1803. This house is now the home of Mrs. Lum Allen.

On the Elihu Road in the yard of Miss Eva Taylor's house, stands the original home which was built on the land that Richard Price bought from Mr. John Gibson, March 10, 1803.

One of the oldest houses in Pulaski County is the one built by Benjamin Sloan, who came from Virginia about 1798 and settled south of the Cumberland River in the community later named for him—Sloans Valley. Although for many years weatherboarding has covered the logs of which the old home was built, most of the original structure has remained unchanged, and the huge stone chimney is in good repair. The house has never been vacant in the century and a half since its construction. For 125 years it remained in the possession of the Sloan heirs, but in later years has passed into other ownerhip.

In the locality of Shopville, and beyond, are some of Pulaski's most interesting landmarks. Near the Shopville post office and store is a very old stone house, the home of Luther Sears. It is said to have been built by one of the James family, who were among the first people to settle in that part of the county. It has recently been reclaimed by a complete renovation inside and the addition of a porch on the front.

On Fishing Creek stands the pioneer home of Socrates Lee, father of William, Thomas, and DeWitt. A log house, it is now covered with weatherboarding. The first floor has a hall twelve feet wide with a room twenty by eighteen feet on either side, with huge fireplaces and high mantels. The room on the left of the entrance is on the hall level, while the room on the right is four steps higher, conforming to the contour of the ground. A boxed-in stairway leads from the hall to the upper story, which is on three levels.

Not far beyond, on the Mt. Vernon Road, a tree-fringed avenue leads to a fascinating old brick house, in earlier days known as the Evans place. At that time it was an imposing two-story brick, but fire damaged the second story which was not replaced. The inter-married families of Evans, Beaty, Farris, Ford, and Gilmore were associated with this house. Supposedly, it was built by Josiah Evans who died in 1836.

Another handsome house in this locality was built by William Owens II, considerably more than a hundred years ago. The unusual brick trim beneath the eaves, the cherry woodwork (now painted white), beautiful mantels, windows, and doors make it the best piece of old architecture in Pulaski County. A story told the writer by Mr. Jack Bobbitt, ninety years of age, who heard it as a lad, goes like this: "The owner would sit on the upper portico and watch and direct the slaves as they tilled the level acres of his large estate."

Romance of more than a hundred years lingers around the ruins of the James place five miles east of Somerset on Highway 80. Part of the thick walls and four crumbling chimneys show the splendid lines of the structure—time has not marred the beauty of the arched doorway and graceful windows.

A tradition handed down in the James family from one generation to another is that the Reverend John James came here from Virginia and built this house with bricks made from clay found on the place. A descendant says, "He himself did not finish it, for the girl he loved married another man."

However, a descendant of one of the old families who spent their lives in the community says, "John James built it and lived in it."

Chapter 10

.... AGRICULTURE ....

EARLY AGRICULTURE

The story of Pulaski County's farming harks back to the beginning of the county when this land was a wilderness. First, the pioneer had to make a clearing. Because of the action of the elements, the land produced well for a few years only. Then the farmer discarded it and cleared another plot. This method was continued many years until fertilizer came into use in the 1870's. Methods were primitive; there was no machinery. Sowing, cutting of grain, and flailing out seed were all done by hand. Farm life was drudgery—all work with little remuneration. There was no accessible market, and, had there been, the farmer knew nothing of perfecting his products.

Pulaski farmers, like those of many other southern Kentucky counties during the "gay nineties" and even until 1908 or 1910, depended heavily upon the forests for stones and railroad ties to supplement farm incomes.

IMPROVED METHODS

The first soil improvement experiment field in Kentucky was established near Burnside in 1908 by Doctor Scovell, director of the Kentucky Experiment Station and was under the supervision of Professor George Roberts, a native of Pulaski County. The results secured at the Burnside Experiment Field showed that an acid phosphate fertilizer and good crop rotation raised the yield of corn from nine bushels per acre in 1909 to fifty bushels per acre in 1915.

The Pulaski County Boys' Corn Club was organized on March 21, 1910, largely through the interest of the late Mr. John C. Ogden, then cashier of the Farmer's National Bank,

135

and the assistance of Professor George Roberts. The Pulaski Boys' Corn Club was the first in the state to gain much recognition. Truesdale Wilson, of Nancy, a member of this corn club, produced 124 bushels of corn per acre at a cost of $20.28 in 1910, the first year a corn-raising contest was held. Another member produced 121 bushels per acre at a cost of $14.67. The average of the 41 boys who entered the contest was 61 bushels per acre. This was a sensational yield when compared to the county average yield of approximately 20 bushels per acre in 1910.

The influence of a progressive group of farmers in the Nancy, Burnetta, and Faubush communities played a big and useful part in the use of soil-building practices and increasing crop yields throughout the county. Among these farmers were: Mr. W. F. Wilson, Mr. William Dalton, and Mr. James Dalton, of Nancy; Mr. L. B. Weddle, of Faubush; Mr. W. C. Pierce and Mr. George Combest, of Burnetta. These farmers were demonstrators of the importance of liberal use of fertilizer and other sound farm management practices long before Agricultural Extension and other farm agencies came to the county. The cooperation of these men and many others like them was used by the first Extension agents to promote better soil and farm management practices throughout the county.

Pulaski for several years has been the leading poultry-producing county in the state. The beginning of better poultry breeding dates back to the time when the late Mr. George P. Taylor, of the George P. Taylor Poultry Company, invested considerable time and money introducing and distributing purebred Barred Rock chickens to farmers in his trade territory. This project was continued for several years by his son Norman I. Taylor and his assistant William "Bill" Ramsey. In the early 1920's the project was stepped up and applied throughout the county in cooperation with Extension workers. The effective result of this work was shown by the fact that Pulaski chickens shipped from Burnside brought a fancy premium on the New York market.

Since 1900 Pulaski County has been a frontier for two groups of settlers. When the coal corporations began to buy coal land and coal rights in Harlan, Letcher, and Pike counties, a number of farmers from those counties settled in Pulaski. The Noes, Skidmores, the Josephus Carter family, and the Farmer family, all from Harlan, bought farms and settled in the Flat Lick neighborhood. The Sanderses, the Mullinses, the Brittons, the Osbornes, and the Varneys, who came from Pike and Letcher counties, bought good-sized farms in the Goodhope, Walnut Grove, and Eubank communities. As a rule, these families prospered in the new location. They were eager to learn and adopt new and better farm practices. Many of these farmers became good cooperators with the Extension workers and made useful leaders in their respective communities, in their farmers' clubs, and 4-H clubs.

Just before, during, and for some time after World War I, farmers from North Carolina, Virginia, and Tennessee bought farms and settled in Pulaski County. Some of these new farmers moved from communities where more intensive methods of farming were used, and they were good disciples of better farming methods. This group of new settlers, as a rule, bought small farms and settled in the central part of the county, around Somerset and Science Hill. Such well-known families as the Frenches, Stallards, Harmons, Grosecloses, Hillenbergs, Mitchels, and Hawks were among them.

AGRICULTURAL EXTENSION

It was not until 1911 or 1912 that Pulaski County had a program of agriculture with a county agent. A few farsighted citizens saw that it would be advantageous to both farmer and businessman for the farmer to learn better methods of soil production, livestock- and poultry-raising, etc. Through their influence the first county agent was employed, although he was retained for one or two years only. That was the beginning of a new era.

Agricultural Extension work was started in Pulaski on January 1, 1914, when W. Clark Wilson was employed as county agent. The group of citizens who pioneered in the new work and donated the county's part of the funds for the first year were Joe H. Gibson, C. M. Langdon, John C. Ogden, W. H. Girdler, A. W. Cain, J. S. Cooper, B. J. Bethurum, Somerset Milling Company, Eli Farmer, T. E. Jasper, and Elbert Wesley. These men should be remembered for their foresight, hopes, and faith in the possibilities of the Pulaski farmers.

Many of these men lived to see the results of the work they helped to start.

On May 8, 1914, the Smith-Lever Law was passed, establishing Agricultural Extension work and enabling fiscal courts and boards of education to appropriate funds to help support Extension work in agriculture and home economics. The following year, 1915, the Pulaski County Fiscal Court made the first appropriation for Extension work. The court was composed of Dr. Jasper, Esq. (as judge); John Sam Stewart, Esq.; A. T. Spears, Esq.; E. Shelby Griffin, Esq.; C. F. Van Hook, Esq.; ——— Piles, Esq.; ——— Bullock, Esq., and Sid Hargis, Esq.

During the first ten years of county agent service in Pulaski the high points of accomplishment were as follows: farmers' clubs were active in buying fertilizer and selling buckwheat cooperatively; banks were active in placing purebred hogs and cattle throughout the county; purebred poultry (Barred Rocks) was greatly improved and increased in the county through cooperation of the Extension and a poultry dealer. Through the cooperation of the Pulaski County Fiscal Court and the Kentucky Department of Agriculture, lime crushers were placed in the county. Farmers learned the use of ground limestone and its beneficial effects on clover and alfalfa. Four-H clubs grew to approximately one thousand members during these first ten years.

Farm men and women learned the value of Extension work, and through voluntary leadership in adult and 4-H work the people themselves expanded Extension work to all parts of the county. The support and services of local leaders have continued to be of invaluable aid to all Extension workers down through the years.

The following are the county agents who have worked in Pulaski County and their tenures of service: W. C. Wilson, 1914-24; A. J. Chadwell, 1924-27; F. B. Wilson, 1927; M. F. Goff, 1928-34; Ben Marsh, 1935-38; Jack Kidd, 1938-42; J. L. Pidcock, 1942-44; and Hugh Hurst, 1944-—.

During the years he served as county agent, Mr. A. J. Chadwell, a poultry specialist, furthered poultry production in the county by helping to develop better laying-strains of poultry and to establish better housing-management practices. Also, Mr. Chadwell strengthened and expanded 4-H club work and trained a state champion demonstration team. He interested the people of Somerset in the value of Extension work, and their support greatly strengthened the program.

Mr. M. F. Goff and Mr. Ben Marsh served as county agents during the first years of the AAA farm program. The AAA program became a law when farm income was at a low ebb. Extension workers had charge of the AAA program from its beginning until July 1, 1937. These agents, especially Mr. Marsh, bore the brunt of the responsibility for proper execution of the AAA. Payments to farmers for reduction in acreage of corn, wheat, and tobacco ran into thousands of dollars annually, not to mention the thousands paid to farmers for reducing the pig crop. Farmers had to be taught the whys and wherefores of the program and this task fell to the lot of the county agent. Pulaski farmers made maximum use of the AAA program because they were already sold on the use of lime and phosphate, which was distributed under the rules and regulations of the AAA.

Mr. Jack S. Kidd and Mr. J. L. Pidcock came into the county after Extension was relieved of total responsibility for the operation of the AAA program. These men devoted their time to regular Extension work with farmers, and 4-H club activities.

Mr. Hugh Hurst, the present agent, came to the county in 1944. Mr. Hurst's tenure of service is noted for the development of sound farmers' organizations through which farmers are able to help themselves. Some of these organizations are as follows: Artificial Breeding Association, Purebred Cattle Breeders Association, Improved 4-H, and Utopia organizations. In 1948, the "baby beeves" fattened, showed, and sold by the boys and girls of these organizations brought over $40,000.

Today, in addition to being educated in modern methods of farming, the farmer and his family live in a modern home, equipped with electricity which brings water, lighting, refrigeration, laundry equipment, radio, and many other modern conveniences. Because of good quality in production the farmer can demand good prices. This increased income enables him to educate his children, own a car and modern farm machinery, and enjoy life.

FROM RECORDS OF THE EXTENSION SERVICE

The yearly reports are so voluminous and varied that there is not enough space to include them all. Enough cannot be said in praise of the work being done through the Agricultural Extension and Home Economics programs and of the splendid accomplishments through the cooperation of civic organizations.

—1947—

In the early part of 1947, the Pulaski Fiscal Court, led by Judge R. C. Tarter, appropriated an additional sum which made it possible to have a full-time Home Demonstration agent, Mrs. Louise Craig, and an assistant county agent most of the time.

Dairying was stressed at district meetings. Interest was shown by 4-H boys and girls in calves; 145 calves were shown and sold at Louisville for $37,363.

—1948—

CORN

1948, county average yield is 37 bushels—Corn Derby contest to teach better practices, there were 42 entries in one acre, and 26 entries in five acres. Nineteen produced over 100 bushels per acre.

Leaders: Charles Roberts, Harry Stigall, H. S. Hail, E. E. Hackey, Robert Chumbley, W. H. Kirby, W. R. Perkins, Jack Kidd, Maurice Baker, John Tuttle, Raymond Cromer, and John Shadoan.

Demonstration in twelve communities.

TOBACCO

Interest by farmers shown in all meetings and methods. Farmers operated closely with Chamber of Commerce in building and opening the first tobacco warehouse in Pulaski County.

Leaders: Oather Randall, Frank Crawford, Drew Bailey, Joe Davidson, C. W. Waddle, Ernest Webb, Rufus Tarter, Harvey Norfleet, Ezra Pierce, Samuel Cox, N. W. Vansant, Irvil Sayer, W. H. Ping, and Ross Gilliland.

FESCUE GROWING

Leaders: Sam Weaver, Clinton Cundiff, A. B. Roberts, Bob Avera, and Ansel Griffin.

POULTRY

Leaders: John Tuttle, Roy McDaniels, John P. Wesley, Clara Pierce, John Shadoan, W. S. Wilson, Hugh P. Daulton, Willard Norfleet, George Best, Robert Warner, Brent Norfleet, Mrs. Vola Trimble, and Mrs. Nichols.

DAIRY PROGRAM

Organized artificial breeding association—many activities.

Leaders: Glenn Loveless, C. V. Weddle, Delmont Cundiff, Charles Roberts, Frank Newell, J. W. Murphy, Dudley Yehning, Ira S. Edwards, William J. Barnes, Ansel Griffin, and D. G. Hurt.

4-H BABY BEEF PROGRAM

Leaders: Charles Correll, Claude Brown, Nile Cundiff, W. J. Tuggle, William Weaver, Bob Chumbley, and E. K. Cooke.

A picture made on Ross Gilliland's farm shows a large group of farmers, on August 4, 1948, in attendance at a showing of different varieties of tobacco, and discussion of control of diseases.

Splendid cooperation given by: Somerset Chamber of Commerce, The *Commonwealth,* The Somerset *Journal,* First National Bank, American Tire Treading Co., Western Auto Store, Kentucky Utilities, Cumberland River Oil Co., Rotary Club, Standard Oil Company, Farmers National Bank, Kiwanis Club, Younger Women's Club, Somerset B. and P. Women's Club, Ross Kreamer-Burnside Veneer Co., Gulf Refining Co., Pulaski Locker Service, Citizens National Bank, Kentucky Oil Co., Blue Grass Ice Cream Co., and Peoples Bank, Science Hill.

HOME DEMONSTRATION

For about one and a half years in 1924 and 1925 Miss Ouida Cundiff was the Home Demonstration agent in Pulaski County. There were clubs in the following communities: Cundiff, Pisgah, Bronston, Oak Hill, Nancy, Cherry Grove, Vaught, Science Hill, and Camp Ground. Mrs. M. A. Dodson, of Science Hill, was the county president, and Mrs. E. C. Andis, of Norwood, the county secretary.

Excerpts from the diary of Mrs. Henry Hail of Pisgah give an idea of the project work at that time.

[An entry dated] August 28, 1924, Thursday, Miss Pedilue the State Clothing Specialist began teaching us to make hats. We worked until four o'clock.

[An entry dated] September 12, 1924, Friday, [concerning the club in Pisgah community]. Had first meeting of women. Planned to organize a club and make hats next Friday.

Friday, September 19, the women met in our house for an all day meeting, organized a club and started fifteen hats. The ladies brought such a good dinner.

Mrs. Hail, recalling some of the hats made in this project, says, "Mrs. Sam Allen's was of brown velvet and she rushed the finishing of it to go to Cincinnati to sing over the radio. Linnie Newell also made a brown velvet and showed it at the school fair. It had to be left on exhibition overnight in the tent. The dew softened the buckram and ruined the hat. She really was mad for her premium money was not enough to buy material for a new hat."

Mrs. Hail continues by saying that they made dress forms and learned to test materials for durability, shrinkage, color, etc.

After this year and half of work the program was discontinued because the necessary funds were not appropriated by the fiscal court. Even though there was no home demonstration agent, the women were still interested and kept in contact with the state office—always working and hoping that eventually they would again have the program in Pulaski (A Home Demonstration agent is available to a county through the cooperation of the University of Kentucky, United States Department of Agriculture, and the local county. Each supplies funds. It is called Cooperative Extension work. The plan for securing a Home Demonstration agent is similar to that of a county Agricultural Extension agent. Both are employees of the University of Kentucky.)

In 1946 the Farm Bureau, interested citizens, and women began a movement for securing the necessary funds. Because the fiscal court did not appropriate the funds at that time, the following business firms and organizations contributed the necessary $800 for one year: Pulaski County Farm Bureau, Pulaski County Board of Education, Engle Furniture and Hardware Store, Hughes Department Store, Somerset Undertaking Company, Denny-Murrell-Ramsey, Somerset Department Store, Kentucky Utilities Company, Farmers National Bank, First National Bank, and the Citizens National Bank. These funds were available July 1, 1946.

A Home Demonstration agent was not secured until January 1, 1947. She was Mrs. Louise Craig, who came from Franklin, Indiana. She was a graduate of Ohio State University and had been a Home Demonstration agent in Hickman and Carlisle counties, Kentucky, previous to her Home Demonstration work in Indiana.

The people of Pulaski County were willing and ready to carry out a Home Demonstration program. The program grew by leaps and bounds. Clubs were organized in or near all the communities, excepting Cherry Grove, which had clubs in 1924. July 1, 1949, there were nineteen clubs. The county officers in 1947 and 1948 were Mrs. E. C. Andis, of Norwood, president; Mrs. Malcome Coomer, of Cundiff, vice president; Mrs. Ray Foster, of Antioch, secretary and treasurer.

Projects studied in 1947 to 1949 were six lessons in "Guides to Make Your Work Easier," six lessons in "A More Livable Home," one or two lessons each in "Flower Arrangement," "Glass Etching," "Salads," "Gift Wrapping," "Poultry," "Small Fruits," and "Garden and Landscaping." The clubs began a reading and citizenship program in 1948.

The specialists from the University of Kentucky and the Home Demonstration agent give the project lessons to one or two leaders from each club, who come to Somerset for the training. These leaders, in turn, present the lessons to their club members in the home community. The attendance at the training school is always good. The leaders are enthusiastic, alert, and willing to put to practice suggestions for better homemaking and housekeeping activities; their spirit of cooperation is excellent.

On May 2, 1949, the Pulaski County Homemakers were hostess to the Wolf Creek Dam District meeting. Three hundred and ninety-seven Homemakers from ten counties attended this meeting held in the First Baptist Church. Too much cannot be written of the genuine interest and enthusiastic participation of members of the Homemakers clubs, as well as all of the people in Somerset and Pulaski County. An indication of the interest was the increased appropriation made by the fiscal court for the Extension work beginning July 1, 1949. This appropriation is for a part-time secretary for the Home Demonstration agent and a full-time associate county Agricultural Extension agent.

The Home Demonstration agent is also responsible for the economics project work in the 4-H clubs. She assists girls with their 4-H demonstrations, "Dress Revue," and participates in many club activities. In 1949, there were thirty-six 4-H clubs, with 352 girls enrolled. Some of these girls carry two or three home economics projects.[1]

VETERINARY MEDICINE

One who has been of invaluable service to the farmers of Wayne, Russell, Rockcastle, Casey, McCreary and Pulaski counties, is Dr. F. E. Tibbals, the first and only graduate veterinarian in this section of southeastern Kentucky for more than fifty years.

He was graduated from the Ontario College of Veterinary Medicine, Toronto, Canada, in 1894; then returned to Somerset where he has practiced for fifty-five years and is still (1949) in active practice.

He has been veterinarian for the Cincinnati Southern Railroad for more than twenty years.

In 1947, he was appointed by Governor Simeon Willis to serve on the State Board of Examiners, but, due to his advanced age, resigned in 1949.

[1]Information supplied by Mrs. Louise Craig, Home Demonstration Agent.

Chapter 11

......MEDICINE, ART, MUSIC.......

EARLY MEDICINE

We find in early marriage records the names of many of the early preachers, showing that they came along with the first people, but there is no mention of doctors. Those early folk had a good knowledge of curative herbs and "teas," and these were not to be taken lightly. As medicine developed those same herbs were found to be the base of many curative medicines. Concerning the "teas," not so much can be said. Some were harmless and helpful if properly used, but others were not sanitary. "Sheep Nanny" tea, taken every hour, was supposed to cause an obstinate case of measles to break out. A helpful poultice was made of cow manure. The little bag of asafetida, swung by a cord around the neck, was a safeguard against communicable diseases. The midwife was an exalted person in every community. Babies were sometimes fed with food premasticated by the mother. These were not customs peculiar to Pulaski County—they were general.

These "old fogy" customs existed for many years after doctors came. The pioneers of medicine in Pulaski County, who struggled so courageously against difficult conditions with so little, have long ago passed to the great beyond, unsung, and unhonored except for the precedent they set.

If they could look upon the present facilities, they would find ample proof that the struggle they waged against disease and suffering provided the spark and inspiration for medical miracles being performed today.

In the possession of Mrs. Charles Oatts, Sr. is a paper, written and read by her grandfather Dr. S. R. Owens before the Eastern Medical Association in Somerset on June 24, 1879, advocating the improvement of medical education, raising the standards of the profession (there were many "quacks" and some who were not from accredited schools), and contributing to the advancement of medical science, which was still in a more or less chaotic state.

The outgrowth of these early struggles has culminated in the present up-to-date Somerset City Hospital, with its staff of competent doctors and surgeons, demonstrating the strides made in medical science in 150 years of Pulaski County's existence.

Those first doctors were men of great heart, with limited knowledge but plenty of experience—depending on old standbys, such as calomel, quinine, opiates, and a limited assortment of other medicines. They were general practitioners—delivering babies, setting broken bones, pulling teeth (with the crudest of tools), occasionally amputating limbs, nursing in extreme cases, and doing everything that presented itself.

MEDICAL MEN

A Tribute to a Family of Doctors

Written by Mrs. Zena Parker Hill, eighty-six years of age, daughter of Dr. J. W. F. Parker, granddaughter of Dr. John A. Caldwell, aunt of Dr. Sam Fletcher Parker, and grandmother of Dr. John Parker Hill.

John Adair Caldwell, son of G. and E. Caldwell, was born January 29, 1801, and died September 29, 1840. He attended lectures at a school of medicine in Louisville in 1825, having gone there from his home in Boyle County, near Danville, where his father and others from Virginia had settled. A few years after finishing his medical education he came to Somerset and opened an office in a small frame building that stood in the southwest corner of the lot where the present post office stands. He married Jane Pickering Fox, daughter of William Fox. To that union were born four daughters and one son. While his children were small, he sickened and died of typhoid fever.

J. W. F. Parker was born in March, 1825 (died December, 1910), and married the eldest daughter of Dr. John A. Caldwell, Sophia E., in the year 1853. He came with his father's family to Pulaski County from Wayne County. His father owned and operated a mill in the Elk Spring Valley, near Monticello. Citizens in Pulaski requested him to come to Pulaski and build a mill down on Pitman Creek, which he did, and for many years the wheat and corn brought to that mill supplied the breadstuff for the people in that section of the county.

I do not know when my father began the study of medicine, he was always a student. I well remember how carefully he studied the cases that came under his care. In the year 1848 he entered the old School of Medicine of Louisville and when he had completed the course he returned to Somerset to take up his life work, and for almost a half century he went in and out—ministering to the needs of the people, answering the calls night and day, going on horseback over roads at times almost impassable. He rode many miles on the back of "Traveler," that faithful friend in horseflesh, then later, in a buggy drawn by "Brownie," another sure-footed and steady horse. His was indeed a busy life. In the early years of his practice his wife often went with him when her services were badly needed. There were no trained nurses then, and few of the many helps the doctors of today have. Going on horseback with his medicine bags thrown over his saddle, out into the country, into homes where he found conditions under which it was hard, indeed, to do the work required, he carried on his professional duties. There is no nobler profession than that of a good family doctor.

Dr. Sam F. Parker, after finishing his course in medicine in Louisville, came back to Somerset; entered the practice of medicine in the office with his grandfather, Dr. J. W. F. Parker; and for a number of years followed in his footsteps, until he felt the call to the service of his country to which he responded and in which he lost his life. [Additional facts are on page 153.]

Now we are looking with much interest to the time when Dr. John Parker Hill (our own Jack Hill) shall have completed his preparation, having graduated from Emory University, Atlanta, Georgia, May 5, 1948. He is now serving his internship at Atlanta. We are expecting him to carry on in the same faithful and efficient way of those who have gone before. This is an aggregate of nearly one hundred and fifty years of service by the family in the practice of medicine.

The following is a list of physicians compiled from records, papers, recollections of families, and personal knowledge. Unfortunately, it has been impossible to get information concerning all of the physicians.[1]

The first doctor of whom we find any record was a Dr. Thompson. Mrs. E. B. Hill, eighty-six years of age, says, "I remember hearing my mother speak of old Dr. Thompson." In the biography of Dr. J. M. Perkins, we find, "Dr. Perkins read medicine under Dr. Thompson." He must have practiced before 1823.

John Milton Perkins was born in Lincoln County, May 13, 1818. He was the son of Elisha Perkins and Sarah Gooch Perkins. At the age of nineteen years he located in Somerset. He received only a common school education and at the age of twenty he commenced to read medicine under Dr. Thompson. He attended lectures at the University of Louisville for a short time and was regarded as a successful physician. His first marriage was to Jane Fitzpatrick. To that marriage was born one son, George. His second wife was Mrs. Elizabeth Taylor Brawner. One child was born to that marriage, Nannie, who married Thomas Thatcher.

Samuel R. Owens was the son of Samuel and Jane Mercer Owens, who were born in Virginia. They came to Kentucky with their parents, who were among the first people to come to Pulaski County. The subject of this sketch was born September 8, 1824, near Bedford, Indiana, where his parents had moved at an earlier date. Receiving his early training and medical education in Indiana, he came to Somerset in 1849 and married Mary Newell, April 22, 1849. The first entry in his account book was "January 19, 1850, to John Simpson, one visit, four miles, $2.00." Like all doctors of that

---

[1] See article on Dr. George Kerns, Chapter 14, p. 198.

early day, he traveled by horseback—through rain and snow, often fording swollen streams, over rugged terrain—day or night. In serious cases he would stay overnight, nursing the patient, administering the medicine, and frequently eating eggs or potatoes roasted in the open fire. He lived to be seventy-four years of age, and was the father of four daughters and five sons.

W. F. Scott, born March 7, 1828, in Lincoln County, was educated at Stanford. In 1848, he read medicine under Dr. Montgomery, of Stanford, and Dr. Reed, of Houstonville, Kentucky, and attended lectures at Transylvania University, Lexington. He was graduated from Transylvania in 1850 and then located in Somerset. He served in the Civil War as surgeon in the Thirty-second Kentucky Infantry under his brother-in-law, Colonel T. Z. Morrow. Dr. Scott married Margaret, daughter of the noted lawyer, Robert Bradley.

George Perkins, the son of Dr. John M. and Jane Fitzpatrick Perkins, was born in Somerset, October 2, 1843. He was educated in Somerset schools, read medicine under his father, attended three full courses of lectures at Bellevue, New York, and was graduated in 1865. He was the first regularly graduated M.D. in Pulaski County. In 1869, he married Miss Sophronia Vickery of Somerset. Dr. Perkins was director of the First National Bank, a member of the American Medical Association, secretary of the Pulaski County Medical Society, surgeon for the Southern Railroad and actively interested in other enterprises. "Doctor George," as he was known to differentiate him from his father, was an able and successful physician, highly respected for his business ability as well as loved by those whom he served until his death.

Dr. Joseph Lowery Owens, born September 22, 1853, in Pulaski County, was the son of Dr. Samuel and Mary Newell Owens, descendants of Pulaski County pioneers. He married Margaret Garnett Van Arsdale of Harrodsburg, on May 25, 1882. He received his early education in select schools taught by his uncle Samuel A. Newell and the Reverend Charles Hill, a Presbyterian minister. He read medicine under his father, attended Louisville Medical School, and was graduated in 1882. March 1, 1882, he received a certificate for a course on children's diseases from the University of Louisville. After he returned to Somerset he opened an office over Mr. John Richardson's drug store (where the Fair Store now is). In 1888, he was called to visit Mrs. Woods Chestnut, mother of Mrs. Cliff Day. Mrs. Chestnut was in her twenties at this time. He found she had an abdominal tumor, and he told her she could not be relieved without an operation. As operations were rare at that early date, there was a consultation of the local doctors—they all disapproved, but Dr. Owens believed he could perform the necessary surgery. With the full consent of Mrs. Chestnut and her husband, he began to prepare the patient. Then one of the doctors endeavored to get an injunction to prevent him from performing the operation. On April 14, 1888, Dr. Owens operated on Mrs. Chestnut, on her kitchen table, removing a twenty-five pound tumor. This was the first abdominal operation in Pulaski County. Mrs. Chestnut in a statement issued shortly before her death, at eighty years, said: "For three weeks before the operation, I did just what Dr. Owens told me to do, and he personally nursed me afterwards until I was out of danger."

Not long after this Dr. Owens himself was stricken with abdominal trouble; he urged an operation which was performed by Dr. McMurty, of Louisville, in Dr. Owens' home. For a time he seemed to recover; then it became necessary to have a second operation. Dr. Johnson, of Danville, operated the second time, but Dr. Owens' health and vitality were wrecked. After many months he resumed his practice, often answering a call when he was sicker than the patient. During that time he operated on himself—making an incision and inserting a tube to drain the abdominal cavity—with the aid of mirrors and lights, held by his wife. Had he kept his health, he doubtless would have made a successful surgeon; and, as it was, he was one of the first in the state to practice surgery. More than fifty years have passed since he served the community. Those who remember him pay him the tribute, "He was a wonderful doctor."

In the 1880's a Dr. Hopkins came here from Ohio, but remained only two or three years.

About this time another doctor came from Ohio, living three miles south of Somerset on what has since been known as Allen's Branch. This was Dr. Allen who had the first telephone installed in the county—a private line from his residence to a hotel in town where he had an office.

Dr. Joseph Baute, homeopathist, was born in Auglege County, Ohio, in 1862, and attended school in Cincinnati. He become a telegrapher in the employ of the Queen and Crescent Railroad for ten years. At a later date he worked as a clerk for a lumber company at Sloans Valley and studied medicine at the same time. He entered Hering Medical School, was graduated, and came to Somerset in 1903, where he practiced until his death.

Dr. "Ike" Warren came to Somerset from Danville in the late 1880's with his brother Sam Warren, a druggist. No record of his life is obtainable; but he is remembered as an educated man, possessing a brilliant mind. While he was still an active practitioner, he was stricken with cancer of the throat.

Joseph Montgomery Owens, son of Major William and Docta Hobbs Owens, was born March 20, 1865 and died August 15, 1926. Dr. Owens received his early education at Pisgah School. He attended medical school and was graduated from Vanderbilt University at Nashville, Tennessee, in 1885. He spent two years at Barren Fork as doctor for the coal mining company there. While he was there he married his cousin, Molly Owens, of McKinney, Kentucky. He later came to Somerset and practiced until his death. His medical associates recognized his marked ability as a diagnostician and consultant.

Dr. George Reddish was born in Franklin County, October 2, 1854, attended school in Franklin County, and was graduated from the city school in Frankfort. He attended the Louisville Medical College from which he was graduated in 1884. He came to Somerset in 1890 and opened a small hospital in South Somerset in 1893. This was principally a railroad hospital, as he had been surgeon for the Southern Railroad for several years. About the turn of the century he moved to north Somerset where he bought the home formerly owned by Dr. George Perkins on Main Street. Shortly after that he and Dr. A. W. Cain opened a hospital in the building across from the post office. He held offices in both the county and state medical associations. He took postgraduate work in New York City, and he attended with regularity the meetings of the American Medical Society.

He led a very busy life, was a conscientious and useful physician, possessed a genial disposition, and was kindly to, and respected by all. He was enormous in size. One tale I have heard about him concerns a small boy crying in the night with a toothache. His father, in desperation, arose and carried the child to Dr. Reddish. When the doctor—standing well over six feet and weighing over three hundred pounds—appeared, he looked like a white giant in a night shirt. When he was told the lad's trouble, he calmly pushed the tooth out with his finger.

Dr. A. A. Weddle, born in 1879 at Waterloo, Pulaski County, attended Berea College and a school in Bowling Green. He was graduated from Louisville Medical School in 1908, and practiced in the western part of the county until 1946 when he came to Somerset.

Dr. Galen Jasper was born November 25, 1864, at Waterloo, Pulaski County. His early education was in the county school at that place. He was graduated July 10, 1902, from the Kentucky School of Medicine, Louisville. He practiced in the vicinity of Nancy, Caintown, Faubush, and Waterloo until February 9, 1906, when he came to Somerset where he has remained. He is now (1949) eighty-four years old and in good health.

Dr. Sam Scott, the son of Dr. W. F. and Maggie Bradley Scott, was born in Somerset. He attended school at the old Masonic College on College Street when Dr. John Montgomery was principal. He married a Miss James in 1892, entered Kentucky School of Medicine, and was graduated in 1892. After practicing in Lexington for six months, he returned to Somerset where he assisted his father.

Dr. Leonidas Hughes, the son of Spencer Boyd and Sarah McBeath Hughes and the youngest of their four children, was born May 15, 1874, in Russell County. His parents, who came to Kentucky from Virginia, both died before he was nine years of age, and he was cared for by an older sister with the help of a former slave family. He taught school for four years in Russell County and entered the old M. and F. College at Columbia, Kentucky, through written examinations. He enrolled in medical school in 1885 at St. Louis, Missouri, received his M.D. in 1889, and returned to Faubush, Pulaski County, where he maintained an active practice until he retired January 1, 1947. During his forty-eight years of strenuous work, he delivered approximately five thousand babies—frequently to three generations of the same family. He married a neighbor girl, Otilla Woolridge, August 27, 1899.

Colonel Sam F. Parker, U.S. Army, the son of Joe Caldwell and Nannie Hines Parker, was born June 2, 1882, at Somerset. He was graduated from Somerset High School, and attended Kentucky State College, now the University of Kentucky. After receiving his degree at the Louisville School of Medicine, he returned to Somerset where he practiced with his grandfather, Dr. J. W. F. Parker. In 1917, he volunteered for the U.S. Army. He served in Hawaii where he commanded the first school of gas warfare for the Hawaiian Department. He then went to Camp Lewis, Washington, and San Francisco, California. In 1923 after the earthquake in Japan, he was detailed to service with the United States Relief Expedition. For a time he was stationed in the Philippines, then at Western Reserve University, Cleveland, Ohio, as an army instructor. He went next to Jackson, Mississippi, where he became the first commanding officer of Foster General Hospital. His wife was Marguerite Sallee of Somerset. His death occurred February 6, 1945.

Dr. W. R. Cundiff, born in Pulaski County, attended the county schools, and was graduated from the old Hospital College of Medicine, Louisville, in 1907, where he specialized in ear, eye, and throat work. He first practiced in Stearns; then came to Somerset to open an office in 1922. He practiced in Somerset until his death in 1952.

Dr. R. C. Sievers, born in Pulaski County, attended school at Nancy, and a normal school. He was graduated from University of Medicine, Louisville, in 1908. He practiced for a coal company at Silersville and the Stearns Coal Company. He came to Somerset in 1921; he was a captain in World War I.

Dr. Brent Weddle, a native of Pulaski County, received his education in the county schools, Berea College, Bowling Green Business University, and the University of Louisville Medical School. He opened an office in Somerset in 1930.

Dr. Volantus Green Trimble, born April 9, 1877, in Somerset, is the son of Henry Green and Colanza Trimble. He married Zada Tate, daughter of Robert M. and Cordelia Hunt Tate. He was graduated from the University of Louisville Medical School in 1909.

Dr. Charles L. Waddle, born 1880 in Pulaski County, is the son of William and Maria Ham Waddle. The youngest of fourteen children, he was nicknamed "Charles the 14th." He received his early education in the Oak Hill county school and was graduated from Somerset High School in 1899. A graduate of the Louisville School of Medicine, he practiced medicine in Somerset until his death in 1946.

Dr. C. E. Farmer, born in Pulaski County, had his early schooling in the common schools, attended Louisville and Chicago Homeopathic Schools, and was graduated in 1909. He located in the county first; then opened an office in Somerset in 1917.

Dr. A. J. Wahle was born in Louisville, attended a Portland parochial school in Louisville, and was graduated from University of Louisville Medical School in 1908. He came to Somerset in 1911 and opened a hospital in 1914 on the corner of Cotter and South Central Avenues.

Dr. Eugene Beard came to Somerset from Bradfordville in 1918. He was a graduate of Transylvania College, Lexington, and of the Louisville School of Medicine. He opened a hospital on College Street known as the Pulaski County Hospital. He was surgeon for the Southern Railroad for several years. He married Valeria Smith, the daughter of Beecher and Mayme Elliot Smith.

Dr. Robert F. Jasper, a native Pulaskian, received his education in the county schools and at Berea College. He was graduated from University of Louisville Medical School in 1908. After practicing for several years in the county, he came to Somerset in 1941. Later, he was graduated from Baptist Theological Seminary with a Th.D. degree. He was county judge in 1914-18, a lieutenant in World War I, and a representative to Frankfort 1947-48. He is a doctor, preacher, lecturer, war veteran, and politician, belonging to the Republican Party.

Dr. E. M. Ewers, born January 20, 1885, at Anchorage, is the son of the Reverend A. E. and Marie Morrison Ewers. He was graduated from Kentucky Institute at Mt. Vernon, in 1902; received a diploma from Maryville, Tennessee, 1909; earned an M.D. degree from University of Louisville, 1915; and interned at Presbyterian Hospital, Puerto Rico, 1915-16. He married Ruth Schaefer in 1916 and was a medical missionary in China, 1916-31. He served as the first health officer of Pulaski County, 1931-33. His days of private practice date from 1933. He is an elder in the Presbyterian Church.

Dr. Robert Gibson Richardson, a descendant of Pulaski County pioneers, was born May 6, 1888, and is the son of John (Jack) M. and Lucy Gibson Richardson and the grandson of Robert and Pamelia Woodcock Gibson. He attended public school in Somerset; at the age of thirteen years, he entered a private school for boys in Cornwall, Connecticut, and later enrolled in Ohio Military Academy, Cincinnati. He received his A.B. degree at Centre College, Danville, graduating in the class of 1908. He took his medical course at Hering School of Medicine in Chicago Homeopathic Hospital. He opened an office in Somerset in 1914 and practiced until 1918 when he volunteered in World War I. He received officers' training at Fort Benjamin Harrison and entered the service as a second lieutenant of infantry. At the end of the war he resumed his practice of medicine in Somerset. In 1942, he married Elizabeth Thatcher Waddle, daughter of Thomas Muir and Nannie Perkins Thatcher.

Dr. M. C. Spradlin, son of William Daniel and Ola Mae Shumate Spradlin, was born August 14, 1909, in Louisville. He was graduated from Louisville School of Medicine in 1931. He married Lillie Thorpe and opened an office in Somerset, 1933. He saw military service with the U.S. AAF, August, 1942 to February, 1946, largely in western Canada and Alaska as station surgeon at bases of the Air Transport Command. He returned to Somerset at the close of the war.

Dr. E. T. Smith, born in McCreary County, received his early education in Stearns High School. Later, he was graduated from Transylvania College, Lexington; and, in 1943, he was graduated from Louisville Medical School. He came to Somerset in 1947.

Dr. Morris Holtsclaw, a surgeon, came to Somerset from Stanford in 1940. Educated at the University of Kentucky, he was graduated from Emory University Medical School, Atlanta, Georgia. He was in the service during World War II, 1940-45. He was discharged with the rank of colonel and returned to Somerset just at the opening of the new hospital in 1945.

Dr. O. L. Herrin was born at Mt. Vernon, was educated at Berea College, and was graduated from Palmer School for Chiropractors, Davenport, Iowa, 1929. He came to Somerset in 1938.

Dr. A. L. Cooper was born at Jefferson City, Tennessee, and was educated at the University of Kentucky, and Rush Medical College, Chicago, in 1922. He served in World War II with the rank of lieutenant colonel. He came to Somerset in 1946.

Dr. R. S. Jasper was born in Pulaski County and attended school at Harlan, 1933-37. He was graduated from University of Louisville Medical School in 1941, and came to Somerset in 1946. He is the son of Dr. Robert Jasper.

Dr. Robert C. Bateman was born at Springfield, April 14, 1913, and received his elementary education in Bradfordville, Lebanon, and Springfield schools. He attended Centre College for one year in 1930-31; four years at University of Kentucky, where he was graduated in 1935 with a B.S. degree; then four years at Tulane Medical School, New Orleans, from which he was graduated in 1939 with an M.D. degree. He interned at French Hospital during his senior year and entered internship at Good Samaritan Hospital, Lexington, 1939-40. He entered the armed forces November 1, 1940, in the Forty-seventh Medical Battalion of the First Armored Division of Fort Knox and went overseas to Iceland in May as battalion surgeon with the First Armored Division of Field Artillery. Later, he went to England, took part in the invasion of Iran, and served through the African campaign. Still later, in a hospital at Biloxi, Mississippi, in conjunction with another doctor, he was in charge of obstetrics and gynecology for over a year. He came to Somerset in December, 1945, and opened his office, January 1, 1946.

Dr. J. F. White, born at Attala, Alabama, was graduated from Attala High School and National School for Chiropractors in Chicago. He came to Somerset in 1939.

Dr. A. B. Morgan was born at Tanksley, Clay County. He is a graduate of Oneida Institute, Kentucky School, Union College, Bowling Green Business University, and University of Louisville Medical School. He came to Somerset in 1946.

Dr. E. V. Weddle was born in Pulaski County in 1911, was graduated from Somerset High School in 1931, and attended University of Kentucky, 1931-32. He finished at Eastern State Teachers College, Richmond, in 1936, and interned at Louisville City Hospital. He opened his office in Somerset in 1945 after serving one and one-half years in the U.S. Medical Corps, World War II.

Dr. McLeod Patterson was born July 18, 1915, at Talladega, Alabama; grew up at Sylacauga, Alabama; was graduated from high school at Miami, Florida, 1932; and attended the University of Florida, 1932-39. He interned at Charity Hospital in 1939-40 and held a residency in medicine three years (1940-43), which was interrupted by five years in the U.S. Army. His principal assignment was as a surgeon on army transport ships with three years' sea duty. He was discharged to the reserves as a lieutenant colonel and opened an office in Somerset in 1949.

Dr. Richard Hunt Weddle, born April 17, 1912, is the son of Claude and Grace Waddle Weddle, of Somerset. He was graduated from Somerset High School, 1930; University of Kentucky, B.S. degree, 1936; University of Cincinnati Medical School, M.D., 1941. He is a Fellow of the American College of Surgeons and American Board of Surgery, saw service in World War II as a major in the U.S. Army Medical Corps, and was awarded the Soldier's Medal and Legion of Merit. He returned to Somerset to practice surgery, November, 1949.

Dr. Robert McCleod, a native of Andalusia, Alabama, was graduated from Davidson College, Davidson, North Carolina, in 1942 and from the University of Pennsylvania Medical School, Philadelphia, in 1945. He interned at Lankenan Hospital and Mary Drexel Children's Hospital in Philadelphia, was in the service from 1946 to 1948, specialized in pediatrics at Walter Reed Hospital, Washington, D.C., and came to Somerset and joined the Clinic Staff, January 1, 1950.

About 1916 or 1917, J. C. Anderson, Negro, came from Tennessee and built a large two-story building a little southeast of Somerset in the edge of Ferguson. He designated this as a sanatorium, and with a corps of nurses, one or more of whom were white, operated it for several years. He was not a registered M.D., but had a reputation for effecting many cures. People from far and wide came to him to be treated for various ills.

After he left Somerset, the building he erected was used as a tuberculosis hospital for many years. After thirty years, there are few people who remember this doctor, although he made a great impression on the community.

During the 1930's, an Indian doctor, known as Dr. Rabbitfoot, located in West Somerset. He did not make the spectacular display that Dr. Anderson did, but sold medicine which he made from native herbs.

Dr. Carl Norfleet, Director of Public Health in Pulaski County, was born in Faubush and graduated in 1905 from the old Hospital College of Medicine, now the University of Louisville Medical School.

After serving as a captain in the Army Medical Corps during World War I, he returned to Pulaski County in 1929 and became surgeon and general manager of the Somerset General Hospital. He held this position for twelve years. In 1946 he became chief of staff of the new Somerset City Hospital and holds that position at this time. Dr. Norfleet has been a member of the Pulaski County Board of Health for over forty years and has been a district councilor of the Kentucky State Medical Association. For over ten years he has served on its medical-economic committee.

On October 3, 1951, the Kentucky State Medical Association conferred their distinguished service award on Dr. Norfleet.

MEDICAL MEN OF BURNSIDE

Dr. Littleton Cook came to Burnside about 1880 as the first licensed Doctor of Medicine to locate in the village. He had the first drug store in the town. While he was building up his practice, he courted and married Miss Lelia Owens, whose sister was the wife of Dr. J. M. Owens of Somerset. Dr. and Mrs. Cook built a big log house on Highland Avenue (the present home of Mrs. John Sloan). This house was erected according to the old custom of a "logrolling with dinner served on the grounds." Later, the house was covered with weather boarding. Anna Cook and Fred Taylor Cook were born in the house next to the Norman Taylor home, but Mary Shepherd Cook was born after the family moved to Stanford. She married Dr. Jesse Perkins, a dentist.

Dr. George M. Reddish moved to Burnside from Greenwood (then in Pulaski County), occupying the Dr. Cook home. Dandridge Reddish, prominent Lexington physician and surgeon, was born in this home.

Dr. Nicholas D. Stigall was born at his parents' farm on the Waitsboro Road near Bronston, February 14, 1863, the son of Fontaine and Fannie Tucker Stigall. Fontaine Stigall, also a native of Pulaski County, was born December 10, 1813, and married Miss Tucker January 22, 1850. Fontaine Stigall, a son of Thomas Stigall (a native of Virginia who married Miriam Harris), was one of the pioneer settlers of the county. Fannie Tucker Stigall, wife of Fontaine, was the daughter of John and Elizabeth Tucker. John Tucker was a soldier in the War of 1812.

Nicholas D. Stigall was the seventh child in a family of ten children: George B., Ballie, Thomas, Nora, Coleman, John, Nicholas, Elizabeth, Mattie, and Will H. Nicholas received a good common school education and at the age of eighteen taught school in the Antioch neighborhood for two years. In 1884 he worked in Burnside's one drug store on Main Street. He married Laura Golden, daughter of John and Celia Gibson Golden, July 15, 1885. She died about 1903, and is buried in Burnside Cemetery. One son, Clarence Golden Stigall, was born to this union.

Dr. Stigall studied medicine with Dr. Littleton B. Cook, the only physician in Burnside, and later attended the Medical College in Louisville. He opened his office in 1891, making a success of his profession. He was known to all citizens as "Doctor Nick."

On June 6, 1906, Dr. Stigall married Grace Virginia Lawrence, of Dayton, Kentucky, the daughter of John King and Patty Beaty Lawrence (the latter was born near Antioch and was a daughter of William Beaty, an early settler in southern Pulaski County). To Dr. Stigall and his wife was born a daughter, Virginia Lawrence Stigall, present postmistress of the Burnside office.

Dr. Stigall was a devoted member of the Burnside Methodist Church, Master Mason, Somerset Knights Templar, and the Mystic Shrine. He died at his home in Burnside, December 2, 1944, and his wife passed away on October 22, 1948. Both are buried in the Burnside Cemetery.

Dr. John Stigall, the sixth child of Fontaine and Fannie Tucker Stigall and the older brother of Dr. Nicholas Stigall, was born at the family home on the Waitsboro Road near Bronston. He received his medical education in Louisville. Known to all as "Doctor John," he began his practice in Burnside in 1888 or 1889, and was known in the surrounding territory as a fine doctor. Although his health was not of the best, nothing prevented him from answering calls, day or night.

He married Nannie Frost, daughter of James Alvin and Lettie Frost. No children were born to this couple. Mrs. Stigall preceded him in death. "Doctor John" passed away in the 1930's and is buried in the cemetery at Somerset.

Dr. T. L. Gamblin, who came from Clinton County to Burnside to reside about 1895, built a small private hospital, practicing there until his death.

Dr. John B. Vigle, who attended Wesleyan Academy in 1896-97 and later entered the Medical College in Louisville, had a large practice in Chattanooga, Tennessee. He practiced for a while in Somerset, then came back to Burnside in the 1930's, and had a large following in the community in 1949.

Dr. Joseph H. Horton came to Burnside in July, 1933, with his wife Mary Louise Cropper Horton and daughter Helen. A son, Joseph Hubert Horton, Jr., was born July 25, 1945. Dr. Horton passed away in October, 1946, as the result of a heart attack.

Dr. Charles Salyer and wife Bobbie Dyche and daughter Patricia came to reside in Burnside in August, 1948. He is a skilled physician, and his wife, who is a nurse, aids him. He is the only M.D. in Burnside in 1952.

Henry Hawkins Bishop, M.D., born in 1882 at Hustonville, is the son of Josiah and Belle Ware Bishop. He married January 24, 1906.

Dr. Lura Lipper, of Hustonville, was graduated from the University of Louisville School of Medicine, June 30, 1905; came to Burnside and was associated with Dr. Gamblin; left Burnside in October, 1909; went to Oklahoma; specialized in urology, New York City; practiced in Louisville, eight years; entered tuberculosis work in 1940; and was located at Western Sanatorium, Arkansas, in 1949.

DRUGGISTS OF SOMERSET

Evidently there were no early drug stores in the county; doctors carried their medicine in "medicine bags" thrown across their saddles, and administered drugs themselves, leaving their patients powders which they measured on the point of a pocket knife. Each dose was folded separately in a paper, like a cigarette paper. The doctor became adept in measuring and folding the doses and cheering the patient at the same time.

It was not until 1888 that registration became a law—thus, this list of druggists is from personal knowledge: John Crawford, 1846; S. R. Owens, 1867; John Richardson, 1882; Ben Neat (later member of Peter, Neat, Richardson, Wholesale Druggists, Louisville), 1884; Tibbals, L. S. and F. E. (Johnson's Block), 1886; Green Cundiff, 1888; C. S. Porter (President of the Kentucky Pharmaceutical Association), 1890; Sam Warren, 1890; R. M. Morrow (South End), 1896; Sam Denham (South End), 1900; J. C. Kelsey, 1930; R. M. Feese, 1934; M. C. Williams and Son, 1904; Tibbals Drug Company (Jas. H. Allen and W. H. Tibbals), 1905; Anderson (Grider)-Wesley (Parker), 1950; Pulaski Drug Company, 1950; Somerset Pharmacy, 1950.

ART AND HANDICRAFTS

Although Pulaski County has never produced any artist of marked ability, there have been some who have done creditable work. The history of this people deals more with their struggle to survive. The rough terrain and lack of communication with outsiders has tended to isolate them in thought and deed. Their contribution to art was more the homely things that made their life comfortable and picturesque.

In old scrapbooks, more than a hundred years old, are found faded water colors. On the walls in many homes hang portraits—some in oil, others in crayon. Also there are paintings of both still life and animals; these were all made by native Pulaskians.

There was an era of china-painting, and at another time the old arts were revived: weaving, knitting, quilting, and hooking rugs. In some homes are found priceless coverlets and counterpanes, the wool and cotton being produced on the farms and the patterns often designed by the weaver. In the earliest days quilts were made for service, from old scraps of calico, but later they became works of art. For the last half-century, quilt-making has progressed from a necessity to a decoration.

The interest in reclaiming old furniture has developed latent talent in cabinet makers. There are many reproductions of the early furniture. A very beautiful reproduction is a grandfather clock made by the late George Elliot. Due to the isolation of many of the early homes the original furniture has been retained and used up to the present time. These early cabinet workers produced furniture which compared well with any made in this country during that period. It is sturdy and of simple Early American design.

MUSIC

Reckoning as far back as the sixties, Pulaski County has been music-minded. The date when the first musical instruments were brought to the county is not definitely known. John G. Lair was said to have bought the first piano and it was hauled by ox teams. As early as stated above there were those who played the dulcimer, guitar, flute, and violin.

With the passing of the years parents become interested in the educational and cultural development of their children. While sons received professional training in colleges; daughters were sent to boarding schools. Here they received special instruction in music.

Before the rural communities and town (because of roads) became closely associated, there were singing schools, or classes, held by itinerant teachers who used a tuning fork to give the "pitch." These classes were held in the churches or schoolhouses.

The heyday of the Masonic College was in the late seventies and eighties. A room on the second floor was set apart as the "music room," and Miss Ellen Ballou, of Stanford, and Miss Lena Long, of Springfield, Illinois, taught piano and voice.

Through the years Somerset has had excellent teachers who have sent out pupils who received recognition elsewhere. Among these teachers have been: Dora Lair Thomas, Nannie Perkins Thatcher, Miss Emma Bash, Mary Morrow Portwood, Miss Ida Tomlinson, Lelia Gooch Reddish, Nancy Waddle Joplin, Mrs. Robert Waddle, Miss Virginia Catron, and Miss Elgie Woods. Burnside has had talented musicians, among whom Miss Virginia Stigall, the present postmistress, is one who has been outstanding in music circles for many years.

There are those who have always called Somerset their home but have received recognition elsewhere: Joe A. Thomas, Sam Adams, and Todd Duncan.

Joe Thomas, the son of William Orlando Thomas and Dora Lair Thomas, was born July 27, 1891, at Somerset in the home (on Harvey's Hill) of his maternal grandparents, Captain John G. Lair and Harriet N. Lair.

Joe's early years were so personally interesting they are worthy of mention. When he was nine years of age he was a newsboy delivering the *Courier-Journal*. At this time his mother attended the Louisville Exposition and one of the main attractions was the famous Liberati, cornet soloist. She was delighted with his solos and hoped that some day her son could play like him. He, Joe, said, "I never reached his peak, but I did play in Liberati's Band, in Lexington at the Blue Grass Fair, August 16, 1913."

When Joe was still a youngster his mother bought him a secondhand bugle. He learned some of the bugle calls, by ear, and practiced on the front porch. The neighbors were very tolerant. The only complaint came from Mr. Jake Weddle, down at the next corner. He said, "How about giving us a rest, Joe?" But Mr. Weddle's daughter Stella banged on the piano, and Vida strummed on the violin, so he could not condemn Joe. The bugle came to grief, and Joe's next instrument was a cornet his mother brought from Cincinnati. He was so delighted with it that he took it to bed with him for some time. Greater grief came to it than to the bugle. Training taken two summers, however, in Warren, Ohio, enabled him to become a member of the Somerset High School Orchestra. The first money he made was for playing in a revival at the M. E. Church.

His first real lead to a colorful musical career was in 1908 when he became band leader for a dramatic company out of Worthington, Indiana. After many successes he was billed with different stock companies from the Pacific to the Atlantic, including Washington, D.C., Atlantic City, Lowell, Massachusetts, New York City, and even in Europe.

He played to millions of people, including such celebrities as the Prince of Wales and Enrico Caruso. According to London papers his company, known as the Joe Thomas Saxotette, made an enormous hit in London. Other tours took him to Scotland, to Paris, and to Spain. After talking pictures came, vaudeville began to limp and then died. This company played its last show on the fairgrounds at Hutchinson, Minnesota.

Sam Adams, the son of Charles Adams and Ida Newell Adams, was born in Somerset, was graduated from Somerset High School and from University of Kentucky in 1924, and attended the Conservatory of Music, Cincinnati, where he studied under Dan Beddoe five years. During this time he was a popular singer over radio station WLW.

He later went to New York and entered Columbia University where he studied under many eminent instructors, and received his Master of Music degree.

He sang with the New Opera Company, New York, and with Rudy Vallee; he appeared in many Broadway shows, including "On the Town."

While in New York, he was much in demand as a church soloist, singing in some of the largest churches. The beauty and pathos of his fine tenor voice was evidenced when, in New York, a passerby heard, stopped, and entered a church where he was singing "The Holy City," and later wrote Sam he was converted by the song.

Besides possessing an excellent tenor voice, he is an accomplished pianist and violinist. At this time, 1950, he is assistant professor of music in Western Michigan College.

Todd Duncan, born in Danville, spent the formative years of his life in the home of his grandfather, Owsley Cooper, a bricklayer, and his step-grandmother Mattie Wheeler Cooper, in Somerset. Here he attended school until, at the age of thirteen, he was sent to Louisville where he attended school.

He was professor of music at Howard University, having received his training at Butler College in Indiana. He later received his Master's degree at Columbia University, New York.

The baritone voice of Todd Duncan has been filling American theaters and concert halls since 1934. In 1935, George Gershwin signed him for the male lead in the musical drama, "Porgy and Bess." As Porgy, he skyrocketed to fame.

He played an eighteen-month run in London's Drury Lane Theater; in 1938, as Bosambo in "The Sun Never Sets"; in 1940, as the Lawd's General in "Cabin in the Sky."

He has toured Canada, Latin America, Scandinavia, Europe, Australia, and New Zealand with brilliant success. He was the first Negro singer in operatic history to sing a white role with a white cast when he was engaged by the New York City Opera Company to sing in "Carmen."

Probably his greatest triumph occurred when, after diligent search by directors, he was sought out in Australia (where he was singing under contract) and asked to return to New York to take the role of Kumala—interpreting, in song and drama, the tragedy of the oppressed people of South Africa—in the production, "Lost in the Stars."

Undoubtedly, a feeling of incomparable pride and humble satisfaction filled the heart of his grandmother when this play was presented in Louisville on October 16, 1950, and she sat in Memorial Auditorium with the cultured and admiring throng. She saw and listened to this man who as a child had slept in her bed, played in her yard, and on whom she had bestowed her love. Through her kindness and training she had influenced the life of a great artist.

Chapter **12**

...THE DEVELOPMENT OF SOMERSET...

After the town of Somerset was located in 1801, it grew slowly. Few important changes were made until later years. In the early days Spring Street (Vine) was the main street and continued so for many years. It was so called because of its nearness to the main water supply, the town spring.

Business, which consisted of a tannery, a wagon factory, carding machine, and a factory for making wool hats, was located along this street; also, the stocks and pillory, and the pound (for stray stock) with a lock and key, were built here.

The first dwellings, which were mostly of log, were erected along Spring Street also. The last of these early houses, the old Jenkins Vickery home, was torn down in September, 1950. The town was incorporated in 1810, but the population must have been very small, as in 1830 it was only 231. It continued to grow until the time of the Civil War at the following rate: in 1840 it was 283; in 1850, 412; in 1860, 662.

Later a few business houses were located south of the Public Square, among them being Silas Hail, and Wait and Withers. Their stock of goods, according to a paper of Cyrenius Wait (in possession of Mrs. Ruth Wait Tuttle), consisted mostly of jeans, old-fashioned calico, a sack of green coffee, a hogshead of sugar, a barrel of New Orleans molasses, powder and lead, and dishes.

The first raw silk in Kentucky was produced at Somerset, January 10, 1842,[1] by Cyrenius Wait. It was said to have been made at the George Shadoan place (now "The Pines") on East Mt. Vernon Street, which Mr. Wait built and where he lived until he moved to the top of Wait's Hill.

The first public well was dug in the town in 1865 in the middle of the Public Square. Old inhabitants say this well

---

[1]Collins, *Ibid.*, Vol. I, page 47.

furnished water for families living as far away as the top of Harvey's Hill. It furnished water until cisterns came into use in the early 1870's.

In 1870, Somerset contained a courthouse, jail, clerk's office, six churches, an excellent school (Masonic College), seven stores, one hat shop (owned by Mrs. Sarah Jane Gossett), one drug store, and three hotels. Six lawyers and five physicians had offices in Somerset. All of these places had a stile block and a pile of wood in front of them.

The first walks were made on the Square about 1842, but there is no mention of what type they were. In 1880, there were some worn brick walks, some boardwalks, and some cinder walks. (This information was furnished by Mrs. George Elliot.)

Somerset was incorporated as a city March 13, 1888, by an Act of the General Assembly, and its form of government changed from the trustee system to that of mayor and board of council.

On March 15, the same year, voters chose Abe Wolfe, a Jewish butcher, to become Somerset's mayor. The following is a list of Somerset's mayors and their terms of office:[2] Abe Wolfe, 1888-90; Barney Higgins, 1890-92; James Colyer, 1892-94; T. R. Griffin, 1894-98; Dr. J. W. F. Parker, 1898-1902; T. R. Griffin, 1902-14; James L. Waddle, 1914-18; George Cruse, 1918-22; W. C. Norfleet, 1922-46; and Andrew Offutt, 1946——.

CITY SERVICES

Until the early nineties, Somerset depended on springs, wells, and cisterns for water, and on kerosene lamps for lighting. The first information regarding the installation of water and lights is vague. Some old citizens recall the year 1891 or 1892 as being the time the work was done, but the first authentic information found is from a notice in the *Somerset Reporter,* dated July 5, 1894, "All water rent will be due July 1st. The collector will call at the house of the consumer by the 4th. [Signed] JOHN A. GEARY."

Captain Geary was the man who installed the water system for Somerset.

[2]From the city clerk's records.

In the city clerk's records are claims for attendance at fires in February, March, and July, 1898. "An ordinance was adopted January 28, 1908 for a Horse and Buggy Fire Department with voluntary firemen." This horse and buggy moved too slowly, and the hose cart, pulled by the volunteers, was more often used.

On August 31, 1905, a twenty-year franchise (the first franchise recorded) was sold to the Somerset Water, Light and Traction Company, with Godfrey Hunter as president. At a later date it was transferred to the Kentucky Utilities.

On February 27, 1905, a franchise by ordinance was granted to O. H. Waddle to operate an electric street railway system in Somerset. This streetcar service ended with the advent of automobiles about 1923; the tracks were removed at a later date.

Before public telephone service came, there was a private line erected in the eighties by a Dr. Allen from his home three miles south of Somerset to his office in the hotel which stood on the northeast corner of the Square, probably the Brinkley Hotel.

The first franchise for telephone service was granted August 9, 1897, under the supervision of T. R. Griffin, mayor, to A. D. Shotwell and J. B. Upton to erect and maintain a telephone exchange in Somerset. This is said to have been located in the old Gem Opera House, now the Kentucky Theater, in the rooms over Emil Jarmer's Tailoring Shop.

On September 24, 1906, an ordinance was passed to authorize the city council to accept bids for building sidewalks on all principal streets, with artificial stone or concrete (sidewalks previously were made of brick), under the supervision of Mayor T. R. Griffin.

Permanent streets of rock asphalt were constructed under the supervision of W. C. Norfleet, mayor. Work on them was started in the year 1922, but inclement weather delayed their completion until 1926.

The first natural gas franchise was sold November 24, 1930, to the Keengreen Utilities Company of Kentucky under the supervision of Mayor Norfleet.

An ordinance was adopted January 6, 1940, for the building of a sewage system and disposal plant. About 70 per cent of the work had been done when World War II interrupted it, but at the close of the war, construction was completed.

Somerset's development for more than fifty years has fluctuated. The town has seen good times and bad times. She has passed through depressions: probably the one following the national bank crisis in the year 1930 was the worst. The upswing following World War II brought her to her peak of growth and achievement.

While the corporate limit has never been changed, building has spread in every direction. Business has encroached on residential streets, until the peace and serenity of the porch is gone.

An unofficial census of 1940 was a conservative 8000. An official census of 1950 was 7,068; but the outlying areas, comprising the school district, would place it at an approximate nine thousand.

HOSPITALS

The first hospital in Somerset was started by Dr. George M. Reddish in 1893 in South Somerset.

A small hospital on Main Street, almost opposite the present post office, was operated by Dr. J. W. F. Parker and Dr. A. W. Cain.

The Somerset General Hospital, on the corner of Main and Columbia, opposite the post office, was operated by Dr. Cain and Dr. G. M. Reddish. Dr. Carl Norfleet managed this hospital in later years.

On College Street, Dr. Eugene Beard operated a hospital which was primarily the Southern Railway Hospital. This was opened about 1920.

Dr. Wahle owned and operated a hospital on the corner of South Central and Cotter Avenues for a number of years, closing in 1947.

These have given place to the present ninety-bed City Hospital, which was completed in 1945. It is located at South Central and Bourne Avenues. It is modern in every way and is supplying the needs of McCreary, Wayne, Russell, Casey, and Pulaski counties.

SOUTH SOMERSET

When the railroad came, Somerset extended only to the top of the hill south of the Square. This hill has been known for one hundred years as Wait's Hill, so called for Cyrenius Wait, who owned a large tract of land on both sides of what is now South Main Street. He built and lived in the house on top of that hill, and his descendants occupied it for more than a century.

There were two other houses along the road leading south: a one-room log house which stood in the bend at the foot of the hill; and, at a short distance on the same side of the road, a small frame house where Tom Shepperd and his wife, Elizabeth Porch Shepperd, lived.

Farther on, where Griffin Avenue and Jacksboro Street intersect today, was another log house in which Fount Shepperd and his wife, Elizabeth Withers Shepperd, lived. Here they began rearing a large family which was closely connected with Somerset for nearly one hundred years. Mrs. Maggie Moss, the last of the family in Somerset, died March 1945, at the age of ninety-three years.

Another old house stood at the top of Monticello Hill, near the city limits, and was known as the Hayden, Sam Newell, and Dr. F. E. Tibbals place. It was built of logs, but was weatherboarded and from time to time was added to and modernized until 1926, when it was destroyed by fire. A church stands there today.

To the writer's knowledge these were the only houses in what is now South Somerset until 1878, when the railroad was completed and the first passenger train went through Pulaski County.

The citizens wanted the railway station built nearer the town (of that time), but, because the site for a station, tracks, etc., was donated, it was built a distance of one-half mile from the courthouse.

The tract of land between Wait's Hill and the depot belonged to Cyrenius Wait, who used it for farming purposes for many years. For these reasons the town was divided, becoming known as North and South Somerset.

Railroad employees and transient travel brought more business and additional interests. Houses began to spring up everywhere, and streets were laid off, Bourne and Griffin Avenues being the principal ones for a number of years. A boardwalk connected the two parts of the town. Leading south from Griffin Avenue was a part of the old Jacksboro Road mentioned in Chapter VI under "Roads."

In 1885, R. A. Johnson (Dick) erected a large two-story business building at the intersection of Monticello and South Main Streets, known as Johnson's Block. There were four business rooms, drug store, hardware and furniture store, and two general stores. The second floor was used at different times as an opera house, skating rink, and dance hall. This burned August, 1913.

The growing population called for more conveniently located facilities. A business block took form, across the street from the railroad station, in which were located the McCabe Hotel, a drug store, a bank, a small hospital, several stores, two churches, parochial school, and an elementary school.

In this same part of South Somerset, across the railroad tracks, were the Electric Power Plant, Somerset Ice Plant, George P. Taylor Produce Company, R. J. Smith Wholesale Grocery Company, Hunt's Machine Shop, a coal yard, and another elementary school.

South Somerset was a very busy place in those years. Later the electric streetcar system was built, then the automobile came into universal use. This caused a swing to the main part of town, and many businesses moved nearer.

SOMERSET—1949

If the pioneer forefathers, whose ashes rest in and near this community, could look over the battlements of heaven, they would gaze with astonishment at the development of the little wilderness settlement they called Somerset. We cannot but admire the courage, perseverance, and virtues of our progenitors when we contemplate the obstacles they surmounted, the hardships they endured, and the unshrinking purpose which turned a wilderness into fruitful fields and established a town that has grown to be the "Queen City of the Mountains."

The comparative population, wealth, resources, and progressive improvement in Somerset has made us learn, to some extent, to appreciate the value of those blessings of political and religious freedom secured to us by the sacrifices made by our ancestors. The legacies of the past have made the present bright for us.

Somerset, lying in the foothills of the Cumberlands, is no mushroom growth. It is built in many sections, and in order to get an idea of its magnitude it is necessary to traverse great distances. Many of the oldest houses have been torn down to make way for business progress, or the estates have been subdivided, and where formerly there was only one home, now many new modern houses have been built.

The approaches to the city are an east-west federal highway, a north-south federal highway, and the Cincinnati Southern Railway (this maintains shops near Somerset). A matter of immense significance to Somerset's future is the proposed erection of an airport at an early date. The land for it has been purchased.

Of greatest importance to the city are its schools and churches. In addition to an excellent system of public graded schools for white and colored, the Catholics are completing a parochial school which is not excelled by any such school in the state. As is to be expected in such a quiet, refined, cultivated community there are numerous churches: Baptist, Catholic, Christian, Methodist, Presbyterian, Nazarene, and Church of God. The Christian sentiment pervades every phase of the city's life.

The city scores high in health facilities with a wide-awake, efficient public health director, sanitary inspector, and registered health nurses.

Banks are always good indices of the financial situation and the First National, Farmer's and Citizens Banks, with their capable, energetic, successful officers, and personnel, are business concerns to which the citizens of Somerset may point with pride.

Chain and independent stores do a fine job in meeting the needs, individual whims and tastes of the people. Competition sees to it that service is good and prices are as low as possible.

Economic development in the past five years has been phenomenal.

A radio station was erected in 1947 and its first broadcast was on December 14, of that year.

Other new enterprises important in the growth of the city are the Goodall factory, creamery and ice-cream factory, city disposal plant, International Minerals and Chemicals Corporation, tobacco warehouses, City Hospital, Girl Scout cottage, Medical Clinic, Singer Sewing Machine Center, armory, Pulaski County locker plant, swimming pool, Rural Electric Administration office, Home Demonstration Agent, and the Highway Mobile Post Office started February 1, 1949.

Civic clubs, literary clubs, lodges, Chamber of Commerce, Medical Society, Boy and Girl Scouts all reveal splendid community organizations.

The city government is conducted economically and in a business-like manner by a mayor and six councilmen. Utility service is good and recreational facilities are increasing year by year. When the lake formed by the opening of Wolf Creek Dam is completed new recreational facilities will be available.

I despair of giving in this article an adequate summary of all the advantages to be found in Somerset today. Not only does it offer rare inducements to the investor, but it is a delightful place to call "home."

It remains for capital, combined with public spirit and enterprise, to develop the resources and bring Somerset to an approximation of its possibilities.

May it continue to provide education and enlightenment for aspiring youth, implanting in them lofty ideals and noble purposes, and remain a beacon light to succeeding generations.[3]

[3]Written by Elizabeth Pettus Meadors.

Chapter 13

..... *PULASKI COUNTY CITIZENS* .....

MEN

Sherrod Williams was a popular member of Congress, 1834-41.

Andrew James, a distinguished lawyer, was representative in the Kentucky Legislature, 1855-57, and secretary of state, 1872-75.

Galen Bishop, who went to St. Joseph, Missouri, and became a famous physician and surgeon, was the grandson of Dr. Galen R. Elliott, one of Pulaski's pioneer doctors.

Judge John Sherman Cooper, Sr., served as school superintendent of Pulaski County, as county judge, eight years as collector of Internal Revenue, and four years as railroad commissioner, being chairman of the board.

George Roberts has been Professor of Agronomy, University of Kentucky, for many years.

Gilbert Glass, D.D., Presbyterian minister, in 1915 was appointed director of Religious Education and editor-in-chief of all periodicals in the Presbyterian Church, United States, serving until his death in 1934 at his home in Richmond, Virginia.

Edwin P. Morrow and his twin brother, Charles H., were born in Somerset November 30, 1877, in the house which stood on the site of the present post office. They were identical twins, except for a mole behind Charles's right ear; and, until their divergent careers separated them, it was difficult to identify them correctly. They were educated at St. Mary's School near Lebanon, Kentucky.

At the age of twenty-one they entered service during the Spanish-American War. Edwin was commissioned a second lieutenant, serving with the Fourth Kentucky Regiment.

At the close of the war, he returned to Kentucky, continuing his education in law. He was graduated from the Law Department of the University of Cincinnati in 1902. After coming back to Somerset, he practiced law until 1909, having served as city attorney during that time.

He was appointed United States district attorney for eastern Kentucky by President Taft. In 1912 he was the Republican nominee for the United States Senate, but the Democratic nominee was elected over him. In 1915 he was the Republican candidate for governor, but was defeated by A. O. Stanley by 471 votes. Four years later, in 1918, he was again nominated for governor and was elected over James D. Black by more than 40,000 votes. His administration was considered a very successful and constructive one. He took the penal institutions out of politics by appointing a bi-partisan Board of Charities and Corrections.

Governor Morrow was chosen to notify Calvin Coolidge of his vice-presidential nomination in 1920. He traveled with Mr. Coolidge when he toured Kentucky for the Republican ticket that fall. The members of this touring group were Governor Hughes of Illinois, Governor Morrow, and two or three other notable men.

They had an appointment in Somerset—the place chosen for the meeting was the Gem Opera House (now the Kentucky), the hour, 8 P.M. Long before the hour set, every seat was filled. The time came, but no speakers appeared. Nine o'clock came. A message from the railway station informed the assemblage that the train bearing the party was behind time and it might be two or three hours before it would arrive. This announcement caused a silence to fall over the crowd, but only for a moment; then the cheers went up for "Ed." The result was that the entire house remained. Impromptu speeches were made until eleven o'clock, when a stir at the entrance notified the waiting crowd of the arrival of the touring party. The walls reverberated as they cheered for their favorite son; nor will they forget how he, in his appreciation and happiness, responded to these friends in his home town.

He died of a heart attack in the home of his cousin, Mrs. Christine Bradley South, in Frankfort, June 15, 1935. With his death there vanished from the scene of Kentucky politics one whom nature fashioned for public life. Much is known of his public life, but a tribute to his personal life by James Tandy Ellis is peculiarly touching.

It was a sad realization that former Governor Morrow had slipped from the anchor post of home out upon the great stream of Eternity. Friendship is the only thing in the world concerning the usefulness of which all mankind are agreed. Politics were forgotten when you fell into the company of Ed Morrow—his hearty laugh was contagious, and set an assembled company in good cheer. He had the old-fashioned interpretation of Kentucky life; its coloring; its humor and its pathos; with native oratory he could recall the undying glory of his beloved state ... the vines clinging above the doors of humble cabins; the happy voices of barefooted children; all revived in charming sweetness under his eloquent tongue.

Mr. Ellis further says:

I was his guest at the Belmont Hotel in Chicago once. One morning I said to him, "Governor, it is a great thing to have served as the Governor of Kentucky." He laughed and said, "But my greatest ambition has never been fulfilled." "What is that?" I inquired. "Well," he said as he gave vent to a hearty laugh, "I have always wanted to own a country hotel in Kentucky, where I could carry the market basket, go fishing, and swap yarns on the porch with the drummers."

That was the unique side of Ed Morrow. He married Katherine Waddle, daughter of O. H. Waddle, one of Somerset's leading lawyers.

His body was laid to rest in the historic cemetery at Frankfort.

Charles H. Morrow, as has been stated, entered the Spanish-American War and was commissioned a second lieutenant of Company I of the First Kentucky Volunteer Infantry. At the close of the war, seeking a military career, he re-enlisted and was commissioned second lieutenant of a company of volunteers who served in the Philippine Insurrection, 1899. In

1901, he was commissioned second lieutenant of the United States Army regulars. He made several trips around the world with these soldiers and was stationed for a long time in the Philippines. He, with his regiment, was sent to China as a representative of the United States and the Red Cross to take charge of relief work in one of China's worst floods. During World War I, he was in command of the American Expeditionary Force in Siberia and was highly commended for his treatment of prisoners during the war. During 1932-33, he raised funds to restore Old Fort Niagara. In 1932, he was made commander of Fort Niagara in New York with the rank of colonel.

After the war the bronzed colonel returned, wearing a double row of honorary and campaign medals and ribbons, beginning with the Croix de Guerre and ending with the American Victory Medal.

He died of a heart attack, just as his twin brother had a short time before.

On a day during Ed Morrow's campaign for governor of Kentucky, Charles happened to be in Somerset.

A man from the adjoining county, Wayne, accosted him in a jovial way, but received only a nod. The man was incensed by this curt nod and in an insulting manner said, "When you are in Wayne County, you shake hands with me and eat with me, but when I am in Somerset you do not know me."

Charles, very much taken aback, replied, "I never saw you before." An argument followed, with Charles saying he was not Ed Morrow, and the man refusing to believe him. Whereupon Charles, realizing this episode might injure Ed in the election, said, "Ed is speaking in Louisville today. If you will go with me, I'll take you there and prove I am not Ed Morrow."

The writer was told this was done.

John Sherman Cooper, Jr., the son of John Sherman Cooper and Helen Tarter Cooper (both from native Pulaski families for four generations), and a son of whom Pulaski can justly be proud, was graduated from Somerset High School in 1918, attended Centre College, and was graduated from Yale University and the Harvard Law School. He represented Pulaski County in the legislature one term, served two terms as county judge, volunteered in World War II as a private and was discharged with the rank of captain.

He served three years overseas and, after the war, presided over a European court trying war criminals. While overseas he was elected circuit judge of the Twenty-eighth Judicial District. In 1946 he was nominated and elected United States senator from Kentucky, filling out the unexpired term of Senator Chandler. In the Democratic landslide of 1948, he was defeated by Virgil Chapman.

On September 14, 1949, President Truman appointed him as a delegate to the United Nations Assembly to represent the United States in the settlement of world affairs. No higher commendation could be given than that by his colleagues in the Senate.

Senator Wiley of Wisconsin reviewed his career as county and circuit judge, soldier, and senator, adding: "an able lawyer, a keen thinker, a warm personality, a sincere man with an humble approach to life, a deeply religious man, and a loyal Republican in whom there is nothing of the partisan. I found him to possess a keen mind, a lofty appreciation of what is legally right, and never did he hesitate to throw himself wholeheartedly into his work."

Dr. Arthur W. Allen, internationally famous surgeon, the son of James and Emma Arthur Allen, was born and reared in Somerset. He was graduated from the Somerset High School with the class of 1906; and received his Bachelor of Arts degree from Georgetown, Kentucky. He was graduated from John Hopkins University in 1913 with a Doctor in Medicine degree.

For many years Dr. Allen has resided in Boston, Massachusetts, where he was formerly connected with the Massachusetts State Hospital. Since 1947 he has been President of the Board of Regents of the American College of Surgeons, and President of the Medical Society and Council in Surgery, Massachusetts General Hospital.

He was chosen a Fellow, Royal College of Surgeons in 1947, one of the highest honors that can be paid a member of his profession, and that year was presented at the Court of St. James in London.

He married Miss Vida Weddle, the daughter of Mr. Jacob Weddle and Elizabeth Ware Weddle.

Louis Ware was reared in Somerset where he was graduated from the Somerset High School. He was graduated in Mining Engineering from the University of Kentucky and located for a time in Arizona; from there he was sent to South America as a representative of the Guggenheim Foundation. At the present time, 1949, he is president of International Minerals and Chemical Corporation.

He is the son of Charles P. and Nora Lynn Ware. He married Boyd Morrow, of Somerset, and makes his home in Evanston, Illinois.

George Reddish entered the field of chemistry. He developed mercurochrome and other antiseptics.

W. J. Davidson served as school superintendent of Pulaski County and as state superintendent of Public Instruction.

L. N. Taylor was prominent in educational circles.

Cecil Williams was state commissioner of Rural Highways, 1936-42.

John M. P. Thatcher is a prominent lawyer of New York City.

Gerald Griffin is a prominent journalist.

William Harold Ramsey, Somerset's all-around citizen, was born June 11, 1890, in Burnside, five miles south of Somerset. He is the son of the late James Ramsey of Clinton County, and Louella Lloyd Ramsey, who was born in Russell County. She died when her son was an infant.

William Ramsey received his education in the Burnside and Somerset schools, and was graduated from Somerset High School. His first work was with his father, who was managing a flourishing produce business. He was manager of the George P. Taylor Produce Company for years.

In 1925 William decided to go into business for himself, and obtained the agency for Dodge and Chrysler cars. He also bought an interest in an undertaking business, which was later the Denny, Murrell, Ramsey Funeral Home. He had other business interests and at this time is distributor for the Gulf Refining Company's petroleum products over a large territory, with headquarters at Somerset.

On June 11, 1911, he was married to Mary Ella, daughter of Judge N. L. and Nannie Brinkley Barnett, of Somerset.

Mr. and Mrs. Ramsey have three sons. William Harold Jr., who is associated in business with his father, married Eula Judd, of Somerset. The second son, James B., Instructor in Agriculture, married Mary Elizabeth Andis, of Somerset. The youngest son is Lieutenant Colonel Lloyd B. Ramsey, U.S. Army, Washington, D.C. He married Glenda Burton, the daughter of M. E. Burton, Somerset's present postmaster.

William is an officer of the Baptist Church, where he directed the choir for twenty-five years. His hobby is traveling by auto, and he has covered most of the United States, parts of Mexico and Canada. The adage, "A man is not without honor save in his own country," does not hold good with William Ramsey ("Bill" to everybody in Somerset and Pulaski County). This is shown by his activities in educational, musical and social circles, and in the civic clubs to which he belongs. He has membership in, and has been president of, the following: Rotary Club, Boosters Club, Somerset Boat Club, member of the Board of Education for twelve years, and the Chamber of Commerce. He has led or assisted in many local fund-raising drives—Red Cross, Boy Scouts, and Crippled Children (of which he was chairman for several years). His interest in athletics was not confined to Somerset, but extended elsewhere.

When Centre College played Harvard University, the football fans went by rail, but Mr. and Mrs. Ramsey, with another couple, drove up (auto trips were not common then), and were cited publicly as having driven in their car all the way from Somerset to see the game.

George O. Barnes, a learned divine and noted evangelist of the sixties, seventies, and eighties, was partly reared in the manse of the Pisgah Presbyterian Church, five miles south of Somerset, of which his father the Reverend James C. Barnes was pastor, 1853-60. He studied in England, and on returning to this country he preached to his own people, being termed by some the "Mountain Evangelist." He preached his first sermon in the Pisgah Church from his father's pulpit. After a time he toured the world, without money, on an evangelistic and missionary mission, taking his wife and two daughters with him.

A letter written by his father in 1861, says, "My son George Owen wrote me October 29th, 1860, and that he was in India and suffering from a type of rheumatism contracted from exposure in the mountains where he was doing missionary work. George also says, 'No recovery or relief is offered me if I remain here.'"[1]

After his return to this country, and his bailiwick, George continued his evangelistic work, preaching (sitting because of rheumatism) a doctrine or thought which was not approved by the Presbyterian Church. For this reason he was not invited to preach in churches, but wherever he went over Kentucky he preached to crowds, usually in courthouses. While some attended only through curiosity and to criticize, he had many devoted followers.

If the writer, who was a child when he made his last visit to Somerset in the early eighties, remembers correctly, he preached, "God is love, divine healing, and that none would be lost." An opinion of him, remembered by some of his hearers, was "His platform is too broad." On his world tour and in Kentucky, he took with him a small organ which provided musical accompaniment for him and his two daughters as they sang the old gospel hymns, one of which, the writer recalls after more than sixty years, was "Verily, Verily I say Unto You, You Must Be Born Again."

When the weight of years bore heavily on him and his health was such that he needed rest and a warmer climate, he went, about 1890, to Sanibel Island off the west coast of Florida, where he spent his last days, and there his remains lie beside the sea—typical of his life, restless and turbulent.

James "Red" Roberts, without whose name this list would not be complete, was the football star who played a conspicuous part on the Centre College football team, "The Praying

---

[1]This information was from an old letter in possession of the writer, and a contributed article in the *Courier-Journal,* the date cut off, which has been preserved in an old scrap book.

Colonels," when they defeated Harvard on Harvard's own field in 1922.

Alonzo Currier French was born January 21, 1847, in Canaan, New Hampshire, near the White Mountains. He was the son of Moses and Elizabeth Currier French, who lived to celebrate their fiftieth wedding anniversary, April 4, 1891. He married Martha Jane Locke, daughter of Benjamin Folsom and Charlotte Parker Locke, January 21, 1874, in Manchester, New Hampshire.

They had one daughter, Mable Gertrude French, who married Norman Ingraham Taylor on November 16, 1904.

Mr. and Mrs. French came to live in Point Burnside, June 2, 1886, where he established the Burnside Manufacturing Company on the bank of the South Fork River. This firm made red cedar faucets, posts, and lumber which were used in the States and exported to continental Europe. He sold the business in 1918, and then went into the retail coal business here for the Stearns Coal and Lumber Company, in which he remained until 1930. He was also the local agent for the Burnside Land Company for many years, retiring in 1939, at the age of ninety-two.

He, Captain Geary, of Lexington, and A. B. Massey promoted the Burnside Water Company in 1893. Mr. French, as treasurer, managed the concern until it was sold to John W. Sloan in 1907. Fishing and hunting were among his hobbies and through his efforts the Original Hermitage Camp was organized and built in 1896 on the Cumberland River, five miles east of Burnside. Many of his friends enjoyed the rest and recreation of this camp.

When Point Burnside was incorporated as the town of Burnside in 1889, he was one of the first "City Fathers," thereafter taking a vital interest in the growth and development of his community.

He was commissioned as a colonel on the staff of Governor Edwin P. Morrow, February 5, 1920. He was a Mason, Knights Templar, and a member of the Mystic Shrine.

He and Mrs. French were devout members of the Methodist Church; but, before it was organized in the town, both were instrumental in building the first church in the valley, which was deeded to and dedicated as the Presbyterian

Church in September, 1893, with Dr. Harvey Glass, Somerset, as pastor.

Mrs. French passed away at her home April 3, 1931, and Mr. French spent his remaining years in the home of his daughter and son-in-law.

Mr. French's robust health and long years of life were due to his love of the great outdoors. His sense of humor was well known to all his acquaintances. He died June 12, 1940, at the home of Mr. and Mrs. Norman Taylor. His remains rest beside his wife in Pine Grove Cemetery, New Hampshire.

George Parker Taylor, Sr., was born October 22, 1852, in Herron, Maine, and passed away at his home in Burnside, October 30, 1905. He was the son of Joseph Pickard and Melvina Parker Taylor. As a lad of sixteen he worked in a grocery store in Auburndale, Massachusetts, near Boston. For his courteous attention to the customers, the ladies of Auburndale presented him with a gold watch, engraved with his name and the reason for the presentation. This watch is the prized possession of his son, Norman Ingraham Taylor.

Mr. Taylor left Massachusetts at an early age for Colorado Springs, Colorado, and from there came to Burnside, about 1878, before the Cincinnati Southern Railroad extended to this town. He became a partner of his friend William Irvin in establishing a general store at the junction of the Cumberland and South Fork rivers. This building burned, but later a store building was erected on the site of the Burnside First National Bank Building, later used by the Ayer & Lord Tie Company.

The railroad tunnel and bridge had been completed, which enabled Mr. Taylor to walk to Somerset for his mail at least once a week, a distance of nearly ten miles. All the supplies for the Irvin, Taylor Store were hauled from Somerset; but, when the first freight train passed over the rails into Burnside, February 21, 1880, their supplies were among the first received in the tiny village.

George P. Taylor was the postmaster in 1889. A section of the store was set aside for that purpose. He was the first chairman of the school board, president of the First National Bank, and charter member of the Methodist Church.

On January 1, 1893, he went into the wholesale poultry, egg and feed business in which he was active at the time of his death. The brick used in the erection of the George P. Taylor Co. building was made from red clay on his farm on the Antioch Road and was fired in the ovens on that place. Mr. Taylor was so intent upon raising the standard of fowls in this section of Kentucky that he gave away settings of purebred "Plymouth Rock" eggs for the asking.

In August, 1880, Miss Ella Florence Jones of Portland, Maine, came to visit her friend, Mrs. William Irvin, the wife of Mr. Taylor's partner in business. After a courtship of several months, Mr. Taylor and Miss Jones were married at the Irvin home on Highland Avenue. There the two sons, Norman I. and Philip Parker Taylor, were born. Mrs. Taylor passed away February 29, 1936.

The third generation of Taylors, the grandsons George Parker II and Robert French Taylor, have grown to manhood in this same home; now the fourth generation of the same family may be seen at the old fireside when Richard Brion (son of George P. Taylor II) and Mark Meneghan and Catherine French (son and daughter of Robert Taylor) arrive in Burnside for a visit.

When the men of Somerset launched a contest to vote for the most outstanding citizen in Pulaski County, George P. Taylor was elected to that great honor, a gift richly deserved by this humble man, whose "left hand knew not the good" his right hand dealt to those less fortunate in worldly needs. His family inherited the wealth of his good name.[2]

Ben V. Smith, son of Jonathan and Nancy VanHook Smith, was born 1860 in the Dabney section. As a child he attended the local school, but arriving at the age of decision regarding his future education, he and his father disagreed ... his father wanting him to become a farmer. At this time young men were sent out as book agents, but Ben's father disapproved such a vocation for his son, hoping providence would intervene. However, the young man selected Wayne County as his field and in a few months had made enough money selling books to pay for one year at Transylvania College which he attended

[2]Written by Mrs. Norman Ingraham Taylor.

two years. Then, because the course in Greek was not satisfactory, he entered National Normal School at Lebanon, Ohio, where he was graduated in law. Here he met and married Jennie Dodge of that place.

The following excerpts are from resolutions adopted by the Pulaski County Bar Association, and read before him in his office on the ninety-second anniversary of his birth:

> Ben V. Smith has journeyed beyond the frontiers vouchsafed only for the holy and strong. Advancing years have laid no toll on his mentality, and have been merciful in their penalty on his health and physique. Time and providence have set him upon a pinnacle where few have stood. His life has spanned the most remarkable period in the world's history; under his gaze scattered continents became one world. He has kept step with the march of progress, and in tune with the music of youth.
>
> His record as a lawyer is long and honorable. His service at the bar has been dignified, courteous, and competent and has won for him the respect of many courts, the familiarity of many lawyers, and the respect of his clients. Mr. Smith is not only a lawyer, but he is one of the golden links that bind us to the great historic past.

WOMEN

Miss Venus Ramey, Eubank, Pulaski County, was "Miss America" in 1945.

Mrs. A. E. Gillis, nee Pearl Owens, born in Somerset, but now of Dallas, Texas, was National Mother of 1949.

Hariette Simpson Arnow, born in Wayne County, reared and educated in Burnside, Pulaski County, was the author of *Mountain Path,* a Book-of-the-Month, and *Hunters Horn,* published in 1949, which received nation-wide comment.

Miss Amelia Saunders, the daughter of George Woodard Saunders and Jane Long Saunders, was born in 1860. She early evinced a talent for teaching, which came about as an interviewer said, in this way. "Her lifework came upon her on the high waters of the Cumberland River, when a friend stopped at her father's house and asked Miss Amelia, then about twenty years of age, if she wouldn't like to teach the primary department in the Burnside School nearby, then a private school. She protested that she had never had any idea of teaching, that life in her father's home with nine brothers and sisters, who were still at home, was very pleasant. The school at Burnside needed someone and Miss Amelia, ready to try anything once, went off to teach—thus began her life work."

For nearly sixty years she taught school, first in the county schools, then later in the Somerset Public School, where she was first assigned the fifth and sixth grades. Finally, they let her have the first grade, and she loved it so they never could get her away from it. She taught three generations in several families; for this reason, when a new generation started school, the mother often asked that her child be placed in Miss Saunders' room. This is proof of her ability, love for, and understanding of, children.

She taught until she was eighty-two years of age; then she retired to her cozy brick home on North Main Street, where she devoted herself to the many things she had not had time for before—art, fancywork, and writing her memoirs. She resumed her activity in the Chautauqua Club where she was an active member because of her literary interests. During all these years, she never neglected her work in the First Baptist Church, just across the street from her home. Here she taught in the Sunday school for many years.

At ninety years of age her mind was as clear and scintillating as when she taught a governor, senators, and others who may not have reached the top rung on "Fame's Ladder," but they all loved and revered her.

The people of Somerset are proud of their veteran teacher.

BOY SCOUTS

Most people think of Scouting as having started in 1910. A "good turn" to William D. Boyce, of Chicago, by an unknown Scout in England, so impressed Mr. Boyce that, upon his return to this country in 1909, he began interesting others in the movement; and, on February 8, 1910, the Boy Scout Association was incorporated. Actually, Scouting is as old as chivalry, dating back to the days of gallant knights who set out to give aid to the weak and oppressed.

Sometime before Scouting was incorporated in this country a William Bass and his English wife resided in Burnside. He was an exceptionally good athlete with quite an enviable reputation as a baseball player. His wife organized a little group of neighborhood boys and called them "Sir Arthur's Knights," Learning of the Scout movement in England, she wrote to London and got the necessary information to organize her group into Scouts. The manual caused a bit of confusion in that it specified swearing allegiance to the King.[3]

Somerset is particularly proud of the record of Troop 79, led by Chester Kaiser, and his assistants, "Big Lee" Girdler and Nick Berry. There are four patrols with a registration of forty Scouts.

This troop, organized in 1922, became affiliated with the National Council in March, 1924. As a troop they have received too many awards to list, yet some are too important to overlook. James R. Moore was sent to Europe by the *Courier-Journal* after winning a state oratorial contest, and became International Boy Orator. This was in 1937. Jack Goldenberg was one of the delegates chosen to tour Europe and attend a meeting at Brussels. Incidentally, Jack Goldenberg at that time had the largest number of merit badges of any Scout in Kentucky.

The record of achievement made by Troop 79 is a tribute to the man who used his outstanding talent for leadership and his deep interest in the youth of Somerset to good advantage, Chester Kaiser.

The first Boy Scout Troop in Somerset was organized in 1912, by the Reverend J. B. Parke of the Presbyterian Church. This troop was not chartered as there was no set-up for charters at that date, but many troops existed.[4]

According to Gilmore Bobbitt, a member from the Methodist Church, the first meetings were held in Mr. Parke's room, which was in the old Dr. Parker home, now the Somerset Funeral Home.

Troop 11, non-existent today, was started by the Reverend C. H. Talbot, Presbyterian minister, about 1921 or 1922,

---

[3]The information regarding this first troop in the United States (to our knowledge) was given by Mr. Edgar Garland, of Somerset, who was a member.
[4]National Headquarters, Washington, D.C. This information collected from Chester Kaiser, and members of the older troop.

but, due to some technicality, the application for a charter was delayed. Records in the possession of Ivan Kelly, who was scribe, show it was granted by 1924. This troop comprised boys from the Presbyterian Church and the Methodist Church.

Mr. Talbot continued as leader until a knee operation forced him to appoint the assistant leader, Luther Tibbals, to take his place.

GIRL SCOUTS

In 1942 the first Girl Scouts were organized by the Reverend Floyd Rose, pastor of the Methodist Church, who became their advisor, and Mrs. Nancy Oatts, their leader. A charter was granted February, 1943.

In 1948, through the efforts of the Scouts and the untiring zeal of their leader, they erected a Scout House, located in Crystal Park. The site was donated by Mr. Arthur Prather.[5]

[5]Information by Mrs. Nancy Oatts.

Chapter 14

.... *LOCAL LORE* ....

THE FORTY-NINERS

Pulaski's young men of one hundred years ago were no different from those in other places who, lured by reports of fortunes to be made in the gold mines of California, started the long trek westward. Transportation was slow and routes were circuitous. Among those who went from Pulaski County were: Fountaine Beaty; Crate Lee; David K. Newell; Fountaine Gossett; Sam Cowan; and William Lee, who died on the way and was buried at Fort Larimee, Wyoming.

These men went by steamboat down the Cumberland and Ohio, thence up the Mississippi River to St. Louis. Here they bought covered wagons and oxen for the trip overland. Their final and real start was from Independence, Missouri.

They traveled the northern route through Nebraska, crossing the treacherous Platte River, where many before them had lost their lives in the quicksand and swirling waters. It took six months to make the trip.

On this long journey cattle died, and to replenish their loss the men hunted and picked up strays which had been lost by travelers before them. These cattle, they found, sometimes went four or five miles for water. They had to be hunted as other animals were, having reverted to the wild state.

How long the men stayed or what luck they had in making a fortune is not known today, but from memories of descendants they acquired more experience, saw more country, and brought back a larger store of tales and less money than they started with.

Perhaps Fountaine Beaty, who never married, was remembered longest. School children delighted in gathering around him when he and his dog made noon-hour rounds of the district schools, playing the fiddle and singing "Poor Old Maid" and "Barbara Allen." The writer was told these men made the homeward trip by boat, sailing from San Francisco, coming by Trinidad and the Gulf of Mexico, then up the Mississippi River and home. This means they came by Cape Horn (unlikely) or crossed the Isthmus of Panama on foot, then took a boat bound for Trinidad, and thence home.

Perhaps David Newell was the only one who remained in the West. He had recently been graduated (1845) in law from Centre College; he probably saw better opportunities in his profession than in digging gold. This proved to be true. A suit, between a company who owned a mine and another company who owned the water right for said mine, was pending. The company owning the mine offered Newell one-third interest in it if he would win the suit. He was engaged and did win the suit; the opposing lawyer was James A. Garfield, later President of the United States.

This marked the beginning of a successful professional career. During the Civil War he was sent to England by the Confederacy to secure money and help. The writer has letters written by his wife, who accompanied him, telling of their fruitless trip and deep sorrow over the condition of the Confederacy. One was written from Cuba on the way home.

THE DEER HUNTING CLUB

It is historic fact that all of Kentucky was a hunting ground, that bear and deer abounded. After fifty years inhabitants had become numerous, and these animals sought refuge in the rugged and mountainous sections of the southern part of Kentucky and the eastern part of Tennessee. Roads were mere trails; there was little travel. Therefore, this was a natural habitat for deer, and occasionally a bear was seen.

The Civil War came on and ended. It probably left its impress on the young men of that time. The humdrum life of the early days was undergoing a change. It was at this time, 1868, that a Deer Hunting Club was formed and existed until 1892. It held an annual meet in the month of November.

The members were: Dick Newell, John Newell, Perk Ingram, Clay Wait, Dr. Joe L. Owens, John Woodcock, W.

O. Newell (Big Bill), S. A. Newell (Big Sam), George Wait, Harvey Sloan, Charlie Parker, William Newell, David Owens, John Wait, Ward W. Tate, Joe Parker, and "Old Loge" Newell (colored) the cook.

These men were bankers, lawyers, doctors, merchants, and well-to-do farmers. They hunted around Barren Fork in lower Pulaski; at Shiloh near Cumberland Falls, where they camped in Kelly's rock house; and in Fentress County, Tennessee, where they were met and made "camp comfortable" by Joe Waters, their annual guide. Until 1880, when the railroad was built, men, bedding, and provisions were transported by pack mule.

An oft-told incident (remembered by the writer) which is illustrative of the zest of the start, was related by W. O. Newell about his brother Dick. W. O., who lived on the south side of the river, had his wife to aid him in his preparations; Dick, a bachelor, lived on the north side alone. The day before the start all arrangements were completed. Everyone was ready to leave before daylight the next morning.

At three-thirty in the morning, W. O. hollered across, "Come on, Dick." The take-off was not as well planned and easy for Dick, whose only helper was a Negro cook, called Jennie. W. O. saw the dugout tied to the river bank and Dick making haste from the house to the boat with bedding and food. All was loaded, the last thing put in being an open crock filled with butter. Dick placed this in the bow of the dugout. He then seated himself, picked up the paddle and called to the hounds, who, all ready and anxious for the signal to go, bounded into the wobbly dugout, each one putting his foot into the open crock of butter.

At the finish of this narrative (probably colored to suit the occasion) by his brother, who enjoyed nothing more, Dick would grin, and stammer his only cuss-word "You b-b-b-burned fool."

These hunts lasted about two weeks—the hunters bringing home venison, antlers, deer hides for buggy robes, and many tall tales. The last survivor of this club was Mr. Joe C. Parker (probably the youngest member) who died in 1947 at the age of ninety, and to whom the writer is indebted for the names and dates.

The only visible evidence of this early and interesting bit of sporting history is two pairs of very large deer horns—one in possession of Mrs. Jennie Hail, the granddaughter of William Newell, and the other in possession of Luther Tibbals, the great-nephew of Samuel Newell.

Another relic is a gun used by Dick Newell on these hunts. This gun came by chance into the hands of his family after many years. Clarence Owens, the nephew of Dick Newell, lived in Oklahoma and was engaged in the hardware business. One day a farmer came into the store and inquired where Mr. Owens was from. He then said he owned a gun his father had bought from a Pulaski County man, who was deer hunting in Fentress County, Tennessee. The farmer happened to be the son of Joe Waters (the old guide), and the gun was none other than Dick Newell's gun. Compared with guns today, it is a real curiosity, being a muzzle loader, eight or nine gauge, with a barrel forty inches long, and weighing about fifteen pounds.

THE COUNTY FAIR AND CIRCUS

There were few events that surpassed the county fair in importance. The first one was in the 1870's and was held at the foot of Wait's Hill, on the west side of the dusty road which is now Main Street. The only reminders of that fair are a few silver julep cups which were given as premiums; all are gone who were old enough to remember it.

About 1885 another fair was held on the land now belonging to Beecher Smith on College Street. Subsequent fairs were held on this same plot for many years. There were two grandstands, bandstand, and floral hall (this was used as a pesthouse during the smallpox epidemic of 1900, and then burned). There was the secretary's stand, occupied by Sam Hicks as secretary for many years.

This was the time of Dignity Dare, the beautiful and perfect show horse, and Enoch Arden, the brown pacer. Yes, and the fancy turnouts ladened with Somerset belles. For the benefit of the uninitiated, a fancy turnout was a competition for the prettiest buggy, horse, and girl. In the later days the horse for his part was shined and curried to perfection. The buggy was rubber-tired, very high, and without a top. The girls were beautiful, dressed in the best Somerset could provide, which meant many ribbons that fluttered out behind, and always a very, very beautiful parasol.

The fair was never complete after the days when Mr. Joe Parker, on his dignified bay, and John Bell Jones, on his spirited grey, were ringmasters. I can remember Joe Buzzard and Mary Kendrick doing the cakewalk. How they did dance! The county fair was an event which had only one competitor—the annual circus. I can still feel the thrill which the circus brought to me, a little country girl. Gaudy and interesting billboards advertised it weeks ahead, so we knew when it would come. The night before I might be awakened by the sound of the wagons, and nothing rolling ever made the purr of a circus wheel, or maybe it was a cluck—anyway it was a thrilling noise. The wagons were pulled by horses on ordinary roads, but they were very heavy and occasionally the hills were too steep for them. Wait's Hill was one of these obstacles and the elephants were used to push the wagons to the top. The boys of the town were always there to water these elephants and enjoy the hours of erecting the tent. The noonday parade with calliopes, bands, performers, clowns, beautiful horses, and riders with spangles was just enough to make my heart stand still with rapture. I can shut my eyes and see and smell the dust, noise, and sawdust of those circuses, and I will enjoy the taste of pink lemonade to my dying day.

THE "OLD SWIMMING HOLE"

One of the joys of all the boys in the summer was the "old swimming hole." Every neighborhood had such a meeting place for the small boys. It was their own private hole, naked was the style, and heavenly was the fun. The Ray Hole on Pitman was just such a place for boys for generation after generation. The joker in these places is that they were the best holes on the creek.

THE JOHNNYCAKE

On cold winter evenings after the family had gathered around the big open fire in the dining room, which served as a living room also, and the logs had burned to the red coal stage, my mother would bring in the johnnycake, which she had prepared at supper time, and a pitcher of sweet milk for a bedtime snack.

The first step in making the johnnycake was a hand split oak or hickory shingle, rounded at both ends, and scraped to a satiny smoothness with a piece of broken glass—this was my father's responsibility.

Then mother got out the oblong wooden corn bread tray, sifted the corn meal into it with the old round sieve, added a pinch of salt, a little bacon grease, and enough warm water to make it easy to handle in her hands—shaped it and placed it on the shingle, patting it to a half-inch thickness to fit the board.

It was then placed in front of the fire at a 90-degree angle and supported by a sadiron. When it was browned—now this was the trick—mother bent over the glowing coals and, taking an old case knife, slipped it under the cake (thus loosening it), flipped it over and replaced it until it became brown on that side. It was an art to turn a johnnycake and not have it slide into the ashes. It was good served with butter and sweet milk.

The corn meal was always what we called water-ground meal, ground at Parker's Mill.

WEDDINGS

With early roads often impassable, there was little intermingling between different communities or neighborhoods. Before the railroad was built Burnside was as far from Somerset as Somerset is from Cincinnati today. For this reason young people usually married in their own community. They were better acquainted and it was considered wiser by their parents for it to be this way. Proof of this was found in an old diary of exactly one hundred years ago, regarding a daughter who dared to marry a man from another state. It runs like this:

> April 22, 1849, My dear, my darling daughter has forsaken us and gone, we know not where, with a stranger. Heavenly Father, for Thy dear Son's sake, guide and protect and restore her wandering feet to the path of duty.

Weddings were real occasions; everyone was invited; all remained for the "infare." This was a festive occasion—a meal which took days of preparation by the family and the slaves. It consisted of meats of all kinds, roast pig, venison, wild turkey, and maybe bear meat. There were stacks of pies, pound cake, and gallons of eggnog. Often there was a bucket of whiskey with a dipper in it.

After that the merrymaking began in earnest with dancing lasting all night. If a honeymoon was taken, the couple made a trip, probably back to Tennessee, or even Virginia, on horseback. This usually took place in the fall of the year after the crops were "laid by," and the honeymooners would have time (the entire winter) for the trip.

DISASTERS

The Cumberland River has given cause for distress and loss of property more often than any other natural cause. Normally it is a peaceful stream with much natural beauty, but at floodtime, which occurs every five or six years, it becomes a muddy, boiling, raging torrent, sweeping everything before it. The towns that lie in the lowland bordering the river suffer. The people must move and everything they have suffers from a deluge of water and mud. Farmers try to erect their buildings above high water mark, but the flood ruins fences and soil, and drowns stock. These floods are quite a terrible sight.

The year 1913 was a memorable year for another kind of disaster. In February of that year the river reached the highest stage (seventy-two feet) that old river men recalled. On March 21, a cyclone did great damage. The old Pisgah Church, a solid brick structure, was razed to its foundations. There were many homes, barns, trees, and much public utility equipment blown down and ruined. No one was hurt, probably due to the fact that everyone was in bed.

In 1922 another severe storm hit Somerset, damaging buildings and disrupting electric service and telephones. On May 21, 1949, a tornado did more damage than any of the previous winds. Pulaski's large, new tobacco barn was destroyed. Many homes suffered and a tree fell into a home, killing one woman.

Pulaski County suffered another kind of disaster, a smallpox epidemic, during the winter of 1900-01. Schools were closed and churches also for a time. Brief services for the dead were held at the graves.

The same conditions existed in the "flu" epidemic of 1918-19 during World War I. There were three or more funerals every day in this small community for a period of time. Schools were closed; people were told to stay out of crowds and at home as much as possible. The doctors were worked to death, and it was almost impossible to get one for any reason that was not next to death itself.

GRAHAM FLOUR

A story, told by residents of the county, identifies a world-famous product with the early history of the county.

According to tradition, Dr. Christopher Columbus Graham, who amassed a fortune at Harrodsburg soon after Kentucky separated from Virginia, sold his interests there, in what was known as Graham Springs, for a large sum. He later settled at Crab Orchard and moved sometime later to the west bank of Rockcastle River at a place then known as Sublimity Springs. Here, according to the story, Dr. Graham built a large grain and sawmill, completely spanning the Rockcastle River. Soon the settlers were bringing their wheat to Dr. Graham's mill to be ground and he produced a coarse, dark flour afterwards referred to as Graham flour.[1]

MAY SNOWFALL

Sunday, May 20, 1894, six inches of snow covered the ground. "Never has anything the equal of this happened in my time," said the oldest inhabitant Sunday morning, when that much-favored person looked out and saw the face of the earth wrapped in a thick blanket of snow. Some there were who said they had seen it "spit snow" in May, but for it to lay on the ground, particularly "shoe mouth" deep, not one dared admit it.

So far back as we can trace the climatic history of this country revealed no such phenomena as snow the twentieth of May—only ten days until June and hot summer days.

Think of brushing off snow in order to pick strawberries, of shaking snow from the leaf-laden branches of every kind of tree,

[1]Published article by Enos Swain in the Somerset *Commonwealth*.

of seeing wheat, already developed, lying flat on the earth beneath a load of frozen moisture, of seeing tender corn, high enough to need plowing, peeping from under a blanket of snow.

Write it down young persons, in the book of your memory; but when you become the oldest inhabitant don't run the risk of your reputation, assert that it snowed May 20, 1894, unless you have this story copied in the *Reporter* to prove your statement.

Somerset has one sage who predicted this storm three weeks ago, and he is none other than Prophet Hedgecroft.

When assisting in setting out flowers about May 1st, he insisted that the lady for whom he was working would leave her plants under the trees and in the cellar. "Why?" she asked. "Blackberry winter is bound to come," replied the prophet, "and a snow will fall about the 18th." And it did.[2]

JESSE JAMES'S VISIT

One of Somerset's famous stories concerns a visit of Jesse James to the town for the purpose of robbing the National Bank, of which Samuel Newell was president and Robert Gibson, cashier. This was in 1876 or 1877. According to tradition, two members of the James gang entered the bank during the noon hour while the stores were closed and the streets were deserted, because businessmen were at home for dinner. Three of the gang were left outside as sentinels.

While the James gang awaited a signal from their leader, a large number of men and boys walked through the Square with shotguns. The two bandits immediately left the bank and hurriedly rode away, followed by the other three. The men with their guns had no idea of the service they were rendering; they were simply going on a hunting trip.

DR. KERNS'S DEATH

This short, but tragic story of one of Pulaski's early doctors was told the writer by Mrs. John Denny, of Bronston, whose mother said, "Go to Flat Lick Church graveyard and you will find the grave of the doctor who, on his way to see me when I had measles, was drowned in Buck Creek." At this time, in

[2]From a newspaper clipping, courtesy of Nora Shepperd Humble.

that neatly-kept country cemetery, stands a modest shaft, moldy with age, bearing the name of Dr. George Kerns. The following inscription expresses the love held for the family doctor. "Sacredly treasured in the memory of his friends in the 28 years of his age; drowned in Buck Creek April 9, 1854." This was erected by C. Stigall.

CIVIL WAR STORIES

This story is told of an outpost company (probably Morgan's) stationed somewhere in southern Ohio—the men were poorly fed and, during a brief stop for rest, had the unfortunate experience of seeing a farmer's hog make a raid on their rations. The fellows belonging to the company decided to kill the marauder and enjoy roast pig. No sooner had they killed and dressed it than the sentinel on guard saw the owner approaching the camp. One quick-witted fellow said, "Leave it to me; I'll manage it." The farmer asked if they had seen anything of a stray hog. The soldier replied, "No, have you had smallpox?" Pointing to the blanket-covered hog lying near, he said, "Our brother died this morning." The farmer left at once and preparations for the sumptuous feast continued.

One tale told by Tom Shepperd, who was one of Morgan's men (that daring regiment that the Northern Army dreaded), relates that they were on a raid and, having a period of rest, decided to make a foray for food to replenish their meager rations. With these daring fellows the suggestion was put into immediate action ... a store was emptied of all its hams, a fire was built, hams sliced, and soon the aroma of broiling ham filled the air. Just then it was discovered the enemy was approaching, and the order was given "to mount—get going." The hams were hastily fastened by strings to the saddles; the order was given, "Move, hurry." As they galloped at top speed, the hams flopping from side to side soon broke loose, thereby strewing the road with the delectable supper the boys had planned for themselves.

Zollie Burton, who was named for General Zollicoffer, the Southern general who lost his life in the Battle of Mill Springs (or Logans Crossroads), visited year after year, on Memorial Day, the site where the battle was fought. While crowds gathered around at the National Cemetery near by, she visited the forgotten graves of the unknown soldiers of the Confederate cause and placed a few simple flowers on the mound which covered the more than one hundred who fought and died there. She also girded each year, with a cedar garland, the huge oak tree under which General Zollicoffer died.

In the early years of Pulaski County many settled in the western part and permanent settlements were made at Forbush (now Faubush), Old Harrison, Waterloo, and Caintown. Old deeds and church records show names of the Weddles, Wares, Coopers, Tarters, Logans, Norfleets, Trimbles, Jaspers, and others who have been prominent in political, professional, agricultural, and military circles.

This vicinity came into military prominence because of the Battle of Logan's Cross Roads which turned the tide of the Civil War. For more than fifty years afterward, entrenchments could be seen and musket balls found. Still standing today, 1952, after ninety years, in a neglected bit of woodland, there is a stark reminder of the strong feeling that often existed between friends and members of the same family on the questions of slavery and secession. It is a fifteen-foot cedar pole, called a "stack pole." The story goes that it was planted there by two brothers as a support for stacking hay.

During the late summer of 1862, when feeling ran high, these brothers, as they were at work in the hay field, became involved in an argument over the right as they saw it. Without finishing their job of harvesting their crop, they left home, one to join the Northern Army, the other, the Southern. The years passed and neither of them came home until the war ended, the victor in his uniform of blue and the other in his tattered unform of gray.

The now heavily wooded plot seems to have kept lonely vigil. It was never cultivated again, according to an old resident, and the stack pole, gradually rotting away at the base, still stands as if waiting for the last load of hay.

A RAILROAD LEGEND

During the building of the railroad, an engine had been brought, piece by piece, to the south side of the river at Burnside and was being assembled. On the opposite side was the tunnel which would be at the end of the bridge when it was completed. One day while the workmen were assembling the engine, a man from the hills came among them and asked many questions concerning the strange contraption. When told it would go into the tunnel across the river he answered, "I'll be ----if I can see how that thing can jump the river and hit that hole."

A SCRAP OF FORGOTTEN HISTORY

Near the brink of famous Cumberland Falls, on the Whitley County side of the river, stood for more than three-quarters of a century an L-shaped two-story frame hotel with wide porches running completely around both the upper and lower stories. The kitchen and dining room were apart from the main building and were reached by a wide covered boardwalk. The dining room, a plain but spacious room where vension, wild turkey, quail from the forest, and fish from the river were served, was the scene of gay dances during the many years when it attracted guests from other states.

THE MOONBOW INN FIRE DESTROYED A GENUINE KENTUCKY LANDMARK

The razing of Moonbow Inn recently at Cumberland Falls is of more than passing interest. The writer knew this section intimately during the nineties when Whitley County was as far away from the Bluegrass section as Russia is from us today.

There are few authentic facts recorded about the early history of this section of southeastern Kentucky.

Dr. Thomas Walker who came through the Gap in 1750 gave the name of Cumberland, for the English duke, to the river and mountains. The Long Hunters, early narratives say, camped on the site where Moonbow Inn burned recently.

Years earlier than my discovery of the Falls, Socrates Owens, my father-in-law, came to Whitley County to survey timber and coal lands belonging to his father's estate. He had a brand new degree in surveying from Bacon College, Harrodsburg, afterwards merged with Transylvania. His friend, Sid Myers, owned large tracts of coal and timber land several miles below the falls. They formed a partnership in 1867. Later Mr. Owens bought Mr. Myers' interest and acquired land, including the falls. In 1869 he began cutting timber and preparing to build a hotel. He called it Cumberland Falls Hotel. The falls property was purchased from Parson Louis and "Mammy" Renfro, sometimes written Renfrew. The narrative of Parson Renfro begins as early as 1830 when Matthew Walton and Andrew Sheperd patented 200 acres which included the falls. Renfro, a young Baptist preacher from Tennessee, purchased the rights of the falls properties in 1850. He built the usual log cabin above the falls near where the present highway comes in from Corbin, later added two more lean-to rooms of smaller dimensions. This, except for a small log enclosure for horses and mules, was the extent of Renfro's early inn.

Before the war John Swift stopped for a stay, left his diary and other things in the hands of "Mammy" Renfro, and never returned. The story is, that Swift worked a silver mine at or near Cumberland Falls. The hotel opened as a summer resort in 1871.

Furniture was all made by hand on the premises. Bedding and equipment were shipped from Cincinnati to Parker's Lake Post Office, 14 miles from the falls and forty miles from Somerset, over rugged roads.

During the yellow fever scourge an influx of the Deep South's frightened citizens made for this resort—seeking the clean pure air.

Tobe Walker, merchant at Parker's Lake, says his father sawed some of the lumber at the mouth of Jellico Creek and in rafting it down the river in high tides the whole cut was lost to the "indraw" of the falls, to the amount of $10,000.

The hotel was built of yellow poplar, wide boards being used. All nails and many of the tools were hand wrought on the place. Carpenters were brought in from Lincoln, Pulaski and Wayne. Dominie Gerardi, a noted harpist at that time, brought an orchestra from Louisville for the summer months.

Mr. Owens died in 1890 and the Cumberland Falls Hotel property came to his son, Edward F. Owens, and his widow, Mrs. Nannie Williams Owens. It was operated by them as a hotel until sold to the Cumberland Falls Company in which they were large stockholders. Later it was purchased by the Brunsons.[3]

---

[3] Written by Mrs. Reb Owens Herbert and published in the *Courier-Journal* of March 5, 1949.

Chapter 15

.... WARS ....

REVOLUTIONARY SOLDIERS

The Revolutionary soldiers[1] who settled in Pulaski County are listed below. There are others but records have not been established.

Robert Adams	John Evans	Samuel Newell
Francis Aldridge	Job Gastineau, Sr.	William Owens
Robert Anderson	James Gilmore	John Perry
Samuel Allen, Sr.	Richard Goggin	James Rainey
Thomas Arman	William Hansford	Jesse Richardson
William Barren	James Hamilton	Michael Reagon
John Barren	James Harrell	David Roper
John Barker	William Hays	Robert Sayers
Henry Baugh	William Heath	Thomas Seaton
Michael Beakman	John Hopper	Dorson Sewell
Icabod Blacklege	Nicholas Jasper	Richard Cheek
Robert Buchanan	Thomas Kelley	Swearingen
Michael Burton	James Kennedy	William Sweeney
Andrew Cowan	James Lee	Peter Tarter
Elijah Denny	Joseph McAllister	Nathaniel Tomlinson
John Dick	Moses Martin	William Trimble
Lovell Dogan	John Mayfield	Martin Turpin
Josiah Earp	Barnabas Murry	John Wilson
John Edwards	John Newby	Michael Young

MILITARY OF PULASKI COUNTY

Pulaski was a result of the War for Independence. For this reason patriotism and zeal for military service have continued to be characteristic of the men from generation to generation.

[1]Established by the Somerset Chapter of the Daughters of the American Revolution.

The first problem of the newly-created county was the preservation of law and order at home. For this purpose the court, at the direction of the legislature, divided the county into districts and appointed a company of patrollers in each district. Their duty was to keep down any trouble which might arise.

From the County Order Book II we find the first patrollers in the town of Somerset were: William Fox (captain), William Sallee, and Joseph Porter. Those for the east end of the county were: Henry James (captain), Samuel Tindle, and Benjamin Thurman. In the southern part of the county they were: John Cowan (captain), Isaac Hays, and Charles Moddrell. On Buck Creek they were: John Griffin (captain), Thomas Stigall, and John Jones. In the western end they were: Andrew Davidson (captain), Isaac Muse, and Seton Lee.

One month after the organization of the companies of patrollers, on December 20, 1799, Governor Garrard organized a new regiment of Kentucky Militia, the Forty-fourth, embracing the county of Pulaski.

Jesse Richardson was lieutenant colonel of the regiment with Charles Debrel and William Fox majors of the First and Second Battalion.

Fox resigned May 16, 1800, and Robert Moddrell was appointed to take his place.

In the year 1813, John B. Austin was appointed paymaster to the Forty-fourth Regiment of Kentucky Militia.

In 1816 Josiah Evans was paymaster to the Forty-fourth Regiment of Kentucky Militia with Tunstall Quarles, Jr., and William Fox as securities. In the March court, 1816, William Fox having received his appointment on January 15, 1815, from Governor Shelby, was commissioned paymaster of the Ninety-fifth Regiment of Kentucky Militia, of which Samuel Newell II was captain.

In 1819, the last year in which the Militia served in this capacity, two names were added: John Dishman in Captain Galloway's Company and John Beaty in that part of Pulaski taken off of Wayne and attached to Pulaski by an Act of the General Assembly, approved the fourth day of February, 1817.

THE WAR OF 1812

The fourth day of June, 1812, Congress declared war on England. In September of that same year the war records show Tunstall Quarles of Pulaski County organized and became captain of a company of infantry of the Second Regiment of Kentucky Volunteer Militia. He served through March, 1813.

Another record was of Thomas Dollarhide of Pulaski County. He commanded a company of Kentucky Volunteer Militia of Renick's Mounted Battalion under General Samuel Hopkins. Muster roll was from September 18, 1812, to October 27, 1812.[2]

A third company was formed by Captain Samuel Tate, as follows:

WAR OF 1812

ROLL OF CAPTAIN SAMUEL TATE'S COMPANY OF PULASKI COUNTY KENTUCKY MOUNTED VOLUNTEER MILITIA
7TH REGIMENT COMMANDED BY COLONEL MICHAEL TAUL[3]

Names:	Date and place of muster	To what time engaged or enlisted	Remarks
Samuel Tate, Captain	8/23/1813	11/14/1813	
Robert Gilmore, Lieutenant	"	"	
Jonathan Smith, Ensign	"	"	
Samuel Newell II, First Sergeant	"	"	
William Hays, Second Sergeant	"	"	
Thomas Gibson, Third Sergeant	"	"	
Robert Cowan, Fourth Sergeant	"	"	
Privates			
Barns, Adam	"	"	Left behind
Barrier, James	"	"	Left behind
Beard, Abraham	"	"	
Beaty, James	"	"	
Bell, James	"	"	
Bregis, Edmund	"	"	Deserted 10/16
Buster, William	"	"	
Clarke, Elisha	"	"	
Cooper, Acey	"	"	Left behind with lame horse
Cowan, Isaac	"	"	
Cox, Allen	"	"	
Cundiff, Gregory	"	"	

[2]Photostatic copy in possession of the writer.
[3]War Department, Washington, D.C.

Names:	Date and place of muster	To what time engaged or enlisted	Remarks
Davis, Fields	"	"	
Davidson, Henry	"	"	Left behind, sick
Dishman, John	"	"	
Dunham, Alex	"	"	
Evins, Samuel	"	"	
Garner, Parich	"	"	Left behind, sick
Gasper, Achilles	"	"	
Gibson, Martin	"	"	Promoted to sergeant
Gilmore, John	"	"	
Gilmore, William	"	"	
Hargis, Thomas	"	"	Left behind
Hast, Israel	"	"	
Herring, Joshea	"	"	
Hickman, Lewallin	"	"	Not accounted for
Higgins, James	"	"	
Hines, James	"	"	
Hughes, Hiram	"	"	
Humphries, David	"	"	Left behind
Hunter, Thomas	"	"	
Kelly, Joseph	"	"	
Lankford, Garrard	"	"	
Lewis, John	"	"	
Martin, John	"	"	
Mathews, William	"	"	
Mayfield, Reuben	"	"	
McDonald, Andrew	"	"	
McKinney, James	"	"	
Minton, William	"	"	
Murphy, Bennett	"	"	
Neal, Isaac	"	"	
Nealey, Isaac	"	"	
Owens, John	"	"	
Owens, William	"	"	
Preston, William	"	"	
Richardson, Joel	"	"	Left·behind
Richardson, Stephen	"	"	
Ridge, Robertson	"	"	
Roberts, John	"	"	
Scott, John	"	"	
Short, John	"	"	
Short, Reuben	"	"	
Short, Thomas	"	"	
Smith, James	"	"	
Stogsdill, William	"	"	
St. John, Noah	"	"	
Sutherford, James	"	"	

	Date and place of muster	To what time engaged or enlisted	Remarks
Turley, Standford	"	"	
Vanhook, Sullivan	"	"	
White, John	"	"	Left behind
Willis, Henry	"	"	
Wontland, Thomas	"	"	
Yeams, John	"	"	

WAR OF 1812

COMPANY OF ROCKCASTLE COUNTY, KENTUCKY[4]

Johnston Dysart, Captain
Charles C. Carson, Lieutenant
Joseph Henderson, Ensign
James Wilson, First Sergeant
Jacob Frederick, Second Sergeant
Isaiah Ham, Third Sergeant
Samuel Vance, Fourth Sergeant
John Bustle, First Corporal
John Evans, Second Corporal
George Watkins, Third Corporal
Isaac Dillard, Fourth Corporal

Privates

Alexander, George	Conn, Alexander	Owens, Martin
Bailey, Hannan	Cremon, John	Owens, Presley
Bealey, Reuben	Dearmine, Flenion	Owens, Samuel
Bell, Elijah	Denning, Levi	Roberts, Hiram
Bowen, Jacob	Dysart, Samuel	Roberts, James
Brooks, James	Graves, William	Stewart, James
Brown, Wilson	Haley, John	Tenner, Silvester
Buford, William	Henderson, William	Terrell, James
Callahan, John	Jones, James	Thompson, Joseph
Callons, Andrew	Lawrence, Thomas	Tysah, John
Colyar, Gabriel	McEnturf, Manuel	Warren, Benjamin
Colyar, John	Owens, Allen	White, Joel

MEXICAN WAR, 1847

The Fourth Regiment of Kentucky Volunteers was organized in September, 1847 by Captain John G. Lair in Pulaski

[4]From National Archives 116.

County. It left Pulaski County in September, 1847 and marched to Louisville, where it arrived on the third of October, 1847. This was a distance of 130 miles by the nearest and most practical route.

The Muster Roll of Captain John G. Lair's Company in the Fourth Regiment of Kentucky Volunteers is stated below.

MEXICAN WAR 1847

ROLL OF CAPTAIN JOHN G. LAIR'S COMPANY[5]

Names
Commissioned Officers
John G. Lair, Captain
Milford Elliott, First Lieutenant
Samuel D. Cowan, Second Lieutenant
Cyrenius W. Gilmore, Second Lieutenant

Sergeants	*Age*
Andrew H. Campbell	25
James M. Cowan	37
Erasmus D. Fisher	22
Isaac Smith	19

Corporals	*Age*
Cyrenius W. Collyer	23
Lewis C. Grubb	20
Tunstall Q. Jasper	26
Henry L. Porch	22

Musicians	*Age*
William F. Turpin	44
William S. Turpin	20

Privates	*Age*
Adkins, Benjamin	18
Alexander, Thomas	18
Armstrong, Wiliam H.	25
Arnett, William W.	35
Baker, John A.	22
Barnett, James T. W.	20
Beaty, Addison	22
Black, Calvin	19
Blacklidge, Woodruff	18
Blankenship, Noah	22
Bowyers, James	21
Bratton, Richard C.	18
Brown, William	26
Buckner, Bemat B.	18
Burger, Jackson	20
Carugan, James M.	19
Carugan, John	18
Christian, John C.	20
Cox, Thomas	26
Crain, John L.	18
Cundriff, Martin	22
Dunman, Green	23
Durham, Samuel	19
Durham, William	29
Elder, Jesse T.	20
Estis, Patrick H.	23
Evans, James	21
Faris, Thomas C.	25
Faris, Tunstall Q.	21
Freeman, Green C.	22
Freeman, Stephen L.	25
Fugate, Martin H.	19
Gamis, Thomas	22
Gilmore, James	19
Goggin, David	43
Gunnell, Robert N.	24
Hargis, Thomas	20
Harman, David S.	21

[5]From the National Archives.

Privates	Age		
Harman, William	23	Price, Noah	22
Harris, John L.	19	Pumphery, Anderson	23
Hays, Charles P.	31	Quinton, John Jr.	20
Hays, Isaac	40	Roberts, Montgomery	19
Hendricks, James	19	Rousseau, James A.	20
Higgins, Columbus	28	Rousseau, Lawrence H.	19
Hines, Joel	21	Sadler, Edward	19
Hoskins, Gideon	24	Silvers, Wesley	22
Hunt, Silas	20	Snodgrass, Simeon	18
Jasper, Merrill	22	Stewart, George B.	18
Lamb, James M.	26	Stogsdill, John	23
May, Jesse	23	Stringer, Charles	22
McGinnis, James C.	19	Stringer, Cyrenius W.	20
McKinney, William W.	22	Sumney, David B. F.	20
McLeen, Hosea C.	44	Surben, Galen E.	19
Meece, Harvey J.	19	Tarter, Alvadas	22
Merrick, James T.	21	Tarter, Calet	22
Millz (or s) Samuel F.	21	Taylor, Lewis	20
Morgan, William	39	Taymans, Elisha G.	24
Mounts, Greenup R.	21	Thacker, James	20
Nance, Jesse	25	Vaught, Stephen	28
Nunnelly, William B.	24	Warren, Alexander	19
Owens, David D.	20	Weddle, Daniel	18
Parker, Chrisman H.	19	Wells, John M.	19
Pence, William	21	Williams, George B.	20
Peters, Harrison	24	Wilson, Benjamin G.	20
		Woodall, John	18

THE CIVIL WAR

The purpose in this account is not to give attention to the cause or causes of the War Between the States, but to the part Pulaski County had in this conflict which changed the social and political conditions in the nation. However, it is necessary to bring some things forward which bear on the understanding of points to be mentioned.

President Lincoln was elected in November, 1860. South Carolina seceded from the Union on December 17, 1860.[6]

---

[6]Thomas P. Kettell, *History of the Great Rebellion*, (Cincinnati, Ohio: L. Stebbins [copyright], 1865) p. 35.

Her leaders' intention was to have a new Confederate government in operation before Mr. Lincoln's accession to office. On the fourth of March the president was inaugurated.

After South Carolina seceded she was alone for a time, and it behooved her to seek aid and friends. Commissioners were sent to other state conventions which were called to follow the lead of South Carolina. During this time when war clouds were threatening, Kentucky took no part. She passed no acts of secession but adopted a policy of neutrality.

In April, 1861, President Lincoln issued a Proclamation calling for seventy-five thousand troops. On receipt of the requisition to Kentucky, Governor Magoffin sternly replied, "Kentucky will furnish no troops for the purpose of subduing her sister Southern States." On May 20, the Governor issued a declaration solemnly forbidding any movement of troops upon Kentucky soil. But this did not prevent many Kentuckians from answering the call to arms. Many volunteered in home guards while others reported to recruiting stations for enlistment. Camp Dick Robinson in Garrard County was the most important center for Union activities.

During this summer the First Federal Kentucky Cavalry Regiment was organized in Casey County by Colonel Frank Wolford, who had been appointed by General Nelson at Camp Dick Robinson. The companies under his command were organized from surrounding counties. Pulaski was one of these. Until the last year of operations this regiment was better known as "Wolford's Cavalry." The Colonel did not have an exalted respect for too much "red tape." Though he had had experience in a previous war (Mexican) he had peculiar notions of his own. He cared little for prescribed forms of maneuvering his men, so he got them in shape to suit himself. He believed a soldier's efficiency depended more on his fighting qualities than on his ability to go through fancy maneuvers. He estimated a man, not by his rank or position, but by his real worth.

About eight companies, enough to give type to the regiment, came from the outlying spurs of the Cumberland Mountains. One of these companies was Company L of Pulaski County, which was organized at Somerset, September 11, 1861; arrived at Camp Dick Robinson on September 13, 1861; was mustered into service October 28, 1861; and was mustered out December 31, 1864.

The roll of Captain W. N. Owens' Company[7] of Pulaski County, which is stated above, is as follows:

Commissioned Officers

Captain W. N. Owens, enlisted September 11, 1861, promoted major July 31, 1862
Captain Joe D. Beaty, enlisted September 11, 1861
Captain John B. Fishback
First Lieutenant Matthew H. Blackford
First Lieutenant Robert M. Griffin
Second Lieutenant William A. Lockett
Second Lieutenant Benjamin H. Milton
Second Lieutenant George K. Speed
Second Lieutenant Granville J. Vaught

Non Commissioned Officers

First Sergeant Hampton H. Brinkley
First Sergeant John Rourk
Sergeant Andrew J. Catron
Sergeant Daniel Elliott
Sergeant William B. Gragg
Corporal Archibald B. Campbell
Corporal William H. Cox
Corporal James F. Humphries
Corporal Rufus M. Patterson
Corporal Admice T. Saunders
Corporal Joseph N. Taylor
James B. Harper, Bugler

Privates

Baker, David	Eassepp, James	Green, Marquis D.
Bates, Mitchell	Edwards, Andrew F.	Haynes, Ebenezer T.
Bowling, John H.	Edwards, Jesse	Loveless, John
Bratten, James P.	Elliott, Henry	McDowell, Thomas
Brewes, Orville	Falkner, Richard	Messick, John C.
Burton, William	Farmer, William	Mills, Joseph
Culliss, John F.	Fulcher, Andrew	Moore, Robert H.
Doolien, James D.	Green, Luther C.	Nunnelly, Robert A.

[7]Eastham Tarrant, *The Wild Riders of the First Kentucky Cavalry*, (Louisville, Ky.: R. H. Carothers Press, 1894) pp. 463-69.

Privates

Osborne, William A.	Silvers, Jesse M.	Sowder, Emanuel
Raney, Samuel	Silvers, John P.	Sowder, William
Reynolds, Samuel	Silvers, Wesley H.	Taylor, John
Sewell, Joseph	Smith, Thomas H.	Thacker, John W.

Discharged for Disability

Sergeant G. McLue	Gilmore, John B.	Reynolds, James F.
Ashurst, Henry C.	Mound, Ira R.	Tinsley, William
Burnett, Henry D.	Osborn, John	

Killed and Died

Corporal James H. Adams	Gilmore, Wilford
Corporal George W. Baber	McQuery, Robert
Corporal Charles P. Cox	Parker, John M. W. E.
Corporal John Meece	Raborne, Robert F.
Branch, William	Warn, John
Comstock, John C.	West, James M.
Evans, Killis J.	

Recruits Transferred

Sergeant Christopher C. Kenner   Corporal Peter R. Dobbs

Privates

Ashley, James M.	Gregory, John P.	Mowbray, Henry
Ashley, John	Grider, John W.	Nunnelly, James M.
Ashley, John J.	Grider, William	Pence, James
Barclay, Alexander	Hail, Elias	Perkins, John
Boyd, Aaron	Hank, Miles	Rash, Francis M.
Bumganliner, George	Hartgrove, John W.	Richardson, David
Burton, Robert T.	Henson, John	Sath, Ephraim
Clarke, William	Hunt, Andrew P.	Sears, John
Davis, Constantine C.	Jones, David A.	Smith, William
Denton, Alexander	Jones, James A.	Summers, William
Dungan, John	Large, Walter	Swearinger, William
Edwards, William	Love, John B.	Willis, David
Frost, John	Love, William H.	Woodall, William
Gregory, George G.		

THE BATTLE OF LOGAN'S CROSSROADS
(ERRONUSLY CALLED THE BATTLE OF MILL SPRINGS)

The beginning of war activities in Pulaski County was in September, 1861, when General Felix Zollicoffer entered Kentucky by way of Cumberland Gap and advanced in the direction of Camp Dick Robinson, where the Union forces were stationed.

This news from the mountains of eastern Kentucky demanded attention. Colonel Frank Wolford, with a strong body of his regiment, moved across the Rockcastle River and went into camp. The rugged, wild, and dreary scenery suggested an appropriate name, and he headed a dispatch to General Thomas "Camp Wild Cat," which name it retains today.

It was in this area that General Zollicoffer was repulsed by a command of United States Volunteers from Ohio and Indiana under General Schoeff, supported by Colonel Wolford with his regiment, many of whom were Pulaskians.

About the same time scouts were sent to Clinton County on the state line. It was reported there was a Rebel organization just south of the line known as the "Bull Pups." A scouting party under Captain John A. Morrison went there to see, but the "Bull Pups" were not found. They met a squad of men from Wayne County, scouting for the Rebels, and had a skirmish with them. Captain Morrison's Company (C) was then ordered to Waitsboro on the Cumberland River, five miles south of Somerset, to watch a possible movement of the enemy.

After the battle of Wild Cat, General Thomas was moved to Crab Orchard, thus detaching General Schoeff to London. In the meantime companies A, B, C, D, E, F, G, H, I, J, and L, of the First Kentucky Regiment, were ordered to Somerset and went into camp at the Sam Owens place, which was between Somerset and the river. They were to watch the movements of the enemy south of the Cumberland River.

Zollicoffer, after his repulse at Wild Cat, fell back through Cumberland Gap and commenced reinforcing his troops, preparatory to making another move into central Kentucky by way of Monticello and Somerset. General Thomas had been ordered, with General Schoeff and his brigade, to Somerset. Two days later some of the enemy appeared before Colonel Hoskins' camp near the Cumberland River. On the twenty-seventh of November Colonel Hoskins reported the enemy in force near Monticello. At this time General Zollicoffer advanced to the south side of the river and made his camp at Mill Springs, Wayne County. He determined to occupy the position on the opposite side at Beech Grove. On January 18, 1862, he fortified this place and placed there five regiments of infantry, twelve guns, and several hundred cavalry. At Mill Springs he kept two regiments of infantry and a few hundred horses.

At the same time a Union force under Wolford was at Columbia, twenty-five miles northwest of Beech Grove. General Buell and General Thomas occupied Logan's Crossroads, five miles from Beech Grove. General Schoeff and General Helvetti held Somerset. Between Somerset and Logan's Crossroads runs Fishing Creek, then so swollen from rains that it could not be crossed. Roads were bad. Supplies were running short, and the neighboring county had been exhausted. In this state of affairs General Zollicoffer determined to attack the Union forces at the Crossroads before the force at Somerset and at Columbia should be able to join them.

The morning of Sunday, January 19, was foggy and rainy. General Zollicoffer, with Tennessee troops and two wings of troops from Mississippi and Alabama, advanced and soon encountered a strong picket, who, not being aware the enemy was advancing in force, offered determined resistance. In the meantime Colonel Wolford, whom General Zollicoffer had not reckoned would make such speed over muddy roads, had come from Columbia by way of Wolf Creek, Simith Cain's, Old Harrison, and Forbush (Faubush). Colonel Wolford heard the firing and ordered a company to reinforce the picket. The Confederates opened a galling fire which was returned by the enemy in the same spirit.

During an electrical rain storm this battle raged for four hours. At this time, while resistance was strong and amid the confusion of the storm and the smoke of battle, General Zollicoffer, the handsome and gallant commander of the Confederate forces, fell mortally wounded. Whose shot killed him was never known. It may have been fired by Colonel Fry of the Federal forces, whose story confirms that supposition, or by one Ike Chrisman, who in delirium raved about having done it.

A touching story was told of the Reverend W. H. Honnell, the chaplain of Wolford's Regiment, who was working in the midst of the fight, caring for the wounded and encouraging men to deeds of valor. He dismounted and assisted in removing the body of the Confederate General from the road to prevent its being trampled by the surging mass of combatants.

The loss of their beloved commander was depressing and discouraging to Zollicoffer's men. They soon fell back to their entrenchments on the Cumberland River.

In the evening, after the swollen waters of Fishing Creek went down, General Schoeff came up with additional regiments, and on the following morning advanced in the direction of the Cumberland River. His men began firing; but getting no response, they approached to find the enemy had crossed the river in the night, burning all the boats to avoid pursuit.

Thus ended the Battle of Logan's Crossroads, a decisive battle which was among the first to turn the tide of the Civil War.

After a short rest from the conflict, General Thomas moved his infantry to Somerset, where he completed preparations for again striking the enemy. He was later ordered to Tennessee, and for several months Pulaski County was relatively quiet.[8]

Morgan's Raid Through Central Kentucky

In July, 1862, news came to Somerset that Morgan, famed Confederate Cavalry leader, was at Crab Orchard with his dashing and daring regiment. As one Union officer put it: "He has the best-mounted men in the world."

Morgan's retreat from Kentucky to Tennessee, through Somerset, took place after he had captured and abandoned Cynthiana. The Federal troops were closing in on him, and he retreated by way of Crab Orchard, moving toward Somerset. At Crab Orchard and Somerset 130 government wagons were captured and burned. At Somerset a great many stores of all kinds, blankets, shoes, etc., were found. Several wagons were loaded with as much as could be conveniently carried away and the rest destroyed. He also found arms that had been taken from General Zollicoffer, together with shells and ammunition.[9]

Morgan's Cavalry left Crab Orchard at 11:00 A.M., moving toward Somerset, and reached there at sundown of July 22.

---
[8]General information, *Ibid.*, pp. 41-65.
[9]Swigget, *The Rebel Rider*, (Indianapolis, Ind.: Bobbs-Merrill Company, 1934), p. 69.

The telegraph was taken possession of, and Colonel Morgan instructed his operator to call Stanford and countermand all of General Boyle's orders for pursuit.[10] In a short time Stanford telegraphed, asking if there were any signs of Morgan. Ellsworth, the clever operator, assured the Stanford operator there were none. They arranged a secret code, so as not to be interrupted. Thus reassured, Morgan and his men turned in for a good night's sleep.

The next morning Morgan telegraphed the Union Commander:

> GENERAL J. T. BOYLE, Louisville, Kentucky. Good morning, Jerry. This telegraph is a great institution. You should destroy it as it keeps me too well posted. My friend Ellsworth here has all your dispatches since July 10, on file. Do you wish copies? JOHN HUNT MORGAN, *Commanding Brigade, C.S.A.*

By the time General Boyle's Union forces reached Somerset, Morgan, enjoying the confusion his telegraph operator had caused, had crossed the Cumberland River at Waitsboro and was galloping toward Dixie.

A rare volume[11] still in existance contains the signatures of General John Hunt Morgan and fifty-eight of his officers. These were obtained in August, 1863, while General Morgan and many of his officers were held prisoners at Columbus, Ohio. On the list of signatures was the name of M. B. Perkins, captain of Company C, Sixth Regiment Cavalry, Morgan's Division, C. S. A., Somerset. Captain M. B. Perkins formed this Company C in Somerset and two of the members were Tom Shepherd and Will C. Curd.

The capture of the General and his cavalrymen occurred while they were executing one of the most daring and spectacular movements of the entire War Between the States. This was after a foray into western Kentucky, when Morgan retreated into Tennessee and there made preparations for his advance into Ohio. Proceeding northward and crossing the Cumberland and Ohio rivers, Morgan moved through southern Indiana and Ohio, destroying railroads and cutting off communications. Continuing along the Ohio River, he

---

[10]Basil W. Duke, *History of Morgan's Cavalry* (Cincinnati, Ohio: Miami Printing & Publishing Company, 1867), p. 204.
[11]From *Lexington Leader,* March 12, 1940.

was opposed by large Federal forces when he tried to cross the river at Cincinnati; he pressed eastward toward Wheeling, West Virginia, in search of a place to cross.

Finally, after a skirmish in which he lost a large number of men, his command was surrounded by Federal soldiers, and many of his officers were captured and sent to the Ohio penitentiary at Columbus. His daring escape was effected within a short time and he returned to the South to reorganize his Cavalry for its last invasion of Kentucky in 1864.

Notes and Incidents

In 1864, the First Kentucky Cavalry, now under the command of General Stoneman of the Army of the Ohio, was ordered to Tennessee.[12] He issued many orders which were often impractical in the extreme. The stern iron will of the commander thought to bend the dashing, frolicsome, mountaineer Cavalry into rigid discipline. It was found, on closer acquaintance, that the General, like Colonel Wolford, had certain original tactics and regulations all his own, which he put in force as well as he could. It was to be shown which should yield: the iron will of the General, or the rather free ways of the Cavalry.

The conflict came on the march through the central and southern part of the state to the first objective, Point Burnside. They had orders not to break ranks, but to keep in orderly march. The homes of most of the men were directly on the route to that place. There were various reasons why they desired to make stops. The most important, perhaps, were to see their families and to tell their sweethearts good-by. In passing through Jessamine and Garrard counties, many of the men slipped out of the ranks. Upon reaching Danville, where many roads centered and streets offered opportunities to execute their favorite maneuvers, General Stoneman issued orders to arrest all the men found out of ranks. An officer gave the command for the column to "right face—march!" which order was obeyed with alacrity, [with the men] marching through Stoneman's bodyguard. Companies A and B and parts of C and F composed the columns which broke through Stoneman's lines.

---

[12]Colonel Wolford had been released from the command of the First Kentucky Cavalry.

The main command marched on to Burnside, where a roll call showed only seventy-one men and two officers present out of over eight hundred men. The blameless conduct of these two officers on that occasion deserves that their names be handed down to posterity. They were Lieutenants James E. Chilton and Joe D. Beaty of Company L of Pulaski County. Not a field officer or staff officer was there.[18]

Perhaps it will not be amiss to give the reader a character sketch of Colonel Frank Wolford, in whose regiment many Pulaskians served.

Colonel Wolford was forty-four years of age when he entered the service. He belonged to an intellectual family, but poor in this world's goods. His early life was one of struggle and toil. He acquired a practical education at home; his only tutor was his father. His study was by the light of "pine knots" after the family had retired for the night.

His first occupation was teaching; then he studied law under a crochety Pennsylvanian, who was a frequent visitor in his father's home on Rolling Fork Creek in Casey County.

When the country became involved in war with Mexico, in 1847, a company was made up in Casey County, and he was made captain. On his return from the war he was elected to represent Casey and Russell counties in the legislature. Colonel Wolford was a man of much genius and originality, and acquired fame and popularity in central Kentucky as an orator. Had he had opportunities for classical training in youth, it is impossible to conjecture what he might have been; but there was so much individuality about the man, that it would have been difficult to have confined him to beaten paths. He was a man careless in respect to finances, and in speech and in dress. But he possessed the qualifications of loyalty, patriotism, honesty, determination, and force. His speech was not profane but abounded in colloquialisms such as "thar," and sometimes his orders were said to be "git ready and git going."

He inherited religious tendencies, often conducting the service at the burial of a fellow comrade.

Colonel Wolword was conspicuous in the midst of danger, giving orders and encouraging his men. To add to his unmili-

"Excerpts from Eastham Tarrent, *The Wild Riders of the First Kentucky Cavalry,* (Louisville, Ky.: R. H. Carothers Press, 1894) p. 318.

tary appearance, he rode an ugly roan horse and wore an old red hat and brown homespun coat. His face often had not been defiled by water or razor for some time.[14]

EXCERPTS OF DISPATCHES
(FROM WAR RECORDS)

Relative to the Battle of Duttons Hill, Knoxville, March 1, 1863.
East Tennessee Headquarters Department.
General Pegram will start in a few days on an expedition from Fentress County, Tennessee, through Wayne County.

D. S. DONNELSON, *Brigadier General, Knoxville,*
to GENERAL SAMUEL JONES.

Mt. Sterling, Kentucky, March 5, 1863.
Information received that the Rebels are crossing the Cumberland River at Stigall's Ferry below Somerset.

BENJAMIN P. RUNKLE, *Colonel Commanding 2nd Brigade.*

Lexington, Kentucky, March 21, 1863.
MAJOR GENERAL H. C. WRIGHT, Cincinnati, Ohio
Colonel Wolford says, "Three thousand five hundred Rebels are at Stigall's Ferry ready to cross." Send forward immediately all troops you can spare. Wolford will fight them. Carter and myself will go forward at once.

Q. A. GILLMORE, *Brigadier General.*

Louisville, March 22, 1863.
MAJOR GENERAL W. S. ROSECRANS:
General Fry telegraphs from Stanford 700 Rebel cavalry are moving in direction of Hustonville, 700 in the direction of Stanford. Colonel Hoskins telegraphs 3,000 at Somerset and 5,000 on other side of river. I do not believe the latter reliable.

J. T. BOYLE, *Brigadier General.*

Lexington, Kentucky, March 22, 1863.
COLONEL BENJAMIN J. RUNKLE, Richmond:
The Rebels have crossed the Cumberland and the Somerset operator has again run away. Keep Clay's Ferry in order and be ready to move at a moment's notice.

SAMUEL M. KNEELAND, *Lieutenant and Aide-de-Camp.*

---

[14]*Ibid.*, (from the chaplain of his regiment) p. 20f.

Somerset, Kentucky, March 31, 1863.
A. E. BURNSIDE, *Major General Commanding:*
I attacked the enemy yesterday in strong point of his own selection, defended by six cannon, near this town; fought him for five hours, driving him from one position to another, and finally stormed his position. Whipped him handsomely and drove him toward the river. His loss over 300 killed, wounded and prisoners. The enemy outnumbered us nearly two to one and were commanded by Pegram in person. Night stopped pursuit, which will be resumed in the morning.

GILLMORE, *Brigadier General.*

Stigall's Ferry, April 1, 1863.
A. E. BURNSIDE, *General Commanding:*
During the night the troops recrossed the Cumberland River in three places. We have retaken between 300 and 400 cattle.

GILLMORE, *Brigadier General.*

THE BATTLE OF DUTTON'S HILL

On the first day of March, 1863, Governor Robinson (Governor Magoffin having resigned) notified General Wright, commander of the Ohio at Cincinnati, of information received that a heavy invasion of Kentucky had been determined by the enemy. Also, Generals Marshall and Pegram were to invade the state from Virginia with 7,000 mounted troops, simultaneously with Morgan and Forrest from Tennessee with a like number, the date being the twentieth of March.

The First Kentucky was given orders to advance to Danville where they remained until March 6. This regiment, under Colonel Wolford, later moved to Stanford and then three miles out on the Hustonville Road where it camped until the twenty-second.

Here the men and horses rested for two weeks, only sending out scouts to the Cumberland River and Mt. Vernon. The camp was in a wealthy bluegrass region, and forage and rations were plentiful. There were good Union men in this section, but many of the splendid farmers were Southern sympathizers. No matter on which side their sympathies lay, their hospitable homes were generally opened freely to both men and officers.

This did not last long. As early as March 18, General Q. A. Gillmore received information from spies, who had been sent to Somerset and the Cumberland River, that Southern troops under General Scott, numbering 3,500 men, were in Wayne County. On the twenty-first of March Colonel Wolford, who held the front, telegraphed Gillmore at Stanford, "The Rebels are at Stigall's Ferry ready to cross the river." On the twenty-first and twenty-second, Pegram crossed the Cumberland. Moving in two columns, one by Waynesburg and the other on the Crab Orchard Road, his forces advanced to within three miles of Stanford, driving the pickets back and engaging in occasional skirmishes.

On March 28 General Carter gave orders to advance by Lancaster. General Gillmore started on the same day from Stanford and overtook Carter's command at Buck Creek, ten miles north of Somerset on the Crab Orchard Road. There he learned the enemy had retreated. On the thirtieth, General Gillmore took command as a portion of Garrard's Cavalry stormed the hill. This was done with great coolness and gallantry. Wolford's regiment seemed to be everywhere at the same time. They were on their native soil and knew every foot of the country. They had been trained sketchily in discipline and knew little about drill, but they respected their colonel and he knew their fighting ability.

Colonel Wolford's men, not being in a position to see the movements of the enemy, were now hopeful the bloody work was over. But they were mistaken for, just at this time, Scott's dashing Louisiana Cavalry was seen maneuvering for the capture of the train and horses, then a mile in the rear. Scott with his regiment and Colonel Wolford with his moved up and located on the border of the heavy-timbered land. Soon the fighting became desperate. Fences were scattered; trees were mowed down. There were more men killed here than in any other part of the field. The estimated time of the battle was three hours and the number killed about one hundred and fifty.

This practically ended the Battle of Dutton's Hill, a victory for the Union forces under General Quincy A. Gillmore.

From this point (the Confederates now being in full retreat) a running fight was kept up to near the river where pursuit ended as nightfall came. The Rebels withdrew during the night and recrossed the river.

Major William Owens, who was prominent throughout the fighting, distinguished himself on different parts of the field that day, and had a shoulder strap shot off. The major was in the vicinity of his own home, which was an inspiration to do gallant deeds.[15]

At various times and for indefinite periods, detachments under General Burnside were stationed at Somerset and Burnside (this place was named in honor of General Burnside—it having been known prior to the Civil War as Point Isabel), these points being on a direct route from Cincinnati to the South.

Because of its location on the route and its situation at the juncture of the Cumberland and South Fork rivers, Burnside was a strategic point for reconnaissance and command. On the bottom of Lake Cumberland lie the remains of a house known by old inhabitants as Burnside's headquarters. On the hill on the opposite side of the South Fork River is another house, said to have been his observation headquarters, which is standing today.

The river for many miles above and below Burnside was the rendezvous for the armies. The high wooded hills made scouting easy. Both armies crossed and recrossed the river at the Stigall and Newell ferries below Burnside.

The counties of Wayne and Clinton and parts of Pulaski were on the south side of the Cumberland River. Most of the citizens were intensely partisan, and they furnished a large number of gallant officers and men to both the army of the North and that of the South. Throughout the war this section suffered depredations by both armies. The river divided the two armies, so encampments were made on both sides. It was army tactics to demand food and rations for the men and horses. The country by now was depleted of both food and horses.

Joe B. Newell, a Union man but a Southern sympathizer (of which there were many), had been brought down to his last horse, a flea-bitten roan, which had been locked in the smokehouse. This horse was the only thing left on which to go to the mill. The lock proved to be no safeguard to a soldier who wanted a fresh horse. Mr. Newell's daughter, Mrs.

---

[15]*Ibid.*, p. 153.

S. R. Owens, was not to be outdone by a soldier of either army. She stationed herself in front of the house and, seeing an officer approaching, stepped out and accosted him, telling him what had taken place. The gallant officer called to an orderly, then asked Mrs. Owens if she could pick out the horse. She answered, "Yes," and pointed to the horse and soldier a short distance down the road. The officer directed the orderly to tell the offending soldier to give the horse back to the owner. The soldier refused, saying, "I'll be d—— if I do." Mrs. Owens, who had followed the orderly, had been unconsciously clipping a large pair of scissors she had in the voluminous pocket of her full dress skirt. She must have given the scissors a merciless clip as she replied in his same words. The surrounding soldiers said, "Aye, but she cussed—she'll shoot."

She answered, "Yes, and I'll shoot to kill." The horse was recovered, and she rode it bridleless and bareback to her home.

Those regiments on the north side of the river deeply sympathized with their fellow comrades in arms living on the south side, because of the exposed condition of their families.

At the time when General Carter, Union commander, was on the south side of the river, his force was ordered back to Somerset. As the infantry was crossing over the river on May 6, 1863, an unfortunate accident occurred. They were using two boats, pulled over by means of ropes stretched across, one some distance above the other. The upper rope broke, and as the boat was swept downstream, gaining velocity from the rapid current, the men became excited. As it passed under the lower rope, they rushed to the upper side of the boat and caught the rope; this action threw the most weight to that side, causing the boat to dip, capsize, and throw its passengers into the river. The men, encumbered with knapsacks and unable to swim, drowned before help could reach them. Thirty-two lost their lives. Those whose bodies were recovered were buried in the deep sand along the riverbanks. When the first high tide receded the sand was washed away, and the feet of those unfortunate soldiers were seen protruding from their shallow graves.[16]

---

[16] Authority for this is found in excerpts from Tarrant, *The Wild Riders of the First Kentucky Cavalry*, in Brigadier General Q. A. Gillmore's report of the Battle of Dutton's Hill, and from my mother.

Regiments

The Twelfth Regiment of Infantry, Union Army, was organized by Colonel W. A. Hoskins in October, 1861, at Camp Clio. Captain Lawrence H. Rousseau (Mexican War) was commissioned colonel August 11, 1862. Captain Joe M. Owens of Company B was promoted to major July 15, 1862. Ephraim Hays was adjutant of Company A.[17]

The Thirty-second Kentucky Regiment of Infantry was organized from various detachments and was mustered into service with Thomas Z. Morrow as colonel on the fifteenth of April, 1863, at Camp Burnside.[18]

In the Third Kentucky Infantry Robert Gilmore[19] was commissioned first lieutenant for bravery in battle. When the flag was shot down he ran out, picked it up, waved it, and planted it in the ground. His gun rod was shot off of the end of his gun barrel. Captain R. M. Gilmore, under Colonel Buckner Board of Company M, was promoted to major, May 12, 1865. According to an old letter, he commanded General Sherman's escort in the famous "March" from Atlanta to the sea.

SPANISH-AMERICAN WAR

The echoes of the sinking of the United States battleship "Maine" off the coast of Cuba on February 15, 1898, had scarcely ceased, when, on April 20, President McKinley signed an ultimatum to Spain demanding the immediate withdrawal of her forces from Cuba. This Declaration of War called for 25,000 volunteers.

Pulaski County answered this call with a large quota of men.

WORLD WAR I

The conflict of World War I was in its third year. The realization of the United States government that Germany intended to continue her submarine warfare, that England might become impoverished and be forced into submission,

---

[17]W. H. Perrin, J. H. Battle, G. C. Kniffin, *Kentucky, A History of the State*, (Louisville, Ky.: F. A. Battey and Company, 1887) p. 701.
[18]*Ibid.*, p. 712.
[19]*Ibid.*, p. 695.

that the Germans might then use England's navy in conquering the United States, caused action. After a lengthy and stormy session of Congress on the nights of April 4 and 5, 1917, at eleven minutes past one o'clock, the forbearing and peace-loving president, Woodrow Wilson, made a formal Declaration of War against Germany.

An eloquent statement justifying the United States' entry, made when the first contingent marched to war, was: "The lads that go now, highhearted as they are, go to bleed and do and die in a war that is to be fought under water, on its surface, on the land and in the air above. They go to face all of these; they go to face more; they go to prove that they are the soldiers of a great republic whose people are civilized; they go to write into history that humanity, mercy and justice have their place in war as in peace and they go to win victory."

In this classification, Pulaski soldiers—lawyers, doctors, boys from the farm, from the stores, yes, from every vocation—can be placed.

WORLD WAR II

On Sunday afternoon, December 7, 1941, many who were sitting quietly at home, scanning the *Courier-Journal,* and listening to their radios tuned low to their favorite program, caught strange words. The dial was turned higher and this announcement blared forth: "The Japanese attacked Pearl Harbor." A group of school girls out for an afternoon walk were startled as this announcement, from a small portable radio they were carrying, caught their ears. So it was, not only in Pulaski County, but over the nation. The news was incredible, but too true; the nation was again caught in the maelstrom of war.

There was no time for bickering or red tape. The security of the United States was at stake. Immediate action was necessary. On December 9, President Franklin D. Roosevelt declared war on Japan.

Putting the country on a wartime footing of production of war materials and trained man power was a stupendous task. By May 26 this was accomplished.

The patriotism and zeal of the boys was characteristic of their fathers who fought in World War I, just a short twenty-three years before. Pulaski boys were outstanding, not only because they were among the first to respond to the call to the "colors," but also because of the sterling quality of their service. George Ed Kiser's splendid record as "Eagle" pilot was an example of this trait of Pulaski's soldiers.

Perhaps the deeds of those who dug into Japanese-filled caves on the western front, or of those who were in the invasion of Africa, or the lonely vigil of the forgotten sentinel on the African desert, were not as spectacular as the eagle pilot's sky raids, but they were equally meritorious.

Pulaski's casualties numbered approximately 196, of which Ralph Gardner and Fred Bruce Hill of Somerset were the first; these two were lost when the American forces landed at Casablanca.

It can be said that Pulaski County boys clasped hands around the globe.

The tabulation of Pulaski County's casualties in the Army is:

K. I. A.	(killed in action)	81
D. O. W.	(died of wounds)	10
D. O. I.	(died of injuries)	1
D. N. B.	(died—non-battle)	24
F. O. D.	(finding of death under public law)	3
M.		0

MEMORIALS

In 1893 the court took up the matter of the erection of a public fountain in the Public Square, and justices were appointed to confer with a committee from the Board of Council of the city. In 1908, R. H. Bartells designed and erected in the Square the present little park with the fountain. It was built through the generosity of the citizens of Somerset and Pulaski County. Bronze tablets were placed on each of the pedestals, to the memory of the following citizens who have contributed to Pulaski County's development and have passed on to the Great Beyond, but live in the hearts of a grateful people. These men were: T. R. Griffin, Thomas Z. Morrow, O. H. Waddle, Dr. George Perkins, Dr. J. W. F. Parker, Milford Elliot, and Dr. John Milton Perkins.

On June 14, 1939, the Somerset Chapter of the Daughters of the American Revolution erected and dedicated a monument to those heroes of the Revolution who came here and helped to develop Pulaski County. A bronze tablet, bearing fifty-six names, was placed on two old millstones on a foundation of native stone in the little park in the center of the Public Square.

A monument to the Veterans of Foreign Wars also was erected in the park in the Public Square.

In the plot beside the courthouse, a marker of native stone was erected. A bronze tablet, bearing the names of the war dead and the following inscription – "To the memory of Pulaski County's honored dead who lost their lives in World War II"—was placed on this marker. This marker was erected by the Girl Scout troops of Somerset and by the generous gifts of citizens and organizations.

Zollicoffer Park was set aside in memory of General Felix Zollicoffer and his Confederate followers, and dedicated Oct. 7, 1933. It is located nine miles west of Somerset on an acre of ground surrounding the spot where General Zollicoffer fell. The ground was donated by Mrs. Green Trimble, wife of a one-armed Union soldier.

Erected in 1911, a monument to his memory bears the following inscription:

> On this spot fell General Felix Zollicoffer of Tennessee, Jan. 19, 1862. Lieutenants Bailie Peyton, Jr., H. M. R. Fogg and more than 150 of their Confederate associates in the Battle of Fishing Creek here died, with General Zollicoffer for the right as they saw it. They are a part of the great host who crowned Southern manhood with glorious immortality. They gave their lives, the noblest of all offerings, at Duty's Call and fame will ever point with pride to this sacred place where these heroes now so peacefully sleep.
>
> Erected by Gen. Bennett H. Young, Mrs. L. Z. Duke and James A. Shuttleworth as a tribute to Southern valor.

Near this monument is a mound which covers the remains of about one hundred Confederate soldiers which were thrown into a pit and covered with earth by the Union soldiers after the battle. A marker erected on the mound bears this inscription:

Beneath this mound rest in sleep that knows no waking more than 100 Confederate soldiers from Tennessee, Mississippi and Alabama who were killed in the battle of Fishing Creek (Mill Springs, Logan's Cross Roads), Jan. 19, 1862. We know not who they were, but the whole world knows what they were. These died far from their homes, but they fill heroes' graves and glory keeps ceaseless watch about their tomb.

The National Cemetery, known as the Mill Springs (Nancy) Cemetery, is near the site of this same battlefield. The Union soldiers who were killed in the battle of Logan's Crossroads or Fishing Creek are buried here. In 1940, there were, according to the cemetery custodian, 754 buried there. Since World War II, the remains of those who gave their lives on the foreign fields have been returned and buried there.

.... *CONCLUSION* ....

In reading this book you have learned something of the people who settled Pulaski County, where they came from, why they came, and the privations and hardships they endured. You have learned something, too, of the formation of the county and its government; the names of some who contributed to its birth, infancy, and full grown status; of its growth and development through one hundred and fifty years.

Some of the pioneers who came here moved on and had a part in the settling of the West; others remained to rear large families, the descendants of whom are here today and take great pride in the standards set by their forebears.

Pulaski County today, with its modern highways and automobiles, is a far cry from the year 1750, when Dr. Walker located the Cumberland River, and Daniel Boone went up the Rockcastle River; from 1799, when Michael Stoner, Joshua Jones, and Samuel Forbush were appointed to view the best place for a road from Stoner's Ferry across Beaver Creek; from the time when this land was a wilderness, inhabited only by the redmen and wild animals and traversed by wilderness trails traveled by ox carts and pack horses.

The pine knot flare has given way to rural electricity; the once sparsely settled county now contains four sizable towns —Burnside, Science Hill, Eubank, and Ferguson—in addition to Somerset with its population of nearly ten thousand. The county, with a population of 38,500, is developing rapidly in farming and dairying, with the county seat recognized as the most progressive business town of its size in the state.

Pulaski has contributed of her children to every state in the Union. You may travel over these United States, and rarely will you stop in a city or town where you will not find a native Pulaskian. Wherever you find them, they are warm-hearted individuals having a longing in their hearts for the hills and red clay of old Pulaski.

THE RED CLAY OF PULASKI

There's a sunny hill-girt valley
Where the Cumberland wends its way,
Where the morning glory clambers,
And a cardinal sings all day.

There's a cabin in the clearing,
And a hound dog in the shade;
A scent of woodsmoke in the air,
And sorghum freshly made.

And I know that hazy mornings
Say that frost will be here soon.
There'll be bittersweet and asters,
And a golden harvest moon.

For the mist is on the river,
And it's there that I would go
To that cabin in the clearing,
That was built so long ago.

For the friends I loved are sleeping
Where I would rest some day,
In the shadow of the mountains,
Wrapped in old Pulaski clay.

— Jennie Wirt Hall

..... *LIST OF ILLUSTRATIONS* .....

	Page
Dr. Samuel Richard and Mary Newell Owens	233
Johnson's Block	234
Old National Hotel	235
Flat Lick Baptist Church	235
Stone Chimney, Waitsboro	235
Smokehouse at Lee Home	235
Ruins of James Home	235
Socrates Lee Home	236
Paling Fence Often Found in This Section	236
Home of G. W. Saunders, South of Cumberland	237
Dr. Samuel R. Owens Home	237
Old Newell Home	237
Home of William N. Owens II	237
Lewis Parker	238
Dam at Parker's Mill	238
Parker's Mill	238
Hotel Beecher, Somerset	239
Fourth Pulaski County Courthouse	239

Steamboat, "City of Burnside" 240

World's First Diesel-Electric Road Freight Locomotive 240

Stagecoach, 1910 241

Highway and Railroad Bridges Entering Burnside 241

Cumberland Falls Showing Old Moonbow Inn 242

Hon. Edwin P. Morrow 243

Hon. John Sherman Cooper, Jr. 243

Major William Newell Owens 244

Captain Joseph M. Owens 244

Major Robert McAlister Gilmore 244

Captain Milton Brent Perkins 245

Inscription on Zollicoffer Monument 245

Dr. Joseph Lowery Owens 246

Jerome Tarter 246

George W. Shadoan 246

Mrs. Jerome Tarter 246

George P. Taylor 247

Edwin D. Porch 247

David Kinkead Newell 247

Hon. Thomas Z. Morrow 247

Adolphus Waddle 248

Amelia Saunders 248

Samuel Tate 248

DR. SAMUEL RICHARD AND MARY NEWELL OWENS
PARENTS OF THE AUTHOR
TO WHOSE MEMORY THIS BOOK IS DEDICATED

JOHNSON'S BLOCK

On wagon, Davy Epperson and Harvey Sloan; on horse, William Waddle, grandfather of Ed, Will, Bob, et al; left of post with foot on stone, R. A. (Dick) Johnson and right of post, F. E. Tibbals.

OLD NATIONAL HOTEL

FLAT LICK BAPTIST CHURCH

STONE CHIMNEY, WAITSBORO

SMOKEHOUSE AT LEE HOME

RUINS OF JAMES HOME

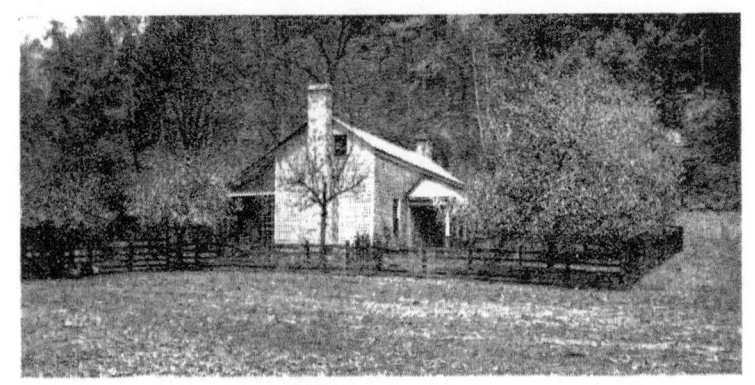

SOCRATES LEE HOME

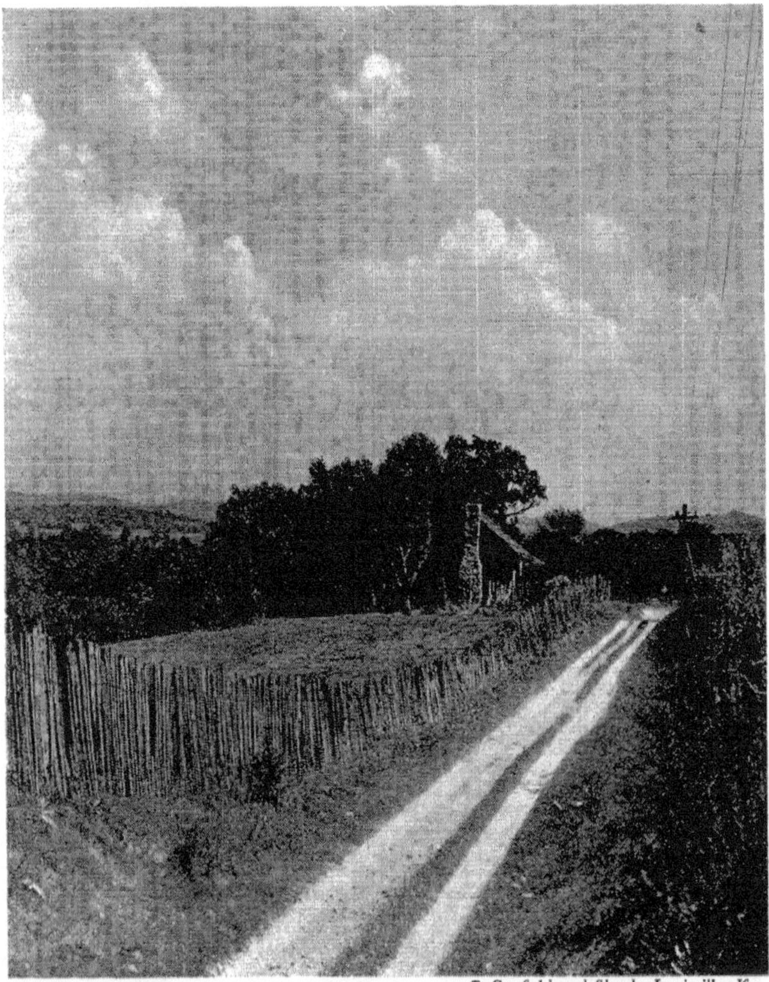

© *Caufield and Shook, Louisville, Ky.*

PALING FENCE OFTEN FOUND IN THIS SECTION

HOME OF
G. W. SAUNDERS
SOUTH OF
CUMBERLAND

DR. SAMUEL R. OWENS
HOME

OLD NEWELL HOME
built circa 1796 by
John and William Beaty
Home of John and
Polly Forgey Beaty

HOME OF
WILLIAM N. OWENS II

LEWIS PARKER

DAM AT PARKER'S MILL

PARKER'S MILL
built more than one hundred
years ago, before 1849

HOTEL BEECHER,
SOMERSET

FOURTH PULASKI
COUNTY COURTHOUSE,
BUILT 1847

STEAMBOAT, "CITY OF BURNSIDE," ON CUMBERLAND RIVER AT WAITSBORO

WORLD'S FIRST DIESEL-ELECTRIC ROAD FREIGHT LOCOMOTIVE SOUTHERN RAILWAY, NEAR BURNSIDE, BEFORE FORMATION OF CUMBERLAND LAKE

STAGECOACH, 1910, OPERATED BETWEEN BURNSIDE AND MONTICELLO
Driver, Charlie Burton, Monticello, Ky.; passengers on lookout seat, Mrs. Alma O. Tibbals, the author, Somerset, and Clara Denham Havemeyer, Chicago, Ill.

HIGHWAY AND RAILROAD BRIDGES ENTERING BURNSIDE
BEFORE FORMATION OF CUMBERLAND LAKE

CUMBERLAND FALLS SHOWING OLD MOONBOW INN

© *Caufield and Shook, Louisville, Ky.*

HON. EDWIN P. MORROW
Governor of Kentucky, 1919-1923

HON. JOHN SHERMAN COOPER, JR.
U. S. Senator from Kentucky, 1947-1948

MAJOR WILLIAM NEWELL OWENS

CAPTAIN JOSEPH M. OWENS

MAJOR ROBERT McALISTER GILMORE,
member of Sherman's escort at the surrender
of the Confederacy

CAPTAIN MILTON BRENT PERKINS
Company C, 6th Regiment
Kentucky Calvary, Morgan's Division, C.S.A.

ON THIS SPOT FELL
GEN'L. FELIX K. ZOLLICOFFER
OF TENNESSEE. JAN. 19, 1862
LIEUTS. BAILIE PEYTON Jr. H. M. R. FOGG
AND MORE THAN 150 OF THEIR CONFEDERATE ASSOCIATES IN THE BATTLE OF FISHING CREEK HERE DIED WITH GEN'L. ZOLLICOFFER FOR RIGHT AS THEY SAW IT THEY ARE PART OF THE GREAT HOST WHO CROWNED SOUTHERN MANHOOD WITH GLORIOUS IMMORTALITY THEY GAVE THEIR LIVES THE NOBLEST OF ALL OFFERINGS AT DUTY'S CALL, AND FAME WILL EVER POINT WITH PRIDE TO THIS SACRED PLACE WHERE THESE HEROES NOW SO PEACEFULLY SLEEP

ERECTED BY GEN'L. BENNETT H. YOUNG,
MRS. L. Z. DUKE AND JAMES A. SHUTTLEWORTH
AS A TRIBUTE TO SOUTHERN VALOR

INSCRIPTION ON ZOLLICOFFER MONUMENT, NEAR SOMERSET

JOSEPH LOWERY OWENS

JEROME TARTER

GEORGE W. SHADOAN,
County Attorney 1878-1902
State Senator and Representative

MRS. JEROME TARTER
Somerset's first and only postmistress

GEORGE P. TAYLOR

EDWIN D. PORCH
COUNTY CLERK 1862-78

DAVID KINKEAD NEWELL

HON. THOMAS Z. MORROW

ADOLPHUS WADDLE,
Prominent citizen, he was influential in the promotion of city water, electric system, and electric railway. He was one of those instituting the Somerset Public School and member of the school board for twenty-five years. Because of his interest in education, he was largely responsible in procuring the gift of the Carnegie Library.

AMELIA SAUNDERS,
prominent citizen on her ninetieth birthday

SAMUEL TATE
Starting in 1853 he served as constable for six years; 1860, magistrate for four years; 1871, appointed deputy sheriff and served three years; 1874, elected sheriff, serving two years; 1876, appointed sheriff and served in 1877, 1880, 1881, and 1882. Refer to vacancies in County Officers List during this period. A highly respected and much loved citizen, remembered as "Uncle Sammy Tate."

INDEX

Able, Rev. Jeremiah, 104
Acts of the General
 Assembly, 6, 9, 23, 28,
 124, 204
Adams, Alexander, 15, 85
Adams, Armstrong, 85
Adams, Charles, 124, 165
Adams, C. W., 108
Adams, Elvin, 103
Adams, Capt. George, 51
Adams House, 130
Adams, Ida Newell
 (Mrs. Charles), 165
Adams, James G., 18
Adams, Corp. James H.,
 212
Adams, John, 15
Adams, J. J., 130
Adams, Nancy, 128
Adams, Nancy, 48;
 see Pettus
Adams, Napier, 19
Adams, Robert, 203
Adams, Sam, 165-66
Addlemus, B. P., 87
Adkins, Benjamin, 208
Adkins, Ben L., 38
Adkins, George M., 19
Adkins, Maria Elliot
 (Mrs. Ben. L.), 24, 38
Agriculture, 135-44
Aldridge, Francis, 105,
 203
Alexander, Dr. E. R., 103
Alexander, George, 207
Alexander House, 130
Alexander, Nicholas, 11
Alexander, Thomas, 208
Allcorn, George, 11, 13
Allcorn, Judge James D.,
 16, 50
Allen, Dr., 151, 169
Allen, Dr. Arthur W.,
 179-80
Allen, Edwin, 47, 117
Allen, Emma Arthur
 (Mrs. James), 179

Allen, Frances, 47;
 see LeHue
Allen, James H., 162, 179
Allen, Mrs. Lum, 47, 133
Allen, Sam, 132
Allen, Samuel, Sr., 203
Allen, Mrs. Sam, 132,
 142
Allen, Sarah, 23;
 see Wade
Allen, Vida Weddle
 (Mrs. Arthur W.), 180
Anderson, Grider, 162
Anderson, Henry, 112
Anderson, J. C., 158-59
Anderson, Robert, 21, 26,
 203
Anderson, William A., 86
Anderson, William L., 85
Andis, Mrs. E. C., 141,
 143
Andis, Mary Elizabeth,
 181; see Ramsey
Andrews, Miss, 113
Arman, Thomas, 203
Armstrong, Rev. David,
 103
Armstrong, Wiliam H.,
 208
Arnett, William W., 208
Arnold, Rev. W. E., 101
Arnow, Hariette
 Simpson, 186-87
Art and Handicrafts,
 162-63
Arthur, Emma, 179;
 see Allen
Arthur, Jane Zachary
 (Mrs. John), 59
Arthur, John, 59
Asbury, J. W., 115
Ashley, James M., 212
Ashley, John, 212
Ashley, John J., 212
Ashurst, Cloda, 117
Ashurst, Henry C., 212
Astel, Rev. W. W., 107

Atkins, Wiatt, 11
Austin, John B., 204
Automobile, first, 81
Avera, Bob, 140

Baber, Corp. George W.,
 212
Bacheller, Mary, 50-51;
 see Porch
Bachellor, O. B., 16, 120
Bailey, Drew, 140
Bailey, Hannan, 207
Bain, Margaret, 105
Baker, 65
Baker, David, 211
Baker, John A., 208
Baker, Maurice, 140
Baldwin vs. Baldwin, 25
Ballou, Ellen, 164
Ballou, Thomas, 16
Bank, first, 123
Banks, Dr. G. W., 101
Banks, Thomas, 32
Baptist Meetinghouse, 13
Barclay, Alexander, 212
Barker, Claude, M., 127
Barker, Frank, 129
Barker House, 129
Barker, John, 203
Barker, Nellie, 103
Barnard, Dr., 61
Barnes, Elijah, 89
Barnes, George O., 181-
 82
Barnes, Rev. James C.,
 106, 181-82
Barnes, Mary, 37;
 see Elliot
Barnes, William, 21
Barnes, William J., 141
Barnett, James T. W.,
 208
Barnett, John, 85
Barnett, John N., 17
Barnett, J. W., 117
Barnett, Leona, 34;
 see Cox

249

Barnett, Mary Ella, 181; see Ramsey
Barnett, M. H., 116
Barnett, Nannie Brinkley (Mrs. N. L.), 181
Barnett, Napoleon, 86
Barnett, Judge N. L., 17-19, 181
Barns, Adam, 205
Barren, John, 203
Barren, William, 203
Barrier, James, 205
Barron, Robert, 121
Barron, Susan McBee, 39; see Gastineau
Bartells, R. H., 226
Bash, Emma, 164
Bash, Mrs. Lucy, 101
Bass, William, 188
Bateman, Dr. Robert C., 157
Bates, Mitchell, 211
Battles
    Dutton's Hill, 219-22
    King's Mountain, 44, 55
    Mill Springs, 199-200, 212-15, 227-28 (also called Fishing Creek and Logan's Cross Roads)
    Thames, 55
    Wild Cat, 213
Baugh, Freda, 117
Baugh, Henry, 203
Baute, Dr. Joseph, 151
Beakman, Michael, 203
Bealey, Reuben, 207
Beard, Abraham, 205
Beard, Dr. Eugene, 154-55, 170
Beard, Valeria Smith (Mrs. Eugene), 155
Beard, William, 76
Beaty, Addison, 208
Beaty and Wait, 122
Beaty, Eliza, 57; see Wait
Beaty family, 134
Beaty, Fountaine, 190-91
Beaty, Frank, 20
Beaty, Henry, 86
Beaty, James, 205
Beaty, James M., 19
Beaty, Capt. Joe D., 211, 218
Beaty, John, 27, 66, 104, 105, 133, 204
Beaty, Kitty, 103
Beaty, Margaret, 46; see Newell

Beaty, Patty, 161; see Lawrence
Beaty, Mary F. (Polly Forgey) (Mrs. John), 66, 105
Beaty, Robert, 22
Beaty Schoolhouse, 67
Beaty, William, 161
Beecher Hotel, 10, 113, 130-31
Bell, Elijah, 207
Bell, James, 205
Bently, Emma B. Hudson (Mrs. W. H.), 61
Bently, Dr. W. H., 60-61
Bernard, Lucinda, 54; see Tarter
Berry, Mae 122; see Williams
Berry, Nick, 188
Best, George, 141
Bethurum, Judge B. J., 125, 137
Bicycle, first, 81
Bilderdeck, Annie Elliot (Mrs. Owen), 38
Bilderdeck, Owen, 38
Bingham, Lee, 20
Bishop, Belle Ware (Mrs. Josiah), 161
Bishop, Galen, 175
Bishop, Dr. Henry Hawkins, 161
Bishop, Josiah, 161
Bishop, Miss, 113
Black, Calvin, 208
Black, Elizabeth Colville, 44; see Newell
Black, James D., 176
Black, Rev. John, 30, 66
Black, W. D., 16
Blackford, Lieut. Matthew H., 211
Blacklege, Icabod, 203
Blacklidge, Woodruff, 208
Blackwell, Capt. William, 37
Blain, C. R., 107
Blankenship, Noah, 208
Board, Col. Buckner, 224
Bobbitt, Gilmore, 189
Bobbitt, Jack, 134
Bobbitt, James L., 86
Bobbitt, John, 85
Bogle, Henry, 41
Bogle, Nancy, 103
Boland, Rev. B. J., 96
Bolin, Mrs. Bannie, 66
Boling, Bettie Cox (Mrs. James), 35
Books, Elizabeth, 27

Books, William, 27
Boone, Daniel, 36, 53, 229
Boone, Kirk, 123
Borden, Prof. Benjamin, 114
Borden, Daniel, 18
Borden, Emma, 114
Borum, W. O., 93
Bowen, Jacob, 207
Bowling, John H., 211
Bowyers, James, 208
Boy Scouts, 187-89
Boyce, William D., 187
Boyd, Aaron, 212
Boyd, H. B., 107
Boyd, Margaret, 43; see Morrow
Boyle, Henry, 41
Boyle, James, 128
Boyle, John, 78
Boyle, Gen. J. J., 216-17, 219
Boyle, Martha Ann Gibson (Mrs. Henry), 41
Boyles, John, 24
Boynton, D. N., 116
Bracken, Mary, 55; see Tate
Bradley, Ellen Totten (Mrs. Robert M.), 44
Bradley, Margaret (Maggie), 149, 152; see Scott
Bradley, Mary, 108, 114; see Newell
Bradley, Robert M., 44, 120, 149
Bradley, Virginia, 44, 103, 108; see Morrow
Bradley, William O., 44
Brady, Rev. A. J., 96
Branch, William, 212
Brandenberg, Rev. D. T., 107
Bratten, James P., 211
Bratton, Richard C., 208
Brawner, Mrs. Elizabeth Taylor, 148; see Perkins
Bray family, 65
Bregis, Edmund, 205
Brent, Lucy, 35; see Curd
Brent, Solomon, 78
Brewes, Orville, 211
Bridges, John L., 23, 78
Brinkley, Hampton H., 85-86, 129, 211
Brinkley Hotel, 169

Brinkley, Nannie, 181;
see Barnett
Brinkley, Sue, 81; see
Owens
Brittons, 137
Brooks, Henry, 90
Brooks, James, 207
Brown, Claude, 141
Brown, Dennis, 82
Brown, Elizabeth
Mercer, 40; see
Gastineau
Brown, Elizabeth
Mercer Smith (Mrs.
John), 40
Brown, Ellen, 67
Brown family, **65**
Brown, John, 40
Brown, Nix, 67
Brown, Robert, 122
Brown, Robert L., 84
Brown, Sarah, 105
Brown, Thomas C., 86
Brown, Tobias, 105
Brown, William, 208
Brown, Wilson, 207
Brouse, J. P. W., 116
Bruce, John G., 119
Brunsons, 202
Buchanan, Robert, 203
Buckner, Bemat B., 208
Buckner, Daniel, 92
Buell, General, 214
Buford, William, 207
Buggy, first, 80
Bullock, 138
Bumganliner, George, 212
Burger, Jackson, 208
Burgin, Lizzie Reynolds, 60
Burk, Patience, 41; see
Gibson
Burke, J. P., 125
Burnett, Henry D., 212
Burnside, Gen. A. E., 62-63, 133, 220-22
Burnside, town of, 2, 8, 61-63, 160, 183, 222
Burton family, 65
Burton, Glenda, 181;
see Ramsey
Burton, John, 79
Burton, M. E., 84, 181
Burton, Michael, 203
Burton, Robert T., 212
Burton, William, 211
Burton, Zollie, 199
Buster, Michael, 41
Buster, Peggy, 41; see
Gibson
Buster, Phebe Gibson
(Mrs. Michael), 41

Buster, W. J., 125
Buster, William, 205
Bustle, John, 207
Butte, D. W., 125
Buzzard, Joe, 194
Byers, Rev. J. H., 106, 108-10, 113
Byers, Mrs. M. J., 108

Cain, Dr. A. W., 116, 126, 137, 152, 170
Cain, Harold "Bucky", 126-27
Cain, Smith, 29, 125
Cain, Smith W., 30
Cain, Mrs. Wilmoth, 66
Cain's Store, 30
Caintown, 29, 54
Caldwell, E., 146
Caldwell, G, 146
Caldwell, Jane Pickering
Fox (Mrs. John
Adair), 38, 108
Caldwell, Dr. John Adair, 14, 146
Caldwell, Sophia E., 146;
see Parker
Callahan, John, 207
Callons, Andrew, 207
Calvert, Lizzie, 81; see
Ogden
Cambel, Mat, 95
Cameron and
Klinginsmith, 70
Cameron Mill, 70
Camp Dick Robinson, 210-13
Campbell, Andrew H., 208
Campbell, Ann, 59; see
Porter
Campbell, Archibald B., 211
Campbell, Col. Arthur, 44-45
Campbell, B. B. (Mrs. "Seph"), 122
Campbell, Flavius
Josephus "Seph", 122-23
Campbell, Josephus, 85-86
Campbell, Martha, 50, 115, 117-18
Campbell, Col. William, 55
Campbell and Stapp, 23
Candler House, 131
Candler, T. J., 130
Candler, Bishop Warren
A., 102
Caney Fork, 21

Caperton, A. C., 92
Carnegie Library, 115, 117
Carson, Charles C., 207
Carson, C. C., 83
Carter, General, 221, 223
Carter, Josephus, 136
Carugan, James M., 208
Carugan, John, 208
Casualties, World War II, 226
Catron, Andrew J., 211
Catron, A. J., 18
Catron, Virginia, 164
Catron, William, 116
Catron, Judge William
M., 17, 18, 84, 97, 116
Chadwell, A. J., 138
Chandler, Senator, 180
Chaney, Amos, 87
Chaplain, Elizabeth
Perkins (Mrs.
William), 35
Chaplin, Helen M., 29, 35; see Curd
Chaplin, William, 35
Chapman, Virgil, 79
Chesney, Ann, 48, 91
see Owens
Chesney, John, 24
Chesney, Polly, 48; see
Owens
Chesney, Robert, 97
Chestnut, Edmund, 54
Chestnut, Mrs. Edmund, 54
Chestnut, Mrs. Woods, 150
Chief Double Head, 2, 75
Childs, Rev. R. L., 94
Chilton, Edward, 87
Chilton, Lieut. James E., 218
Chrisman, Ike, 214
Christian, John C., 208
Christopher, Maurice, 117
Chumbley, Robert, 140, 141
Churches, 88-110
early, 88-89
Alexander's Chapel, 67
Antioch, 88, 98
Baptist Church, 23, 28, 89-95
Baptist Church,
Colored, 94
Bethany, 88
Bethel, 88
Cabin Hollow Church, 90

251

Calvary Baptist Church, 92
Caney Fork Church, 97-8
Catholic Church (St. Mildred's), 96, 173
Christian Church, Somerset, 89, 97-8, 173
Church of God, 174
Davis Chapel A.M.E. Church (colored) 102
Eden, 88
Fellowship, 88
Ferguson Baptist Church, 92
First (Sinking Creek) Baptist Church, 12. 90-1
Fishing Creek Church, 65, 93
Flat Lick Baptist Church (Old Stone Church), 48, 89
Freedom, 88, 98
High Street Baptist Church, 92, 95
Hopeful Church, 65, 93
Main Street Methodist, 99
Methodist Church, an early, 98
Methodist Church, 99-103, 131, 173
Mt. Gilead, 88, 99
Mt. Olive, 88
Mt. Pisgah Baptist Church, 65
Mt. Victory, 88
Mt. Zion, 88
Nazarene, 173
Oil Center Church, 65
"Old Stone Church" (See Flat Lick Baptist)
Pisgah Presbyterian Church, 88, 103-5, 114, 181-82, 196
Pitman Creek Baptist Church, 90
Presbyterian Church, Burnside, 183-84
Presbyterian Church, First, 36, 44, 108-10
Rocklick Baptist Church, 28, 52
Science Hill Baptist Church, 92
Soul's Chapel, 88
Union Church, 98

Churchwell, Ephriam, 11
Cincinnati, New Orleans and Texas Pacific Railroad, 83
Cincinnati Southern Railroad, 9, 174
Circus, 193-94
Citizens, 176
Citizens National Bank, 125
City Services, Somerset, 168-70
City Hospital, 170
Claire, Daniel, 25
Clark, Gen. George Rogers, 51
Clark, Dr. J. L., 101
Clark, James M., 86
Clark, Rev. P. H., 94
Clark, Rev. W. L., 101
Clarke, Elisha, 205
Clarke, William, 212
Claunch, Chrystopher, 15
Claunch, Greenup, 85
Claunch, Joseph C., 84
Claunch, Margaret, 117
Claunch, Virginia, 128
Civil War, 199-200, 209-24
Clelland, Rev. Thomas, 104
Clio, town of, 46, 67, 75
Clough, Polly Hardester (Mrs. Thurston), 34
Clough, Thurston, 34
Coal, 9
shipping of, 71-72
Coffee, Clark, 95
Coffee, Harriet, 103
Coffey, Oliver, 86
Coleman, J. Winston, 78
Coleman, Thomas H., 92
Collier, Charles, 69
Collier, Stephen, 92
Collins, James Polk Knox, 59
Collins, Mary F. Zachary (Mrs. James P. K.), 59
Collyer, Cyrenius W., 208
Columbia School Building, 115
Colville, Captain, 44
Colyar, Gabriel, 207
Colyar, John, 207
Colyer House, 131
Colyer, James, 169
Colyer, James L., 17
Colyer, James P., 85
Colyer, Jennie, 38; see..Elliot

Colyer, J. W., 18
Colyer, W. A., 125
Combest family, 65
Combest, George, 136
Combest, Samuel D., 29
Commonwealth (Somerset), 123, 141
Company L of Pulaski County, 210
Compton family, 65
Comstock, John C., 212
Conn, Alexander, 207
Conveyances, private, 80-81
Cook, Anna, 159
Cook, Fred Taylor, 159
Cook, J. R., 106
Cook, Lelia Owens (Mrs. Littleton), 159
Cook, Dr. Littleton, 159-60-61
Cook, Mary Shepherd, 159; see Perkins
Cook stove, first, 4
Cooke, E. K., 141
Coomer, Mrs. Malcome, 143
Cooper, Abner, 30
Cooper, Acey, 205
Cooper, Dr. A. L., 156
Cooper, E., 93
Cooper, Edward, 32
Cooper family, 93
Cooper, George, 106
Cooper, George B., 33, 104-5
Cooper, Mrs. Helen, 117
Cooper, Helen Tarter (Mrs. John Sherman, Sr.), 178
Cooper, Jacob, 26
Cooper, James, 65, 93, 94
Cooper, John, 30, 64
Cooper, John Sherman, Jr., 19, 178-79
Cooper, John Sherman, Sr., 19, 58, 126, 175, 178
Cooper, J. S., 18, 137
Cooper, Levi, 65
Cooper, Malikiah, 11
Cooper, Margaret, 105
Cooper, Mattie Wheeler (Mrs. Owsley), 166
Cooper, Owsley, 166
Cooper, Patsy, 30; see McNish
Cooper, Polly McCowan (Mrs. John), 30
Cooper, Polly Spencer (Mrs. Abner), 30
Cooper, Quarles M., 87

Cooper, R. O., 103
Cooper, Robert, 85
Cooper, William, 18
Corn Club, Boys', 135-36
Correll, Charles, 141
Cosson, J. E., 33, 124
Cosson, J. S., 17
Cosson, John E., 84
Costello, Miss, 79
County clerk, first, 10
County
  boundary changes, 6-7
  buildings, 13-15
  clerk's office, 13
  courthouses, 13-15
  creation of, 6
  geography, 6-7
  natural resources, 9
  population, 7
  topography, 7
County fair, 193-94
County officers, 15-20
  pay of early officers, 15
County seat, 11-13
  name of, 12
  plan for town, 12-13
  selection of, 11
Courier-Journal
  (Louisville), 164, 188
Court orders, first, 128
Court records, early, 21-33
Court sessions, early, 21-33
Courts of Quarter Sessions, 9-10
  first, 11
Cowan, Andrew, 203
Cowan, Campbell, 103
Cowan, D., 108
Cowan, Elizabeth, 41; see Gibson
Cowan, Elizabeth Gibson, (Mrs. — — —), 41
Cowan, Elizabeth, 41; see Smith
Cowan, Hattie, 38
Cowan, Isaac, 106, 205
Cowan, Jacob, 26
Cowan, James M., 208
Cowan, Jane, 106
Cowan, Jim, 41
Cowan, John, 26, 32, 33, 204
Cowan, Louisa Gibson (Mrs. William), 41
Cowan, Polly Ann, 106
Cowan, Robert, 205
Cowan, Sam, 103, 190
Cowan, Samuel D., 208
Cowan, Thomas, 11, 23, 26

Cowan, William, 41, 105
Cowan, William G., 104
Cowan, Zeralda, 106
Cox, Allen, 205
Cox, Amanda Goggin Fitzpatrick (Mrs. Jefferson), 34
Cox, Amanda Jane, 34; see Owens
Cox, Ann Elizabeth, 35; see Jenkins
Cox, Bettie, 35; see Boling
Cox, Catherine, 34
Cox, Catherine Hughes (Mrs. John), 34
Cox, Corp. Charles P., 212
Cox, Clay Hughes, 35
Cox, Cyrenius, 34
Cox, Daniel Harrison, 34
Cox, Daniel Webster, 34
Cox, Dora King (Mrs. Joseph Porter), 35
Cox, Elizabeth Hampton (Kempton?) (Mrs. James Madison), 34
Cox family, 34, 35
Cox, Francis Marion, 34, 35, 59
Cox, George Washington, 34
Cox, Henry, 34
Cox, James, 34
Cox, James Madison, 34
Cox, James Zachary, 35
Cox, Jefferson, 34
Cox, John, 34
Cox, John William, 34
Cox, Joseph Porter, 35; see Crutchlow
Cox, Josephine, 35;
Cox, Kate, 34; see Hines
Cox, Leona Barnett (Mrs. John William), 34
Cox, Lula Neil, 35
Cox, Mariah, 34; see Wesley
Cox, Martha Ann Zachary (Mrs. Francis Marion), 34, 59
Cox, Martha Frances, 35; see Rice
Cox, Mary, 35
Cox, Mary Florinda, 34
Cox, Mary Hoff (Mrs. William), 34
Cox, Pamelia Catherine, 35; see Hendricks

Cox, Sallie Lester (Mrs. James), 34
Cox, Sally, 34
Cox, Samuel, 140
Cox, Thomas, 208
Cox, William, 34
Cox, William H., 211
Cox, William Jefferson, 34
Crab Orchard, 1, 22
Crabtree, Isaac, 22
Craig, Louise, 140, 143
Crain, John L., 208
Crawford, A. J., 103
Crawford, Andrew J., 35
Crawford, Bettie, 101
Crawford, Brent, 35
Crawford, Elizabeth, 35, 113; see Whinnery
Crawford, Elizabeth Curd (Mrs. John), 35
Crawford family, 35
Crawford, Flora, 35
Crawford, Frank, 125, 127, 140
Crawford, Frankie, 103
Crawford, John, 35, 131, 162
Crawford, Katherine Stokes (Mrs. Andrew J.), 35
Crawford, Mary Helen, 35, 109
Crawford, —— —— Kendrick (Mrs. Brent), 35
Cremon, John, 207
Crockett, Dr. O. B., 101
Croley, Dr. L. B., 38
Croley, Nancy P. Elliot (Mrs. L. B.), 38
Cromer, Raymond, 140
Cropper, Col. John, 37
Cropper, Mary Louise, 161; see Horton
Crow, Rev. William, Sr., 106, 110
Crozier, Mrs. Hugh, 76
Crozier, Capt. William, 76
Cruse, George, 168
Crutchlow, Josephine Cox (Mrs. Lloyd), 35
Crutchlow, Lloyd, 35
C.S.A. Sixth Regiment Cavalry, Company C, 216
Culliss, John F., 211
Cumberland Falls, 9, 200-2
Cumberland Falls Hotel, 201-2
Cumberland Hotel, 130

253

Cumberland National Park, 9
Cumberland River, 196, 201
  settlements south of, 66-68
Cumberland River Association, 90, 94
Cummins, Mrs. Betsy Elliot, 37; *see* Jones
Cummins, John, 37
Cummins, Moses, 37
Cundiff, Mrs. Betty Zachary, 58
Cundiff, Clinton, 140
Cundiff, Dave, 59
Cundiff, Delmont, 141
Cundiff, Dickey F., 17, 59
Cundiff, Gregory, 205
Cundiff, Green, 162
Cundiff, John, 97
Cundiff, Louisa Zachary (Mrs. Dave), 59
Cundiff, Nile, 141
Cundiff, Ouida, 141
Cundiff, Permelia Zachary (Mrs. Dickey F.), 59
Cundiff, Dr. W. R., 153
Cundiff's Mill, 69-70
Cundriff, Martin, 208
Cunningham, Charles, 33
Cunningham, Charles M., 33
Curd, Belle O. Saunders (Mrs. William Chaplin), 35, 36
Curd, Daniel, 35
Curd, Elizabeth, 35; *see* Crawford
Curd family, 35
Curd, Fannie Trigg (Mrs. Daniel), 35
Curd, Fox, 117; *see* Morrow
Curd, Helen M. Chaplin (Mrs. John B.), 29, 35
Curd, Rev. Henry, 94
Curd, John, 35
Curd, John B., 28, 29, 35, 99, 101, 124
Curd, Lucy Brent (Mrs. John), 35
Curd, Mattie, 35; *see* Gragg
Curd, Sallie, 35; *see* Keene
Curd, Will C., 17, 216
Curd, William Chaplin, 35, 36
Current, Rev. J. N., 100

Currier, Elizabeth, 183; *see* French
Curtis, Will, 128

Dabney, 185
Dalton, James, 136
Dalton, William, 136
Darlington, Bishop U. V. W., 102
Darus, John, 24
Daugherty, Elizabeth, 106
Daugherty, Joseph, 106
Daughters of American Revolution, Somerset Chapter, 203, 227
Daulton, Hugh P., 141
Davidson, 65
Davidson, Andrew, 204
Davidson, Henry, 206
Davidson, Joe, 140
Davidson, W. J., 114, 180
Davis, Constantine C., 212
Davis, Fields, 206
Davis, Rev. James, 98
Davis, J. Newton, 112
Davis, Will B., 16
Davis, Rev. Robert, 103
Day, Mrs. Cliff, 150
Dearmine, Flenion, 207
Debrel, Charles, 204
Decker, Ted, 19, 20
Deeds, early, 27-30
Deer Hunting Club, 191-93
DeFrees, Lida, 115
DeHuff, James, 102
Denham, Charles, 82
Denham, Sam, 162
Denning, Levi, 207
Denny, Charles, 82
Denny, Bishop Collins, 102
Denny, Elijah, 4, 203
Denny, Mrs. John, 198
Denton, Alec, 36
Denton, Alexander, 212
Denton, Anna Fox Goggin (Mrs. James), 36
Denton, Judge Dudley H., 16, 36, 120, 125
Denton, Emma Tate (Mrs. Lincoln), 36
Denton family, 36
Denton, Gertrude, 36
Denton, Henry, 36, 38
Denton, James, 10, 17, 36, 116
Denton, John, 36
Denton, Lincoln, 36

Denton, Nancy McKee (Mrs. Dudley H.), 36
Denton, Rebecca P., 50; *see* Porch
Denton, Sallie Elliot (Mrs. Henry), 36, 38
Deposit Bank of Somerset, 124
DeRake, Pearl Catron, 56
Dick, John, 203
Dick, Marshall, 87
Dick, Orville, 19
Dick, Thomas D., 87
Dickey, Rev. C. F., 101
Dickson, Rev. William, 104-6
Diesel engine, first, 83
Dillard, Isaac, 207
Dishman, Jeremiah, 27
Dishman, John, 204, 206
Divorce, first, 25
Dobbs, Peter R., 212
Dobbs, Phebe (*see* Hobbs), 41
Dodge, Jennie, 186; *see* Smith
Dodson, Mrs. M. A., 141
Dodson, William, 12
Dogan, Lovell, 203
Dollarhide, Thomas, 32-3, 46, 205
Donnelson, Gen. D. S., 219
Doolin, James, 85
Doolien, James D., 211
Dorsey, Adele, 117
Doss, Ayers, 22
Doss, Joel, 22
Double Head Gap, 2, 75
Douglas, Ann, 40; *see* Gastineau
Douglas, Elizabeth Gastineau (Mrs. John), 40
Douglas, John, 40
Downes, J. M. N., 115-116
Drummond, Mr., 112
Duck, Josiah, 85
Duke, Basil W., 216
Duke, Mrs. L. Z., 227
Duke, Rev. T. C., 95
Duncan, Samuel, 11, 32
Duncan, Todd, 164, 166
Dungan, John, 212
Dunham, Alex, 206
Dunman, Green, 208
Dunn, James A., 120
Dunn, Timothy, 26
Durham, Samuel, 208
Durham, William, 27, 208
Dutton, Jonathan, 97
Dutton, J. S., 120

Dutton, Mary Gastineau (Mrs. William), 39
Dutton, Rufus M., 85
Dutton, William, 39
Dyche, Bobbie, 161; see Salyer
Dye family, 93
Dye, J. H., 125
Dysart, Johnston, 207
Dysart, Katherine, 41; see Gibson
Dysart, Samuel, 207

Early courts, 21
Earp, Josiah, 203
Eassepp, James, 211
Eastham, 65
Eastham, Willis, 97
Edge, Larkin, 78
Education, early, 111
Edwards, Andrew F., 211
Edwards, Ira S., 141
Edwards, Jack, 19
Edwards, Jesse, 211
Edwards, John, 203
Edwards, Linville W., 86
Edwards, William, 212
Eighth Judicial District, 25
Electric Power Plant, 172
Electric street railway, 169
Elder, Jesse T., 208
Elihu, town of, 47, 63-64
Elkin, Reuben, 85
Elkins, Mr., 61
Elliot; see also Elliott
Elliot, Amanda, 37
Elliot, Annie, 38; see Bilderdech
Elliot, Asa, 37
Elliot, Betsy, 37; see Cummins and Jones
Elliot, Cyrus, 37
Elliot, Dan, 37
Elliot, Dorinda Kirkpatrick (Mrs. Cyrus), 37
Elliot family, 36-38
Elliot, Dr. Galen R., 37, 175
Elliot, George, 37-38, 116, 163
Elliot, George L., 10
Elliot, Hattie Cowan (Mrs. George), 38, 168
Elliot, Jennie Colyer (Mrs. Robert T.), 38
Elliot, John, 37
Elliot, Josiah, 37
Elliot, Kate, 38; see Pettus

Elliot, Maria, 24, 38; see Adkins
Elliot, Maria F. Porter (Mrs. Tunstall Q.), 37-38
Elliot, Mary Barnes (Mrs. John), 37
Elliot, Mary Oldham (Mrs. Samuel), 37
Elliot, Mattie Helen, 38
Elliot, Mayme, 155; see Smith
Elliot (Elliott), Milford, 33, 124-5, 208, 226
Elliot, Nancy Elliot (Mrs. Galen R.), 37
Elliot, Nancy P., 38; see Croley
Elliot, Nancy Taylor (Mrs. George), 38
Elliot, Nathan, 37
Elliot, Polly Kirkpatrick (Mrs. Robert), 37
Elliot, Rhoda, 38; see Roberts
Elliot, Robert, 37
Elliot, Robert Tunstall, 38
Elliot, Sallie, 36, 38; see Denton
Elliot, Samuel, 36-37
Elliot, Tunstall Quarles, 37-38
Elliot, William, 37
Elliott, Daniel, 37, 211
Elliott, Henry, 211
Ellis, George S., 116
Ellis, James Tandy, 177
Ellis, Mildred, 117
Ellsworth, ———, 216
Elrod, Walter, 17
Emerson family, 65-66
Emerson, Rev., 100
Enoch, Ora, 117
Ensel, G. H., 122
Epidemics
  "flu", 197
  yellow fever, 200
  small pox, 193, 196-97
Erickson, Rev. A., 107
Estis, Patrick H., 208
Eubanks, John W., 85
Evans family, 134
Evans, Andrew, 16, 21, 26, 46
Evans, James, 46, 208
Evans, Jean Newell (Mrs. James), 46
Evans, John, 33, 203, 207
Evans, Josiah, 25, 134, 204

Evans Killis J., 212
Evans, Rev. Morris, 100
Evans, Susannah Newell (Mrs. Andrew), 46
Evans, Zacharia, 15
Evins, Benjamin, 24
Evins, Samuel, 206
Ewers, Rev. A. E., 155
Ewers, Dr. E. M., 155
Ewers, MarieMorrison (Mrs. A. E.), 155
Ewers, Ruth Schaefer, (Mrs. E. M.), 155

Fain, Paulina ("Pelina"), 46; see Newell
Falkner, Richard, 211
Faris, Ephraim C., 33
Faris, Thomas C., 208
Faris, Tunstall Q., 208
Farmer, Dr. C. E., 154
Farmer, Eli, 87, 137
Farmer family, 137
Farmer, John, 25
Farmer, William, 211
Farmer's Bank, 123
Farmer's Bank of Kentucky, (Farmer's Bank, Somerset Branch), 35, 57, 123-24
Farmer's National Bank, 126-28, 135, 173
Farris, Ernest, 20
Farris family, 134
Farris, Henry C., 86
Farris, William, 85
Faubush (Forbush), 64, 135, 162
Fears, James, 23, 89
Feese, R. M., 123, 162
Ferguson, town of, 82
Ferrell, T. V., 81
Ferry license, first, 23
Finley, Hon. Frank, 54
Fire department, horse and buggy, 169
First county court, 9-11
First court, 9
First Federal Kentucky Cavalry, 210, 217-20
First Kentucky Regiment, 213, 220
First land grant, 23
First licensed inspection, 23
First National Bank, 15, 42, 125, 173
Fishback, Capt. John B., 211
Fisher, Erasmus D., 208

255

Fisher, Rev. Lee Davis, 98
Fisher, Margaret, 105
Fitchues, 40
Fitzpatrick, Amanda Goggin, 34; see Cox
Fitzpatrick, Anderson, 105-6
Fitzpatrick, Mrs. Elizabeth Fox, 38
Fitzpatrick, Fountain, 109
Fitzpatrick, Jane, 105, 148-49; see Perkins
Fitzpatrick, John, 16, 104
Fitzpatrick, Josie, 103
Fitzpatrick, Rev. Lewis, 102
Fitzpatrick, Lizzie, 103
Fitzpatrick, Malinda, 106
Fitzpatrick, Margaret, 58; see Neikirk
Fitzpatrick, Margery, 109
Fitzpatrick, Matilda Zachary (Mrs. Will), 58
Fitzpatrick, Sam, 103
Fitzpatrick, William, 16, 58, 106
Flour, first licensed inspection of, 23
Floyd, J. W., 87
Floyd, Viletha, 42; see Girdler
Fogg, H. M. R., 227
Forbush; see Faubush
Forbush, Samuel, 74, 229
Ford, Andrew J., Jr., 87
Ford family, 134
Ford, Rev. Gerald K., 95
Ford, John C., 86
Forgey, Mary (Polly), 66, 105; see Beaty
Forrest, General, 220
Fortune, Benjamin, 98
Forty-niners, the, 190-91
Foster, Allyn K., 92
Foster, Mrs. Ray, 143
Four-H Clubs, 138
Fourth Regiment of Ky. Volunteers, 207-9
Fox, Amanda, 38; see Goggin
Fox, Elizabeth, 38; see Fitzpatrick
Fox, Fountain T., 32-33, 38, 131
Fox, Jane Pickering, 38, 108, 146; see Caldwell
Fox, Sophia (Mrs. William), 39
Fox, Sophia Ann, 38; see Kendrick

Fox, William, 10, 12-16, 24-25, 28-29, 38-39, 111, 128, 131, 146, 204
Fox, Col. William, 36
Fox, William McKee, 32, 38, 54, 108-9
Francis, Henry, 11, 13, 16, 21-23, 128
Francis, John, 76
Franklin, independent state of, 45
Frazure, Jane Gibson (Mrs. John), 41
Frazure, John, 41
Frazure, Mary Jane Gibson (Mrs. Thomas), 41
Frazure, Thomas, 41, 108
Freancy, Mr., 61
Frederici, F., 83
Frederick, Jacob, 207
Freeman, Green C., 208
Freeman, John, 41
Freeman, Mary Gibson (Mrs. John), 41
Freeman, Stephen L., 208
French, Alonzo Currier, 183-84
French, Elizabeth Currier (Mrs. Moses), 183
French family, 137
French, Mabel Gertrude, 183-85; see Taylor
French, Martha Jane Locke (Mrs. Alonzo C.), 183-84
French, Moses, 183
Frost, James Alvin, 161
Frost, John, 212
Frost, Lettie (Mrs. James A.), 161
Frost, Nannie, 161; see Stigall
Fry, General (Colonel), 214, 219
Fryman, Dr. W. P., 101
Fulcher, Andrew, 211
Fugate, Martin H., 208

Gadberry, 65
Gaines, John, 102
Gaines Precinct, 64
Galloway, Captain, 204
Gamble, Rev. B. C., 101
Gamblin, Dr. T. L., 160-61
Gamis, Thomas, 208
Gann, H. C., 81
Gann, "Preacher", 80
Gardner, Ralph, 226
Garland, Edgar, 188
Garner, George W., 29

Garner, Howard, 85
Garner, Parich, 206
Garner, Vincent, 21
Garrard, Gov. James, 10-11, 204
Garrard's Cavalry, 221
Gasper, Achilles, 206
Gastineau, Ann Douglas (Mrs. Charles), 40
Gastineau, Betsy, 39; see Lee
Gastineau, Charles, 40
Gastineau, Christley, 39
Gastineau, Eliza Ann, 39; see Smith
Gastineau, Elizabeth, 40; see Douglas
Gastineau, Elizabeth, 39; see Phelps
Gastineau, Elizabeth Mercer
Gastineau, Elizabeth Mercer Brown (Mrs. Job, Sr.), 40
Gastineau, Elizabeth Todd (Mrs. Christley), 39
Gastineau family, 39-41
Gastineau, Frances Ann Hubble (Mrs. George), 39
Gastineau, George, 39, 97
Gastineau, Henry, 40
Gastineau, Isaac, 39
Gastineau, James, 39
Gastineau, James P. R., 39
Gastineau, Jessie, 40
Gastineau, Job, Jr., 39-40
Gastineau, Job, Sr., 39-40 203
Gastineau, John, 39
Gastineau, Josiah, 39
Gastineau, Marion, 40
Gastineau, Mary, 39; see Dutton
Gastineau, Mary Frances, 39
Gastineau, Matilda Godby (Mrs. William), 39
Gastineau, Matilda Jane, 39; see Isaacs
Gastineau, Polly Todd (Mrs. Isaac), 39
Gastineau, Rachel, 39; see Newman
Gastineau, Reuben Menifee, 39
Gastineau, Sarah, 39; see Lee

Gastineau, Sarah Hays (Saryann) (Mrs. Job, Jr.), 39-40
Gastineau, Sarah Hays (Mrs. William), 39
Gastineau, Susan McBee Barron (Mrs. James), 39
Gastineau, Susie, 39; see Price
Gastineau, Thomas Jefferson, 39
Gastineau, William, 39-40
Gastineau, William Harrison, 39
Gastineau, Wiston, 39
Geary, Captain, 183
Geary, John A., 168
George, William, 129
Gibson, Amanda, 41, 113; see Newell
Gibson, Andrew, 41, 59, 108
Gibson, Ann Ramsey (Mrs. Stephen), 42
Gibson, Anna, 42; see Robinson
Gibson, Ben T., 41
Gibson, Celia, 160; see Golden
Gibson, Daniel, 95
Gibson, David O., 86
Gibson, Edward, 42
Gibson, Effie Wright (Mrs. Samuel), 41
Gibson, Elizabeth, 41; see Cowan
Gibson, Elizabeth Cowan (Mrs. Thomas), 41
Gibson family, 35, 41-42
Gibson, Fannie Wright (Mrs. Thomas), 41
Gibson, Galen, 102-3
Gibson, Grethe (Geretta), 103
Gibson, Henry, 35, 42
Gibson, Jane, 41; see Frazure
Gibson, Joe H., 42, 81, 101, 125, 137
Gibson, John, 15, 41, 133
Gibson, Kate Wright (Mrs. Ben T.), 41
Gibson, Katherine Dysart (Mrs. Samuel), 41
Gibson, Louisa, 41
Gibson, Lucy, 42, 97, 155; see Richardson
Gibson, Martha Ann, 41; see Boyle

Gibson, Martin, 27, 41, 206
Gibson, Mary, 41; see Freeman
Gibson, Mary Ham (Mrs. John), 41
Gibson, Mary Helen Crawford (Mrs. Henry), 35, 42
Gibson, Mary Jane, 41; see Frazure
Gibson, Mrs. M. H., 101
Gibson, Nancy, 41
Gibson, Nancy Hayden (Mrs. Andrew), 41
Gibson, Pamelia Woodcock (Mrs. Robert), 42, 97, 155
Gibson, Patience Burk (Mrs. Martin), 41
Gibson, Peggy Buster (Mrs. John), 41
Gibson, Phebe, 41; see Buster
Gibson, Phebe Hobbs (Mrs. John), 41
Gibson, Polly, 41; see Roberts
Gibson, Polly Ann, 41
Gibson, Polly Zachary (Mrs. Andrew), 41, 59
Gibson, Robert, 42, 124-25, 156, 198
Gibson, Samuel, 41
Gibson, Sarah, 41; see Richardson
Gibson, Sarah Elizabeth, 41; see Jones
Gibson, Stephen, 42
Gibson, Thomas, 41, 108, 205
Gibson, William, 27, 42, 125
Gibson, Willie, 42
Gibson, Zerelda, 41; see Nunnelly
Gifford, Rev. E. P., 101
Gilliland, Ross, 140-41
Gillis, Pearl, 186; see Owens
Gillmore, Gen. Q. A., 219-21
Gilmore, 134
Gilmore, Cyrenius W., 33, 208
Gilmore, James, 24, 26, 106, 128, 203, 208
Gilmore, John, 206
Gilmore, John B., 212
Gilmore, Martha, 106

Gilmore, Robert (Capt. R. M.), 33, 106, 205, 224
Gilmore, Samuel, 10, 11, 15
Gilmore, Sophia, 43; see Girdler
Gilmore, Wilford, 212
Gilmore, William, 206
Girdler, Atticus Monroe, 42-43
Girdler, Roland (Big Lee), 188
Girdler family, 42-43
Girdler, J. B., 124
Girdler, James (Wee Jimmie), 43
Girdler, Joel Hayden, 42-43
Girdler, John Everette, 42-43, 102
Girdler, Lula Richardson (Mrs. Atticus M.), 43
Girdler, Maude Elizabeth, 43
Girdler, Sophia Gilmore (Mrs. John E.), 43
Girdler, Viletha Floyd (Mrs. Joel H.), 42
Girdler, W. H., 137
Girl Scouts, 175, 189, 227
Glass, Dr. Gilbert, 175
Glass, Rev. Harvey, 106, 109-10, 184
Godby, Matilda, 39; see Gastineau
Goff, M. F., 138-39
Goggin, Amanda Fox, 38
Goggin, Anna Fox, 36; see Denton
Goggin, Bourne, 14, 33, 124, 132
Goggin, Christopher, 132
Goggin, David, 208
Goggin, Jane, 132; see Newell
Goggin, Rev. John, 94
Goggin, Nancy, 106
Goggin, Richard, 104, 106, 203
Goggin, William, 124
Golden, Celia Gibson (Mrs. John), 160
Golden, John, 160
Golden, Laura, 160; see Stigall
Goldenberg, Jack, 188
Gooch, Cecil, 117
Gooch, Sarah, 148; see Perkins
Gooch, Wilson, 86
Goodall Factory, 175

257

Goodin, Eleanor, 86
Goodwin, Jeremiah, 86
Goodwin, W. J., 125
Goodwin, William T., 86
Gossett, Christopher, 85
Gossett, Fountaine, 190
Gossett, Mrs. Sarah Jane, 168
Gover, Claude, 19
Gover family, 66
Gover, Wesley, 86, 87
Gover, Wesley Bruce, 87
Gover, Mrs. Willie, 103
Graff, Barbara, 52; see Holstiener
Gragg family, 35
Gragg, Hiram, 16, 85
Gragg, John B., 35
Gragg, Mattie Curd (Mrs. John B.), 35, 101
Gragg, Viola, 99, 117
Gragg, W. B., 99, 116
Gragg, Mrs. H. H., 101
Gragg, William Brent, 16, 86, 211
Graham, Dr. Christopher Columbus, 197
Graham flour, 197
Grand jury, first, 11
Gravery, ———, 22
Graves, Robert, 85
Graves, William, 207
Great Temperance Reform, 119
Green, John, 25
Green, Luther C., 211
Green, Marquis D., 211
Gregory, George G., 87, 212
Gregory, John P., 212
Gregory, Starling, 102
Grey, Dick, 112
Grey, Mrs. Dick, 112-13
Grider, John, W., 212
Grider, William, 212
Griffin, ———, 61
Griffin, Ansel, 140-41
Griffin, E. Shelby, 138
Griffin, Elizabeth, 130
Griffin, Gerald, 180
Griffin, John, 27, 32-33, 204
Griffin, John, Jr., 33
Griffin, Nellie, 130
Griffin, Lieut. Robert M., 211
Griffin, T. R., 122, 168-69, 226
Grigsby, Colonel, 35
Groseclose family, 137
Grubb, Lewis C., 208

Grundy, town of, 60
Guffey, Clara, 117
Gumelson, John, 84
Gunnell, Robert N., 208

Hackey, E. E., 140
Hail, Elias, 212
Hail, George, 16
Hail, Henry S., 133, 140
Hail, Jennie Newell (Mrs. Henry S.), 75, 133, 141-42, 193
Hail, J. W., 120, 122
Hail, John, 124
Hail, Lawrence, 19
Hail, Lucy A., 97
Hail, Mae, 117
Hail, Micajah, 84
Hail, Robert, 73, 125
Hail, Schuyler, 116
Hail, Silas, 167
Hail, Stephen, 16
Hail, S. M., 120, 124
Hail, William, 86
Haley, John, 207
Haley, Walker W., 32
Hall, C. B., 116
Hall, Darrell, 20
Hall, Dick, 78, 81
Hall, John, 78, 81
Hall, Willard, 128
Ham, Isaiah, 207
Ham, Maria, 154; see Waddle
Ham, Mary, 41; see Gibson
Hamilton, James, 26, 203
Hamilton, Jim, 122
Hamilton, O. P., 19
Hammonds, Jack, 64
Hampton (Kempton), Elizabeth, 34; see Cox
Hands, Moses, 12
Haney, 132
Haney, William D. C., 94
Hanks, Miles, 212
Hanks, Moses, 22
Hansford, Essie H., 121-22
Hansford, June, 18
Hansford, J. M., 122
Hansford, J. W., 85
Hansford, Martha, 91
Hansford, Thomas, 3, 10, 23, 32, 85, 89-92, 98, 120
Hansford, W. F., 121
Hansford, William B., 121-22, 203
Hardester, Benjamin, 34
Hardester, Polly, 34; see Clough

Hardester, Sabra, 34; see Hughes
Hardgrove, Captain, 2
Hardgrove, James, 12-13, 111
Hardgrove, John, 11
Hargis, George, 85
Hargis, Sid, 138
Hargis, Thomas, 206, 208
Hargis, William, 85
Harman, David S., 208
Harman, William, 209
Harmon family, 137
Harper, James B., 211
Harper, John, 23
Harper, Rev. J. Harrell, 107, 109-10
Harrell, James, 203
Harris, Bob, 131
Harris House, 78, 129
Harris, John L., 209
Harris, Miriam, 160; see Stigall
Harris, W. M., 92
"Harrison, Old", town of, 54, 58, 60, 65
Harry, James, Sr., 31
Hart, ———, 129
Hartgrove, John W., 212
Harvey, Anna, 113; see Mourning
Harvey and Newell, 122
Harvey, Mrs. Barthenia, 108
Harvey, Elizabeth, 117
Harvey, Sarah, 112; see Sallee
Harvey, William, 108, 113-15, 124
Harvey's Hill, 164, 168
Hast, Israel, 206
Hatch, Mrs., 131
Hawks family, 137
Hayden, Nancy, 41
Haynes, Ebenezer T., 211
Hays, Charles, 15, 104
Hays, Charles P., 209
Hays, Elizabeth Lemon (Mrs. James), 39
Hays, Ephraim, 224
Hays, Isaac, 204, 209
Hays, James, 39
Hays, Reverend, 101
Hays, Sarah (Saryann), 40; see Gastineau
Hays, Sarah, 39; see Gastineau
Hays, William, 132, 203, 205
Heath, Clate, 80
Heath, Dave, 80

258

Heath, William, 203
Hedgecroft, "Prophet," 198
Helvetti, General, 214
Hemp, first licensed inspection of, 23
Henderson family, 65
Henderson, Joseph, 207
Henderson, Robert, 11
Henderson, Rev. William, 104
Henderson, William, 207
Hendricks, James, 209
Hendricks, Pamelia C. Cox (Mrs. T. A.), 35
Henson, John, 212
Herbert, Mrs. Reb Owens, 202
Herrin, Dr. O. L., 156
Herring, Joshea, 206
Hickman, Lewellen (Lewallin), 25, 206
Hicks, Mrs. Amanda, 80, 111
Hicks House, 129
Hicks, Sam, 193
Hicks, Judge Sim, 129
Higgins, Barney, 168
Higgins, Columbus, 209
Higgins, James, 206
Higgins, John V., 85
Highway Mobile Post Office, 174
Hill, Rev. Charles, 106, 110, 112, 149
Hill, D. L., 93
Hill, Fred Bruce, 226
Hill, Rev. F. M., 101
Hill, John, 33
Hill, Dr. John Parker "Jack", 146-48
Hill, Kathleen, 128
Hill, Mrs. Ralph, 117
Hill, Reubin, 12
Hill, R. E., 116
Hill, Rev. Thomas, 23, 30, 66
Hill, Zena Parker (Mrs. E. B.), 14, 146-48
Hillenberg family, 137
Hind, Joseph, 76
Hines, Ben F., 18
Hines, Frank, 18
Hines, James, 206
Hines, Joel, 209
Hines, J. F., 18
Hines, Kate Cox (Mrs. James), 34
Hines, Nannie, 153; see Parker
Hitchcock, John, 87

Hitner, Rev. John K., 106, 110
Hobbs, Docta, 151; see Owens
Hobbs (Dobbs), Phebe, 41; see Gibson
Hoff, Mary, 34; see Cox
Hogue, Rev. A. A., 106, 108
Holloway, Middleton B., 86
Holstiener, Barbara Graff (Mrs. John L.), 52
Holstiener, George Michael, 52; see Michael Stoner
Holstiener, John Leonhardt, 52
Holtsclaw, Dr. Morris, 156
Homemakers Club, 143-44
Home Demonstration, 142-44, 174
Honnell, Rev. W. H., 214
Hope, Mourning, 59; see Vaughan
Hopeful, town of, 64
Hopkins, Doctor, 150
Hopkins, P. H., 116
Hopkins, General Samuel, 205
Hopper, John, 203
Hopper, Rev. William H., 107
Hornet, The, 123
Horton, Helen, 161
Horton, Dr. Joseph Hubert, 161
Horton, Joseph Hubert, Jr., 161
Horton, Mary Louise Cropper (Mrs. Joseph H.), 161
Hoskins, Gideon, 209
Hoskins, Col. W. A., 213, 219, 224
Hospital, first, 170
Hotels, 128-31
Hotel Beecher; see Beecher.
Houses, old, 131-34
Houston, Esther, 44; see Montgomery
Houston, Sam, 44
Hubble, Frances Ann, 39; see Gastineau
Hubble, Clyde, 19
Hubble, David, 86
Hubble, Joel, 85
Hubble, William, 86, 125
Hudson family, 65

Hudson, Rev., 100
Hudson, Mrs. Emma Bell, 61; see Bentley
Huey, O. M., 93
Hughes, Catherine, 34; see Cox
Hughes, Hiram, 206
Hughes, John, 34
Hughes, Dr. Leonidas, 153
Hughes, Mariah, 34; see Love
Hughes, Otilla Woolridge (Mrs. Leonidas), 153
Hughes, Sabra, 34; see Thurman
Hughes, Sabra Hardester (Mrs. John), 34
Hughes, Sarah McBeath (Mrs. Spencer B.), 153
Hughes, Spencer Boyd, 153
Humphries, David, 206
Humphries, James F., 211
Hunt, Andrew P., 212
Hunt, Cordelia, 154; see Tate
Hunt, Fred, 122-23
Hunt, L. E., 122
Hunt, Silas, 209
Hunter, Godfrey, 169
Hunter, James G., 24
Hunter, Polly, 105
Hunter, Thomas, 206
Hunter, Dr. W. E., 93, 95
Hunt's Machine Shop, 172
Hurse, Peter, 95
Hurst, Hugh, 138-39
Hurt, D. G., 141
Huskinson House, 131
Hutchinson, Elizabeth, 49; see Pettus
Hyden, William, 85

Ignatius, Reverend, 96
Incorporation of Somerset, 168
Incorporations, 60
Ingram, Addie E. Zachary (Mrs. Mit), 59
Ingram, Ben Zachary, 109
Ingram, G. W., 125
Ingram House, 129
Ingram, Isaac, 32
Ingram, J. R., 125
Ingram, John, 126
Ingram, Mrs. Lou, 108
Ingram, M. E., 33, 129

259

Ingram, Mrs. Maggie, 126
Ingram, Mit, 59
Ingram, Perk, 191
Ingram, Samuel, 125
Inman, John, 84, 126
International Minerals & Chemical Corp., 174
Iron furnaces, 74
Iron ore, 9, 73-74
Irvin, William, 184
Irvin, Mrs. William, 185
Irvine, Hiram, 80
Irvine, William, 25
Isaacs, Matilda Jane Gastineau, 39; see Gastineau

Jackson, Joel, 14
Jackson, John, 25
Jail, first, 14, 23
James, Andrew J., 33, 36, 124, 175
James family, 133
James, Henry, 11, 24, 32, 204
James, Jesse, 198
James, Joe Martin, 89
James, John, 21, 23-24, 32, 69
James, Rev. John, 89, 92, 134
James, John R., 92
James, Miss (Mrs. Sam Scott), 152
January, John, 24
Jarmer, Emil, 169
Jasper, Abe, 43, 64
Jasper, Achilles, 32
Jasper, Andrew, 30, 54, 64
Jasper, Chas., 33
Jasper family, 43
Jasper, Dr. Galen, 43, 152
Jasper, James, 43
Jasper, James B., 19, 20
Jasper, John, 11
Jasper, John Abe, 43
Jasper, J. A. L., 18
Jasper, Merrill, 209
Jasper, Nicholas, 3, 12-13, 203
Jasper, Oliver P., 16
Jasper, Dr. Robert F. (Judge), 18, 43, 76, 138, 155, 157
Jasper Dr. R. S., 156-57
Jasper, Thos., 33
Jasper, T. E., 116, 137
Jasper, Tunstall Q., 208

Jenkins, Ann Elizabeth Cox (Mrs. Richard), 35
Jeffrey, H. F., 116
Jesse, George, 19
Johnson, Rev. E. B., 94
Johnson, John T., 97
Johnson, R. A. (Dick), 96, 172
Johnsons Block, 173
Jones, Allen, 33, 59
Jones, Alvin, 41
Jones, A. G., 102
Jones, Betsy Elliot Cummins, 37
Jones, Bettie Zachary (Mrs. Will), 59
Jones, David A., 212
Jones, Dorinda Ann, 37
Jones, Mrs. Eliza, 56; see Tate
Jones, Elizabeth Zachary (Mrs. Allen), 59
Jones, Ella Florence, 185; see Taylor
Jones, James, 207
Jones, James A., 212
Jones, James L., 87
Jones, Joshua, 22, 74, 229
Jones, John, 204
Jones, John Bell, 194
Jones, J. D., 18
Jones, Louise, 37
Jones, Milton E., 33
Jones, Nancy, 37
Jones, Reuben, 81
Jones, Russell, 19
Jones, Gen. Samuel, 219
Jones, Sarah Elizabeth (Mrs. Alvin), 41
Jones, Will, 59
Jones, W. B., 117
Johnnycake, the, 194-95
Joplin, George A., Jr., 123
Joplin, Nancy Waddle, 164
Judd, Eula, 181; see Ramsey
Jugernot, 60

Kaiser, Chester, 188
Keene, Major A. T., 35
Keene family, 35
Keene, Sallie Curd (Mrs. A. T.), 35
Keeney, Mrs. Adele, 117
Keeney, Moses, 28
Keife, Catherine, 117
Kelley, Thomas, 203
Kelly, Charles, 132
Kelly, Clinton, 98

Kelly, Edwil, 85
Kelly, Rev. E., 103
Kelly, Ivan, 189
Kelly, Joseph, 206
Kelly, Nancy (Mrs. Samuel), 98
Kelly, Samuel, 98
Kelsey, J. C., 162
Kempton, Elizabeth; see Hampton
Kendrick, ———, 35; see Crawford
Kendrick, John S., 14, 16
Kendrick, Mrs. Kate, 108
Kendrick, Mary, 194
Kendrick, Mrs. Sophia Ann Fox, 38
Kennedy, Judge H. C., 132
Kennedy, Mrs. H. C., 79, 132
Kennedy, James, 203
Kennedy, Lt. Joseph, 51
Kennedy, Sarah, 106
Kenner, Christopher C., 212
Kentucky Cavalry, First, 217
Kentucky Militia, Forty-fourth Regiment, 204
Fourth Regiment, 207
Second Regiment, 205
Ninety-fifth, 204
Kentucky Mounted Volunteer Militia, Seventh Regiment, 205
Kentucky Utilities, 169
Kenwick Hotel, 130
Kerns, Dr. George, 198-9
Kidd, Jack, 138-40
Kilgo, Bishop J. C., 102
Kincaid, John, 25
King, Dora, 35; see Cox
Kinkead, Jane, 46; see Newell
Kirby, W. H., 140
Kirkpatrick, Dorinda, 37; see Elliot
Kirkpatrick, Polly, 37; see Elliot
Kiser, George Ed, 226
Kizzee family, 65
Klingman, Mrs. Emma, 108
Kneeland, Lieut. Samuel M,. 219
Knox, Reverend, 94
Koger, Mrs. J. D., 132
Kolker, Mrs. Robert, 130

Lackey, Rev. J. W., 94

Lair, Dora, 113, 164;
  see Thomas
Lair, Harriet N.
  (Mrs. John G.), 164
Lair, Capt. John G., 33,
  51, 91, 120, 124,
  163-64, 207-8
Lamb, James M., 209
Langdon, C. B., 18
Langdon, C. M., 18-19,
  137
Langdon, C. W., 18
Lankford, Garrard, 206
Langford, Jocy, 27
Lankford, Stephen, 6
Lapsley, Rev. J. T., 106,
  109
Large, Walter, 212
Lawrence, Grace
  Virginia, 160;
  see Stigall
Lawrence, John King,
  160
Lawrence, Patty Beaty
  (Mrs. John K.), 160
Lawrence, Thomas, 207
Lawson, Aaron, 32
Lea, Francis, 91
Lea, John B., 91
Leak (Leake), Rev.
  Josiah, 92, 121
Lear, Andrew, 26
Ledford, Rev. Joseph B.,
  107, 109-10
Lee, Betsy Gastineau
  (Mrs. Noah), 39
Lee, DeWitt, 134
Lee, Drury, 21, 32
Lee, George, 26
Lee, James, 203
Lee, Noah, 39
Lee, Richard, 26
Lee, Sarah Gastineau, 39
Lee, Seton, 64, 204
Lee, Socrates (Crate),
  134, 190
Lee, Thomas, 26, 134
Lee, William, 134, 190
Legislators from Pulaski
  County, 32-3
LeHue (Lehew), Frances
  Allen (Mrs. Peter), 47
LeHue (Lehew), Peter,
  47
LeHue (Lehew),
  Winifred, 47;
  see Owens
Lemon, Elizabeth, 39;
  see Hays
Lester, George, 86
Lester, Sallie, 34;
  see Cox

Lewis, John, 206
Lewis, Mose, 69
Lincoln, President
  Abraham, 209-10
Linville, F. B., 17
Linville, Francis, 86
Lipper, Dr. Lura, 162
Little Inn, 131
Livingston, A., 116
Lloyd, Louella, 180;
  see Ramsey
Locke, Benjamin Folsom,
  183
Locke, Charlotte Parker
  (Mrs. Benjamin F.),
  183
Locke, Martha Jane, 183;
  see French
Lockett, Lieut. William
  A., 211
Lockhart, Sally, 48;
  see Owens
Logan, Col. Benjamin, 51
Logan, Bill, 65
Logan family, 200
Logan, Rev. James
  Venable, 109-10
Logan, Nancy S., 87
Logan, Rev. Sanford, 107
Logan, Volantis K., 87
Logan, William, 24, 78
Logan, William H., 85
Long family, 46
Long Hunters, 1, 201
Long, Jane, 36, 186;
  see Saunders
Long, John, 66, 69, 105,
  133
Long, Lena, 115, 164
Long, Nancy, 105
Longsworth, Mrs. Ralph,
  43
Louisiana Cavalry, 221
Love, John B., 212
Love, Mariah Hughes
  (Mrs. William), 34
Love, William, 34
Love, William H, 212
Loveless, Glenn, 141
Loveless, John, 211
Lynch, William, 21, 26
Lynn, Nora, 180;
  see Ware

Maderil, Robert, 32; see
  also Moddrell, Moderell
Magoffin, Governor, 210,
  220
Mahale, Miss, 121
Marriage book, first, 30
Marriage license, first, 23
Marsh, Ben, 138-39

Marshall, Capt. John, 37
Marshall, General, 220
Martin, Rev. A. F., 94
Martin, John, 206
Martin, Joseph, 92
Marsee family, 65
Martin, Minerva, 56;
  see Tate
Martin, Moses, 203
Mason, W. F., 122
Masonic College, 36, 54,
  113-115, 164, 168
Massey, A. B., 183
Massey, "Commodore",
  80
Mathews, William, 206
Matthews, Joseph, 11
Maxey, Virgil, 92
Maxson, William S., 116
May, Jesse, 209
May John S., 17-18
May, Woodson, 122
Mayfield, J. F., 18
Mayfield, John, 203
Mayfield, Reuben, 206
Mayhern, James D., 120
Mayor of Somerset, first,
  169
May Snowfall, 197-98
Meadows, Isaac, 69
McAlister (McAllister),
  Joseph, 11, 203
McAllister, Green, 97
McAllister (McAlister),
  Robert, 15, 28, 89
McBeath, Hugh Frank,
  65, 86
McBeath, Joseph, 85
McBeath, Joseph H., 84
McBeath, Lee, 103
McBeath, Sarah, 153;
  see Hughes
McCabe Hotel, 96, 172
McCabe, Mrs. Kate, 130
McCarty, A. J., 116
McCleod, Dr. Robert, 158
McClure, M. L., 121
McClure, Nathan, 2
McCowan, Francis, 22
McCowan, Polly, 30;
  see Cooper
McCurty, Dr., 151
McDaniel, Andrew, 32
McDaniel, Billy, 32
McDaniel, Daniel, 30-31
McDaniel, Polly, 30-31,
  58; see Weddell
McDaniel, Sol, 64
McDaniel, Spencer,
  30-31, 32, 58, 64
McDaniels, Roy, 141
McDonald, Andrew, 206

261

McDowell, Thomas, 211
McElmer, David, 32
McElroy, Rev. William T., 106, 110
McEnturf, Manuel, 207
McFall, John, 24
McGee, James, 125
McGinnis, James C., 209
McGinty, John, 125
McHargue, John, 86
McHenry, John, 32
McIntire, Rev. F. T., 101
McKechnie, John, 86
McKechnie, Robert, 86
McKee, ———, 33
McKee, Nancy, 36; see Denton
McKee, Samuel, 10, 12, 16
McKee, W., 124
McKinney, James, 206
McKinney, William W., 209
McLaughlin, Reverend, 107
McLeen, Hosea C., 209
McLue, Serg. G., 212
McMullins, David, 21
McMurry, Bishop W. F., 102
McNish, John, 30
McNish, Patsy Cooper (Mrs. John), 30
McQueary, Christopher, 87
McQuery, Robert, 212
McVey, Joseph, 25
McWhorter, George, 69
McWhorter, John, 21
Meadors, Cary, 95
Meadors, Mrs. Gilcin F., 50
Meadows, Issac, 69
Medicine, 145-62
   early, 145-6
   medical men, 146-62
Medical clinic, 174
Meece, George L., 19
Meece, Harvey J., 209
Meece, Corp. John, 212
Meece, Ula Hail, 128
Memorials, **226-28**
Mercer, Ann Mounce (Mrs. Robert II), 40
Mercer, Elizabeth, 40; see Brown and Smith
Mercer, Elizabeth (Mrs. Thomas), 40
Mercer, Jane, 148; see Owens
Mercer, John, 41
Mercer, Jonathan, 41

Mercer, Robert II, 40
Mercer, Sarah Ann Moore (Mrs. John), 41
Mercer, Thomas, 40-41
Merrick, James T., 209
Messick, John C., 211
Metcalf farm, 76
Mexican War, 1847, 207-9
Middlesboro, 4
Military claims, 32
Miller, Clay, 117
Millican, W. O., 92
Mill Springs (Nancy) Cemetery, 228
Mills, 69-71
Mills, Archibald E., 15, 22-24, 33, 78
Mills, Henry L., 84
Mills, Joseph, 211
Mill's Mill, 70
Millz (Mills), Samuel F., 209
Milton, Lieut. Benjamin H., 211
Milton, Caroline (Carrie), 108, 124
Milton, Eben, 97, 108, 124
Milton, Mary B., 49
Milton, Mollie, 113; see Pettus
Milton, Sallie, 108, 124
Milton, T., 108
Minton, William, 206
Mitchel family, 137
Moberly, Benjamin, 26
Mobley, Edward, 21, 133
Moddrell, Charles, 204
Moddrell, James, 85
Moddrell, Robert, 204
   see also Maderil, Moderell, Modrell
Moderell, Robert, 13, 32
Modrell, Robert, 105, 111
Moffett, Harry, 107
Molen family, 65
Montgomery, Esther Houston (Mrs. John), 44
Montgomery, Jean, 44, 46; see Newell
Montgomery, John, 44
Montgomery, Dr. (Stamford), 149
Montgomery, Prof. John, D.D., 114, 152
Montgomery, Mrs. John, 114
Montgomery, Thomas, 25, 78
Montgomery, ———, 106

Moonbow, 9
Moonbow Inn, 201-2
Moore, Arthur, 22
Moore, Henry, 32
Moore, James R., 188
Moore, Louise, 59; see Zachary
Moore, O. L., 122
Moore, Robert H., 211
Moore, Sarah Ann, 41; see Mercer
Moore, U. P., 125
Moore, Lieut. William, 51
Morgan, Dr. A. B., 157
Morgan, Col. Daniel, 37
Morgan, Gen. John Hunt, 35, 52, 199, 215-17, 220
Morgan's Raid, 215-17
Morgan, William, 209
Morris, Mrs. Mae Pinnell, 81
Morrison, Bishop Henry C., 102
Morrison, Capt. John A., 213
Morrison, Marie, 155; see Ewers
Morrow, Alexander, 43
Morrow, Boyd, 44, 127, 180; see Ware
Morrow, Charles H., 44, 175-8
Morrow, Gov. Edwin P., 44, 76, 103, 175-8, 183
Morrow family, 43
Morrow, Katherine Waddle (Mrs. Edwin P.), 177
Morrow, Margaret Boyd (Mrs. Alexander), 43
Morrow, Mary, 44, 164
Morrow, Robert, 44, 162
Morrow, Samuel, 44
Morrow, Fox Curd (Mrs. Samuel), 117
Morrow, Thomas, 44
Morrow, Col. Thomas Z., 16, 32-33, 43-44, 108, 149, 224, 226
Morrow, Virginia (Jennie) Bradley (Mrs. Thomas Z.), 44, 103, 108
Morrow, Judge W. B., 127
Morrow, William, 44
Moss, Dill, 52
Moss, Margaret Shepperd (Maggie) (Mrs. Dill), 52, 113, 171

Mounce, Ann, 40;
  see Mercer
Mounce, A. M., 18
Mounce, Christopher, 40
Mounce, Martha
  (Mrs. Christopher), 40
Mound, Ira R., 212
Mounts, Greenup R., 209
Mourning, Anna Harvey
  (Mrs. Tom), 113-14
Mourning, Professor
  Tom, 114
Mowbray, Henry, 212
Mt. Gilead, 12, 60, 99
Mullins family, 137
Munford, Mrs., 103
Mundy, Rev. W. H., 103
Murder, first in county, 24
Murphy, Bennett, 206
Murphy, J. W., 141
Murphy, Robert, 17
Murphy, William C., 84
Murrell, Edgar, 98, 127
Murry, Barnabas, 203
Muse family, 65
Muse, Isaac, 204
Myers, Sid, 202

Nance, Jesse, 209
Nancy, town of, 64
National Bank of
  Somerset, 42, 198
National Cemetery, 228
National Hotel, 78,
  130-31
Natural bridge, 8
Natural gas, first franchise
  for, 169
Natural resources, 9
  development of, 71-74
Neal, Charles, 3, 10
Neal, Isaac, 206
Nealey, Isaac, 206
Neat, Ben, 162
Neikirk, Henry, 58
Neikirk, Homer, 20
Neikirk, Margaret
  Fitzpatrick (Mrs.
  Henry), 58
Nelson, General, 210
Nelson, James, 86
Nelson, Lillian, 117
Nelson, Major, 102-3
Newby, John, 3, 15, 21,
  203
Newell, Adam, 103
Newell, Amanda Gibson
  (Mrs. Bourne), 41, 113
Newell, Bourne, 41
Newell, David K., 190-91
Newell, Dick, 191-93

Newell, Dorcas, 46
Newell, Elizabeth, 44, 106
Newell, Elizabeth Colville
  Black (Mrs. Samuel),
  44
Newell, Elizabeth
  Colville, 46
Newell family, 44-47
Newell, Frank, 141
Newell, Henry Clay, 85
Newell, Ida, 165;
  see Adams
Newell, Capt. James, 47,
  51, 80
Newell, Jane, 106
Newell, Jane Goggin
  (Mrs. William), 132
Newell, Jane Kinkead
  (Mrs. Joseph B.), 46
Newell, Jean, 46;
  see Evans
Newell, Jean Montgomery
  (Mrs. Samuel I), 44,
  46, 105
Newell, Jennie, 133;
  see Hail
Newell, Joe B., 222
Newell, John, 191
Newell, John
  Montgomery, 46, 67,
  132
Newell, Joseph Black, 46,
  67, 85, 121
Newell, Linnie, 142
Newell, Mrs. Lizzie
  Sallee, 132
Newell, Mack, 86
Newell, Margaret, 46, 48,
  105; see Owens
Newell, Margaret Beaty
  (Mrs. John M.), 46
Newell, Mary, 108, 148;
  see Owens
Newell, Mary Bradley
  (Mrs. Samuel III), 114
Newell, Mary Jane, 57;
  see Wait
Newell, Nancy Owens
  (Mrs. Samuel II), 46,
  48
Newell, "Old Loge", 192
Newell, Paulina (Pelina)
  Fain (Mrs. William
  T.), 46
Newell, Samuel, 3, 15, 21,
  26, 44, 88, 105, 128, 203
Newell, Samuel I, 10, 23,
  44-48, 67, 75, 83
Newell, Samuel II, 108-9,
  204-5

Newell, Samuel III (S.A.,
  "Big Sam"), 67, 108,
  112, 114, 124-25, 149,
  171, 192-93, 198
Newell, Sam B., 67
Newell, Susannah, 46;
  see Evans
Newell, W. M., 108
Newell, W. O. ("Big
  Bill"), 191-92
Newell, Mrs. W. O., 113
Newell, William, 132,
  192-93
Newell, William O. I.
  ("Clio Bill"), 67, 85
Newell, William O. II, 66
Newell, William T., 46
Newland, Rev. C. F., 107
Newland, Isaac, 90
Newman, Rachel
  Gastineau (Mrs.
  William), 39
Newman, William, 39
New Market, 23
New opera company, 166
Newspapers, in Somerset,
  119-123
Newton, Abe, 129
Newton, Rev. C. C., 100-1
Newton, Robert, 129
Newton, Sylvester, 129
Newtonian Hotel, 129
Nichols, Mrs., 141
Noe family, 136
Noel, Professor, 114
Norfleet, Brent, 141
Norfleet, Dr. Carl, 159,
  170
Norfleet, Mrs. Carl, 43
Norfleet family, 65, 200
Norfleet, Harvey, 140
Norfleet, Jesse, 86
Norfleet, Sophia, 106
Norfleet, Willard, 141
Norfleet W. C., 168-69
North Somerset, 171
Nunnelly, Anderson, 23
Nunnelly, James M., 212
Nunnelly, Lee, 41
Nunnelly, Robert A., 211
Nunnelly, William B., 209
Nunnelly, Zerelda Gibson
  (Mrs. Lee), 41

Oatts, Mrs. Charles Sr.,
  145
Oatts, Mrs. Nancy, 189
O'Bryan, Rev. J. A., 96
Offutt, Andrew, 168
Ogden, John C., 116,
  126, 135, 137

Ogden, Lizzie Calvert (Mrs. Ellis), 81
Oldham, Mary, 37; see Elliot
Oney, Rev. C. P., 101
Ordinaries, 128-31
Orwin, George, 126
Osborn, John, 212
Osborne family, 137
Osborne, William A., 212
Overstreet, Rev. W. T., 107
Owen, George, 182
Owens, Allen, 207
Owens, Amanda Jane Cox (Mrs. W. C.), 34
Owens, Ann Chesney (Mrs. John), 48, 91
Owens, Avy, 48; see Short
Owens, Clarence, 193
Owens, David D., 192, 209
Owens, Docta Hobbs (Mrs. Wm.), 151
Owens, Edward F., 202
Owens family, 47-48
Owens, James, 92
Owens, Jane, 48, 56; see Tate
Owens, Jane Mercer (Mrs. Samuel), 148
Owens, John, 48, 91, 206
Owens, Capt. Joe M., 224
Owens, Dr. Joseph Lowery, 149-50, 191
Owens, Dr. Joseph Montgomery, 151, 159
Owens, Judah, 48
Owens, Jude (Mrs. William), 47
Owens, Keziah, 91
Owens, Lavina, 48; see Short
Owens, Lelia, 159; see Cook
Owens, Margaret, 105
Owens, Margaret G. Van Arsdale (Mrs. Joseph L.), 149
Owens, Margaret Newell (Mrs. William), 46, 48
Owens, Martin, 48, 89, 92, 207
Owens, Mary Newell (Mrs. Samuel R.), 148-49, 222-23
Owens, Molly (Mrs. John M.), 151
Owens, Nancy, 46, 48, 91; see Newell
Owens, Nancy Owens (Mrs. William), 47

Owens, Nannie Williams (Mrs. Edward F.), 202
Owens, Pearl Gillis (Mrs. A. E.), 186; see Gillis
Owens, Polly Chesney (Mrs. Martin), 48
Owens, Presley, 207
Owens, Rebecca, 48; see Short
Owens, Reuben, 48
Owens, S. A., 108, 125
Owens, Sally Lockhart (Mrs. Reuben), 48
Owens, Samuel, 108, 148, 207, 213
Owens, Dr. Samuel R., 86, 106, 145-46, 148-49, 162
Owens, Sarah, 48; see Price
Owens, Socrates, 201
Owens, Sue Brinkley (Mrs. Cabel, Sr.), 81
Owens, Vincent, 47
Owens, W. Colvin ("Red Bill"), 121-22
Owens, William, 3, 46-48, 91, 124, 133, 203, 206
Owens, Winifred LeHue (Mrs. Vincent), 47
Owens, William II, 124
Owens, Major (Capt.) William N. III, 33, 151, 211, 222
Owsley family, 132
Owsley, Charles, 104
Owsley, Sam, 27
Owsley, Thomas, 27
Owsley, Walter, 124
Owsley, William, 78
Owsley, W. M., 124

Painter, H. M., 106
Parke, Rev. J. B., 109-10, 188
Parker, Charlie, 192
Parker, Charlotte, 184; see Locke
Parker, Chrisman H., 209
Parker, Elisha, 71
Parker, Joe Caldwell, 70, 153, 192, 194
Parker, John M. W. E., 212
Parker, Dr. John W. F., 32, 73, 82, 115, 146-47, 153, 168, 170, 188, 226
Parker, L., 120
Parker, Lewis, 70

Parker, Marguerite Sallee (Mrs. Sam F.), 153
Parker, Melvina, 184; see Taylor
Parker, Nannie Hines (Mrs. Joe C.), 153
Parker, Col. Sam Fletcher, M. D., 147-48, 153
Parker, Sophia Caldwell (Mrs. John W. F.), 146
Parker, T. A., 115, 117
Parker, Zena, 146-48; see Hill
Parker's Lake, 9
Parker's Lake Post Office, 201
Parker's Mill, 69-71, 195
Parks, Rev. John, 110
Parsons, A. M., 17
Parsons, Mrs. Sallie Sandifer, 113
Patten, J. C., 33
Patterson, Lewis, 91
Patterson, Dr. McLeod, 158
Patterson, Rufus M., 211
Pawling, William, 106
Payne, Reubin, 14
Pearce family, 65
Pearce, Jesse, 31
Pearce, Polly, 31; see Tarter
Pedilue, Miss, 142
Pegram, General, 219-21
Pence, James, 212
Pence, William, 209
Peoples, Rev. John, 100
Peoples, Rev. S. W., 101
Perkins, Dr. A. R., 101
Perkins, Benjamin H., 28-29
Perkins, Elisha, 148
Perkins, Elizabeth, 35; see Chaplain
Perkins, Elizabeth Taylor B. (Mrs. John M.), 148
Perkins, Dr. George, 70, 125, 148-49, 152, 226
Perkins, Jane Fitzpatrick (Mrs. John M.), 148-49
Perkins, Dr. Jesse, 159
Perkins, John, 212
Perkins, Dr. John Milton, 124-25, 148-49, 226
Perkins, Capt. M. B., 35, 216
Perkins, Mary S. Cook (Mrs. Jesse), 159

Perkins, Nannie, 113, 148, 156, 164; see Thatcher
Perkins, Sarah Gooch (Mrs. Elisha), 148
Perkins, Sophronia Vickery (Mrs. George), 113, 149
Perkins, W. A., 127
Perkins, W. R., 140
Perry, John, 203
Peter, Thomas, 28
Peters, Harrison, 209
Peters, Serelda, 103
Pettus, Eben Milton, 49
Pettus, Elizabeth Hutchinson (Mrs. William H.), 49
Pettus family, 48-50
Pettus, Joseph, 48
Pettus, Kate Elliot (Mrs. Will), 38
Pettus, Katherine, 50
Pettus, Lillie, 49, 117
Pettus, Mary, 49-50
Pettus, Mary B. (Molly) Milton (Mrs. William H.), 49
Pettus, Nancy, 124
Pettus, Nancy Adams (Mrs. Richard G.), 48-49
Pettus, Nannie E., 49
Pettus, R. H., 125
Pettus, Richard, 49
Pettus, Richard Grover, 48-49
Pettus, Sallie, 49, 117
Pettus, Walter, 49
Pettus, Will, 38
Pettus, Judge William Henry, 16, 33, 49-50, 113, 124-25
Peyton, Lieut. Bailie, Jr., 227
Phelps, Mrs. Elizabeth Gastineau, 39
Phillips, John, 117
Phipps, Rebecca Weddle (Mrs. Thomas), 31
Phipps, Thomas, 31
Piano, first, 163
Pidcock, J. L., 138-39
Pierce, Rev. C. H., 101
Pierce, Clara, 141
Pierce, Ezra, 140
Pierce family, 66
Pierce, Hugh, 26
Pierce, W. C., 136
Piles, ———, 138
Pinnell, Mae, 81; see Morris

Ping, W. H., 140
Pioneer customs, 3-5
Pioneers, 1
Pitman family, 3
Platt, Joseph, 106
Point Isabel, 62, 222; see also Burnside
Popplewell, Aunt Ellen, 130
Popplewell Hotel, 130
Popplewell, Uncle Jeff, 130
Porch, Charles B., 17, 51
Porch, E. D., 16-17, 108, 120
Porch, Edwin D., 51
Porch, Elizabeth, 52, 113, 171; see Shepperd
Porch, Ezekial Abbot, 16, 50-51
Porch family, 50-51
Porch, Henry, 50
Porch, Henry L., 208
Porch, Henry S., 51
Porch, Lina, 117
Porch, Mary Bacheller (Mrs. Ezekial A.), 50-51
Porch, Rebecca Denton (Mrs. Henry), 50-51
Porter family, 65
Porter, Ann, 91
Porter, Ann Campbell (Mrs. Joseph), 59
Porter, C. S., 162
Porter, James, 66
Porter, John, 31, 66
Porter, Joseph, 33, 37-38, 59, 91, 112, 204
Porter, Rev. J. W., 38
Porter, Maria Foster, 37; see Elliot
Porter, Pamelia Q., 34, 59; see Zachary
Porter, Paul, 66
Porter, Thomas, 66
Porter, William, 66
Portwood, Mary Morrow, 164
Postal service, 83-87, 175
Postmasters, Somerset, 84
Post offices, county, 85-87
Powell, I. B., 116
Prather family, 3, 10, 132
Prather, Arthur, 189
Prather, E., 25
Prather, Edward, 21
Prather, Elizabeth, 105
Prather, Gideon, 25, 33, 86

Prather, John, 11-13, 24, 26
Prather, J. F., Jr., 127
Preston, Col., 47, 51
Preston, William, 206
Price, Hansford, 48
Price, Jackson, 87
Price, James, 39
Price, Noah, 209
Price, Owens, 64, 125
Price, Richard, 133
Price, Sarah Owens (Mrs. Hansford), 48
Price, Susie Gastineau (Mrs. James), 39
Price, W. R., 18
Probert, T. O., 92
Progressive Home Journal, 122
Pulaski, Count Casimir, XV-VII, 6
Pulaski County locker plant, 174
Pulaski Drug Company, 162
Puller, Rev. A. W., 94
Pumphery, Anderson, 209
Purdom, C. W., 117

Quarles family, 104
Quarles, John T., 33
Quarles, Tunstall, 15, 25, 32, 47, 83, 123, 205
Quarles, Tunstall, Jr., 25, 204
Queen and Crescent Railroad, 83
Quinton, John, Jr., 209

Rabbitfoot, Dr., 160
Raborne, Robert F., 212
Radio station, first, 173
Ragon, Grace, 117
Railroads, 78-79, 81-83, 171-72
  Burnside railroad, 200
Rainey, James, 203
Rainwater family, 65
Rainwater, V. M., 19
Ramey, Clarice Payne, 118
Ramey, Venus, 186
Ramsey, Adella, 117
Ramsey, Ann, 42; see Gibson
Ramsey, Eula Judd (Mrs. William H., Jr.), 181
Ramsey, Glenda Burton (Mrs. Lloyd B.), 181
Ramsey, James, 180-81
Ramsey, James B., 181

265

Ramsey, Col. Lloyd B., 181
Ramsey, Logan, 80
Ramsey, Louella Lloyd (Mrs. James), 180
Ramsey, Mary Elizabeth Andis (Mrs. James B.), 181
Ramsey, Mary Ella Barnett (Mrs. William H.), 181
Ramsey, Preston L., 93
Ramsey, Robert, 42
Ramsey, William Harold "Bill," 136, 180-81
Ramsey, William Harold, Jr., 181
Randall, Oather, 140
Raney, Samuel, 212
Rankin, James, 132
Rankin, Robert, 106
Rankin, Mrs. Robert, 106
Rankin, Tom, 132
Rash, Francis M., 212
Rawles, J. W., 93
Raw silk, first in Kentucky, 167
Ray Hole, the, 194
Read, Rev. Clarence, 100
Reagon, Michael, 203
Red Clay of Pulaski, 230
Reddish, Dr. Dandridge, 160
Reddish, George, 180
Reddish, Dr. George M., 116, 151-52, 160, 170
Reddish, Lelia Gooch, 164
Reed, Dr., 149
Renfrew; *see* Renfro
Renfro, "Mammy," 202
Renfro, Parson Louis, 202
Renfro, Samuel, 85
Renick's Mounted Battalion, 205
Reporter, the, 121-22, 168, 198
Reppert, Prof. Frank, 114
Rese, Danil, 73
Revolutionary War, American, 203-04
Rexroat, V. H., 19
Reynolds, James F., 212
Reynolds, Josephus, 87
Reynolds, Richard, 16
Reynolds, Samuel, 212
Reynolds, Sherod, 27
Reynolds, Thomas, 28
Rhodes, Rev. Dan, 107

Rice, Martha Frances Cox (Mrs. L. C.), 35
Richardson, Aimy, 51
Richardson, Amanda Zachary (Mrs. James), 59
Richardson, Amos, 51
Richardson, Ann (Mrs. Jonathan), 51
Richardson, Cyrenius W., 84, 124
Richardson, David, 212
Richardson, Elizabeth Thatcher Waddle (Mrs. Robert G.), 156
Richardson family, 51-2
Richardson, James, 21, 59
Richardson, Jesse, 3, 13, 24, 27-28, 32, 51-52, 111, 203-4
Richardson, Joel, 206
Richardson, John (Jack) M., 38, 42, 125, 150, 155, 162
Richardson, John R., 84, 124
Richardson, Jonathan, 51
Richardson, Joseph, 51
Richardson, Lucy, 34, 52; *see* Thurman
Richardson, Lucy Gibson (Mrs. John M.), 42, 97, 101, 155
Richardson, Lula, 43; *see* Girdler
Richardson, Mary, 51
Richardson, Mrs. Mary, 109, 117
Richardson, Meridith G., 16
Richardson, Nancy, 51
Richardson place, 131
Richardson, Robert, 156
Richardson, Dr. Robert Gibson, 155
Richardson, Sarah Gibson (Mrs. William), 41
Richardson, Stephen, 206
Richardson, Thomas, 51, 95
Richardson, William, 41
Rice, Martha Frances Cox (Mrs. L. C.), 35
Richeson *see* Richardson
Riddle, John, 87
Ridge, Robertson, 206
Roads, 21, 74-77
Roberts, A. B., 140
Roberts, Charles, 140-41

Roberts, Prof. George, 38, 135-36, 175
Roberts, Hiram, 207
Roberts, James, 207
Roberts, James "Red," 182-83
Roberts, Joel, 41
Roberts, John, 206
Roberts, Mae Thurman
Roberts, Montgomery, 209
(Mrs. V. D.), 52
Roberts, Polly Gibson (Mrs. Joel), 41
Roberts, Rhoda Elliot (Mrs. George), 38
Roberts, V. D., 102
Roberts, William, 15, 23
Robertson, Rev. Samuel, 104
Robinson, Anna Gibson (Mrs. Charles), 42
Robinson, Charles, 42
Robinson, Governor, 220
Robinson, H. S., 126
Robinson, Rev. — — —, 106
Root, T., 106
Roper, David, 203
Rose, Rev. Floyd, 189
Rose, Dr. F. D., 101
Rosecrans, Gen. W. S., 219
Roseman, H. C., 92
Ross, C. I., 19-20
Roth, Sarah, 109
Rousseau, James G., 209
Rousseau, Capt. Lawrence H., 209, 224
Rourk, John, 211
Roy family, 93
Rucker family, 99
Rucker, Joseph B., 97, 121
Rucker, Mrs. Joseph B. (Smith), 97
Runkle, Col. Benjamin P., 219
Rural Electric Administration office, 124
Russel, Denton, 128
Russell, Andrew, 13
Ruth, town of, 51-52
Ryan, Captain Tom, 80

Sadler, Edward, 209
St. John, Noah, 206
Salem, 98
Sallee, George P., 116, 13
Sallee, Mrs. George, 112-13

Sallee, Joel W., 16, 33, 85
Sallee, John M., 92
Sallee, Lizzie, 132;
   see Newell
Sallee, Marguerite, 153;
   see Parker
Sallee, M. P., 125
Sallee, Mrs. Sarah
   Harvey (Mrs. George),
   112-13, 118
Sallee, William, 204
Sallee, William A., 84
Sallee, William J., 25, 84
Salt, 4, 57, 71
Salyer, Bobbie Dyche
   (Mrs. Charles), 161
Salyer, Dr. Charles, 161
Salyer, Patricia, 161
Sanders family, 138
Sanders, George, 27
Sandifer, Jennie, 113;
   see White
Sandifer, Sallie, 113;
   see Parsons
Sandusky, Evelyn, 117
Sandy, Robert W., 106
Sargent, A., 93
Sath, Ephraim, 212
Saunders, Admice T., 211
Saunders, Amelia, 66,
   116, 186-87
Saunders, Belle O.,
   35-36; see Curd
Saunders family, 46
Saunders, George
   Woodard, 36, 46,
   67-68, 132, 186
Saunders home, 133
Saunders, James, 68
Saunders, Jane Long
   (Mrs. George W.), 36,
   186
Saunders, Julius, 46, 83
Savage, Rev. J. R., 101
Sawyer, Thomas W., 87
Sayer, Irvil, 141
Sayers, Robert, 203
Schaefer, Ruth, 155;
   see Ewers
Schoeff, General, 213-15
Schooler, William, 123
Schools
   early, 112-13
   school districts, first,
     112
   schools in Somerset,
   schools, public, 114-18
Science Hill, 229
Scott, Agnes, 117
Scott, Alex, 103
Scott, General, 221
Scott, John, 206

Scott, Katherine, 103
Scott, Margaret Bradley
   (Mrs. W. F.), 149,
   152
Scott, Mary, 103
Scott, Dr. Sam, 152
Scott, Mrs. Sam, 152;
   see James
Scott, Stephen, 105
Scott, Thomas M., 84
Scott, Rev. William, 104
Scott, Dr. William F.,
   124, 149, 150
Scovell, Doctor, 135
Sears, A. T., 19
Sears, James L., 87
Sears, John, 212
Sears, Luther, 133
Seaton, Thomas, 203
Seventh Regiment,
   Kentucky Mounted
   Volunteer Militia, 32,
   205-7
Sewage system, first
   (Somerset), 169-70
Sewell, Dorson, 203
Sewell, Joseph, 212
Sewell, J. K., 122
Sewing machine, first, 3
Shadoan, George W.,
   17-19, 73, 111,
   113-14, 167; (also
   spelled Shadoin)
Shadoan, John, 140-41
Shadoan, R. J., 18
Shears, Rev. — — —, 94
Shelburne, Rev. James,
   47
Shelby, General (Gov.),
   55, 204
Shepard, Betty Tarter, 30
Sheperd, Andrew, 202
Shepherd, Tom, 216
Shepperd, Elizabeth
   Porch (Mrs. Thomas
   H.), 52, 113, 171
Shepperd, Elizabeth
   Withers (Mrs. Fount),
   52, 171
Shepperd family, 52;
   (see also Shepard,
   Sheperd)
Shepperd, Fount, 52, 171
Shepperd, Margaret
   (Mag), 52, 113;
   see Moses
Shepperd, Thomas
   Hansford, 52, 171,
   199, 216
Shepperd, William S., 17,
   52
Sheriff, first, 10

Sherman, General, 224
Shopville, town of, 133
Short, Avy Owens
   (Mrs. John), 48
Short, John, 48, 206
Short, Lavina Owens
   (Mrs. Reuben), 48
Short, Rebecca Owens
   (Mrs. Wesley), 48
Short, Reuben, 48, 206
Short, Thomas, 206
Short, Wesley, 48
Shotwell, A. D., 169
Shumate, Ola Mae, 156;
   see Spradlin
Shuttleworth, James A.,
   227
Sidewalks, first, 168
Sievers, Christian, 65
Sievers, Dr. Robert C.,
   65, 116, 154
Silk industry, 57, 167
Silver mine, 201
Silvers, Jesse M., 212
Silvers, John, 17
Sivers, John P., 212
Silvers, Neal, 18
Silvers, Wesley, 209
Silvers, Wesley H., 212
Simpson family, 65
Simpson, John, 148
Simpson, Rev. J. M., 101
Simpson, Thomas, 26
Singer Sewing Machine
   Center, 175
Singleton, Moses L., 18
Singing schools, 163
Sinking Creek, 12-13
Skidmore family, 136
Sloan, Benjamin, 133
Sloan, Harvey, 192
Sloan, John W., 183
Sloan, Mrs. John, 159
Sloans Valley, 8, 133
Smiley, George, 11
Smith, Beecher, 131, 155,
   193
Smith, Ben V., 116,
   185-86
Smith, Berry, 32-33
Smith, Daniel, 40
Smith, Dr. E. T., 156
Smith, Eliza Ann
   Gastineau, 39
Smith, Elizabeth Cowan
   (Mrs. Thomas), 41
Smith, Elizabeth Mercer
   (Mrs. Daniel), 40
Smith, George, 26
Smith, Green Clay, 92
Smith, H. G., 86
Smith, Isaac, 208

Smith, James, 95, 206
Smith, James T., 105-6
Smith, Jennie Dodge
   (Mrs. Ben V.), 186
Smith, John, 24
Smith, John
   ("Raccoon"), 97
Smith, Jonathan, 185, 205
Smith, J. Rockwell, 107
Smith, Lettie, 103
Smith, Margaret, 57;
   see Wait
Smith, Mayme Elliot
   (Mrs. Beecher), 155
Smith, Nancy VanHook
   (Mrs. Johnathan), 185
Smith, Rev. ———, 100
Smith, R. J., Wholesale
   Grocery Co., 173
Smith's Shoals, 72
Smith, Thomas H., 212
Smith, Thomas J., 85
Smith, Thomas, 41, 97
Smith, Valeria;
   see Beard, 155
Smith, Virgil P., 116
Smith, William, 212
Snively, Rev. W. H., 100
Snodgrass, Simeon, 209
Somerset, 10-13, 38, 167-74
   city services, 168-70
   development, 167
   early days in, 167-68
   named, 12
   plan for town, 12-13
   population of, 170
   selection of site, 11-12
Somerset Academy, 27, 31-32, 111
Somerset Banking
   Company, 41, 125-26
Somerset Chamber of
   Commerce, 174
Somerset Democrat, 57, 119, 120-21
Somerset Gazette, 78, 119-20, 123
Somerset General
   Hospital, 38, 170
Somerset Graded School, 114
Somerset Ice Plant, 172
Somerset Journal, 122-23, 141
Somerset Paragon, 121
Somerset Pharmacy, 162
Somerset Republican, 122
Somerset Vocational
   School, 116, 118

Somerset Water, Light &
   Traction Co., 169
Sons of Temperance, 119-20
South Carolina, secession
   of, 209-10
South, Mrs. Christine
   Bradley, 177
South Kentucky
   Association of United
   Baptists, 90
South Somerset, 171-72
Southerland, Rev. John
   O., 65, 90, 92, 94
Southern Railway
   System, 82-83
Sowder, Emanuel, 212
Sowder, William, 212
Spanish-American War, 224
Spears, A. T., 138
Spears, James W., 17
Speed, Lieut. George K., 211
Spencer, Elizabeth;
   see Weddle, 30
Spencer, James, 30
Spencer, Polly;
   see Cooper, 30
Spradlin, Lillie Thorpe
   (Mrs. M. C.), 156
Spradlin, Dr. M. C., 156
Spradlin, Ola Mae
   Shumate (Mrs.
   William D.), 156
Spradlin, William Daniel, 156
Stagecoach days, 77-79
Stallard family, 137
Stanley, A. O., 176
Steamboats, 70-80
Stewart, George B., 209
Stewart, James, 207
Stewart, John Sam, 138
Stephenson, Jane, 102
Stigall, Ballie, 159
Stigall, C., 199
Stigall, Clarence Golden, 160
Stigall, Coleman, 160
Stigall, D. H., 107
Stigall, Elizabeth, 160
Stigall family, 67
Stigall, Fannie Tucker
   (Mrs. Fontaine), 160-61
Stigall, Fontaine, 160-1
Stigall, George B., 160
Stigall, Grace Virginia
   Lawrence (Mrs.
   Nicholas D.), 160
Stigall, Harry, 140

Stigall, Dr. John, 160-61
Stigall, Laura Golden
   (Mrs. Nicholas D.), 160
Stigall, Mattie, 160
Stigall, Mrs. Minnie, 103
Stigall, Miriam Harris
   (Mrs. Thomas), 160
Stigall, Nannie Frost
   (Mrs. John), 161
Stigall, Dr. Nicholas D., 2, 160-61
Stigall, Nora, 160
Stigall, Thomas, 160, 204
Stigall, Virginia
   Lawrence, 160, 164
Stigall, William, 104
Stigall, Will H., 160
Stogsdill, John, 209
Stogsdill, William, 206
Stokes, Katherine;
   see Crawford, 35
Stoneman, General, 217
Stoner family, 52-53
Stoner's Ferry, 74, 76, 229
Stoner Ferry Road, 75
Stoner, Frances Tribble
   (Mrs. Michael), 53
Stoner, Michael (George
   Michael Holstiener), 26, 32, 52-53, 74-75, 229
Stonestreet, ———, 106
Stout Hotel, 131
Stray pen, 23
Street railway, first, 169
Streets, first hard-
   surfaced (Somerset), 169
Stringer, Charles, 209
Stringer, Cyrenius W. 209
Strother, Rev. J. P., 101
Stroud, Ansill, 15
Stylesville, town of, 60
Sublette, Phillip A., 13-14, 16, 84
Sublimity, town of, 60
Sublitte, Archibald M., 84
Sugg, Thomas, 11
Summers, William, 212
Sumney, David B. F., 209
Surben, Galen E., 209
Surber, Green Lee, 97
Surber, Isaac, 121
Surber, Thomas, 16
Surveyor, first county, 10
Sutherford, James, 206
Sutton, Micajah, 33
Swain, Enos, 197

268

Swearingen, Richard Cheek, 203
Swearinger, William, 212
Sweeney, John S., 98
Sweeney, William, 203
Swift, John, 201

Talbot, Rev. Charles H., 109-10, 188
Talbot, Rev. Thomas B., 107
Tannery, 168
Tarter, Alfred, 31
Tarter, Alvadas, 209
Tarter, Betsy Trimble (Mrs. Christian L.), 30, 53-54
Tarter, Calet, 209
Tarter, Celia, 31; see Weddle
Tarter, E. L., 30
Tarter, Chris L., 58, 66, 84
Tarter, Chrisley, 29, 31
Tarter, Chrisley (Christley), Jr., 27, 31
Tarter, Christian, 30
Tarter, Christian Logan, 53-54
Tarter, C. L., 19
Tarter, Eliza Todd (Mrs. Alfred), 31
Tarter, Elizabeth (Betsy) Trimble (Mrs. Chrisley), 29, 31
Tarter, Elizabeth T. (Mrs. John, Jr.), 31
Tarter, Enis, 31, 64
Tarter, Enoch, 54
Tarter family, 53, 200
Tarter, Finley, 127
Tarter, Helen, 178; see Cooper
Tarter, Jacob, 31, 53
Tarter, Jerome, 58, 66
Tarter, Jerome Terrell, 54
Tarter, Jesse, 27, 31, 53
Tarter, John, 31-32, 53-54, 64
Tarter, John, Jr., 31
Tarter, J. T., 17, 30
Tarter, Laban, 31
Tarter, Lucinda Bernard (Mrs. Enoch L.), 54
Tarter, Margaret Weddle (Mrs. Jerome T.), 54, 84
Tarter, Nancy (Mrs. John), 31, 64
Tarter, Patsy, 31; see Weddle

Tarter, Peter, 31-32, 64-5, 203
Tarter, Polly Pearce (Mrs. Peter), 31
Tarter, Judge Roscoe C., 18-19, 58, 66, 140
Tarter, Rufus, 140
Tarter, Sally Weddle (Mrs. Jesse), 31
Tarter, William, 53-54
Tate, Bowan Goggin, 56
Tate, Cordelia Hunt (Mrs. Robert), 154
Tate, Eliza Jones (Mrs. Samuel), 56
Tate, Emma; 36; see Denton
Tate family, 55-56
Tate, Hannah, 55
Tate, Isaac, 55
Tate, Jane, 55
Tate, Jane Owens (Mrs. Samuel B.), 48, 56
Tate, John, 55
Tate, Lydia, 55
Tate, Martha, 55
Tate, Mary Bracken (Mrs. John), 55
Tate, Minerva Martin (Mrs. Samuel), 56
Tate, Robert M., 55, 154
Tate, Samuel, 48, 56
Tate, Capt. Samuel, 32, 205
Tate, Samuel Bracken, 55-56
Tate, S. H., 125
Tate, Ward W., 192
Tate, Zada; see Trimble, 154
Tateville, town of, 55
Taul, Col. Micah (Michael), 32, 205
Taverns, 128-31
Tax commissioner, first, 26
Tax lists, early, 25-27
Taylor, Catherine French, 185
Taylor, Elihu, 64, 87
Taylor, Ella Florence Jones (Mrs. George P., Sr.), 185
Taylor, Emma, 117
Taylor, Eva, 63, 133
Taylor family, 65
Taylor, George Parker, Sr., 86, 136, 184-5
Taylor, George Parker II, 185

Taylor, Geo. P., Produce Co., 173
Taylor, John, 212
Taylor, Joseph N., 211
Taylor, Joseph Pickard, 184
Taylor, Joshua, 65, 100
Taylor, Lewis, 209
Taylor, L.N., 180
Taylor, Mabel G. French (Mrs. Norman I.), 183-84
Taylor, Mark Meneghan, 185
Taylor, Melvina Parker (Mrs. Joseph P.), 184
Taylor, Nancy; see Elliot, 38
Taylor, Norman Ingraham, 136, 183-85
Taylor, Philip Parker, 185
Taylor, Richard Brion, 185
Taylor, Robert French, 185
Taylor, Col. William Solander, 127
Taylor, William S., 92
Taymans, Elisha G., 209
Telephone, first, 151, 169
Tenner, Silvester, 207
Terrell, James, 207
Thacker, James, 209
Thacker, John W., 212
Thatcher, Elizabeth, 156; see Richardson and Waddle
Thatcher, John M. P., 180
Thatcher, Nannie Perkins (Mrs. Thomas), 113, 148, 156, 164
Thatcher, Thomas Muir, 148, 156
Third Kentucky Infantry, 224
Thirty-second Kentucky Regiment of Infantry, 224
Thomas, Dora Lair (Mrs. William O.), 113, 164
Thomas, General, 213-15
Thomas, Joe A, 164
Thomas, Joseph, 26
Thomas, William Orlando, 164
Thompson, Dr., 149
Thompson, Henry, 106
Thompson, Joseph, 207
Thompson, Thomas, 15
Thompson, William, 106

269

Thorpe, Lillie, 156;
  see Spradlin
Thurman, Benjamin, 34,
  52, 204
Thurman, J. H., 52
Thurman, Joseph, 34
Thurman, Joshua, 34
Thurman, Lucy
  Richardson (Mrs.
  Benjamin), 34, 52
Thurman, Mae, 52;
  see Roberts
Thurman, Sabra Hughes
  (Mrs. Joshua), 34
Thurston, "Boomer", 80
Timber, 9, 72-73
Tibbals Drug Company,
  162
Tibbals, Dr. F. E., 144,
  162, 171
Tibbals, L. S., 162
Tibbals, Luther, 189, 193
Tibbals, W. H., 162
Tindle, Samuel, 204
Tinsley, William, 212
Tobacco, first licensed
  inspection of, 23
Todd, Eliza, 31;
  see Tarter
Todd, Elizabeth, 39;
  see Gastineau
Todd, Polly, 39;
  see Gastineau
Tomlinson, Charles, 85
Tomlinson, Ida, 164
Tomlinson, John, 84
Tomlinson, Mercy, 106
Tomlinson, Nathaniel,
  203
Tomlinson, Samuel, 124
Tomlinson, William, 86
Tompkins, Chrystopher,
  24
Tornado (1949), 196
Totten, Ellen, 44;
  see Bradley
Transportation, means of,
  74-83
  conveyances, 80-81
  railroads, 80-81
  stagecoach, 77-79
  steamboat, 79-80
Trap, John, 11
Travel, means of,
  rail, 81-83
  roads, 74-77
  water, 79-80
Tribble, Rev. Andrew, 53
Tribble, Frances, 53;
  see Stoner
Tribble, Sarah Ann Burris
  (Mrs. Andrew), 53

Trigg, Fannie, 35;
  see Curd
Trimble, Betsy, 30-31;
  53; see Tarter
Trimble, Colanza
  (Mrs. Henry Green),
  154, 227
Trimble family, 200
Trimble, Henry Green,
  84, 154
Trimble, Dr. Volantus
  (Vola) Green 65, 154
Trimble, William, 30, 53,
  64, 203
Trimble, Zada Tate
  (Mrs. Volantus), 141,
  154
Trolley, first, 169
Tucker, Elizabeth, 159
Tucker, Fannie, 159-60;
  see Stigall
Tucker, John, 159
Tuggle, William, 132
Tuggle, Mrs. William,
  132
Tuggle, W. J., 142
Tummelson, John, 14, 25,
  84
Turley, Standford, 207
Turner, Andrew, 69
Turner, Edward, 11-12
Turner, John, 90
Turpin, Martin, 203
Turpin, Solomon, 84
Turpin, Wiley, 84
Turpin, William F., 208
Turpin, William S., 208
Tustison, M. A., 117
Tuttle, John, 140-41
Tuttle, Mrs. Ruth Wait,
  56, 167
Twelfth Regiment of
  Infantry, Union Army,
  224
Tysah, John, 207

Upton, J. B., 169
U. S. Highway 27, 76-77

Van Arsdale, Margaret
  Garnett, 149;
  see Owens
Vance, Samuel, 207
VanHook, C. F., 138
VanHook, Nancy;
  see Smith
Vanhook, Sullivan, 207
Vansant, N. W., 140
Van Winkle, John S., 122
Varney family, 137
Vaughan, Frances, 59;
  see Zachary

Vaughan, Mourning Hope
  (Mrs. Samuel), 59
Vaughan, Samuel, 59
Vaughan, Rev. W. F., 101
Vaught, Lieut. Granville
  J., 211
Vaught, Stephen, 209
Veterinary medicine, 144
Vickery House, 131
Vickery, Jenkins, 97, 120,
  124, 131
Vickery, Jenkins home,
  167
Vickery, Sophronia
  (Fromia), 113, 149;
  see Perkins
Vigle, Dr. John B., 161
Volk, Reverend, 96

Waddle, Dr. Charles L.,
  154
Waddle, C. W., 140
Waddle, Elizabeth
  Thatcher, 156; see
  Richardson and
  Thatcher
Waddle, Grace, 158;
  see Weddle
Waddle, Henry, 32
Waddle, James L., 168
Waddle, James S., 16
Waddle, Katherine, 177;
  see Morrow
Waddle, Maria Ham
  (Mrs. William), 154
Waddle, Neil, 102
Waddle, O. H., 116, 125,
  169, 177, 226
Waddle, Mrs. Robert, 164
Waddle, R. B., 18
Waddle, Robert L., 84
Waddle, William, 154
Waddle, W. Dennis, 18
Waddle, W. O., 116
Wade, Sarah Allen
  (Mrs. William), 23
Wade, William, 23
Wagon (Somerset)
  factory, 168
Wahle, Dr. A. J., 154, 170
Wait, Benjamin Franklin,
  58
Wait, Clay, 191
Wait, Cyrenius, 28-29, 32,
  56-58, 71, 79, 112-13,
  124, 167, 171
Wait, Eliza Beaty
  (Mrs. Cyrenius), 57
Wait family, 56-58
Wait, G. Harry, 73

Wait, George Washington, 58, 116, 125, 192
Wait, Harry, 56, 83
Wait, Mrs. Harry, 29, 56
Wait, Henry Clay, 58
Wait, John, 192
Wait, John Quincy, 58
Wait, Jonathan, 57
Wait, Margaret Smith (Mrs. Jonathan), 57
Wait, Margaret, 58
Wait, Mary Jane Newell (Mrs. Cyrenius), 57
Wait, Millard Fillmore, 58
Wait Mill, 70
Wait, M. C., 73
Wait, Ruth, 167; see Tuttle
Wait, Webb, 58
Wait, William, 56, 85
Wait and Withers, 167
Waitsboro, town of, 57, 60
Wait's Hill, 171, 194
Walder's Daguerrean Gallery, 120
Walker, Dr. Thomas, 201, 229
Walker, Tobe, 201
Wallace, Frederick, 86
Walton, Matthew, 201
Ward, A. J., 92
Ward, William, 98, 124
Ware, Belle, 161; See Bishop
Ware, Boyd Morrow (Mrs. Louis), 180
Ware, Charles P., 180
Ware, Elizabeth, 180; see Weddle
Ware family, 93, 200
Ware, Louis, 180
Ware, Nora Lynn (Mrs. Charles P.), 180
Warn, John, 212
Warner, Charles, 85
Warner family, 65
Warner, Jake, 65
Warner, Robert, 141
War of 1812, 205-7
Warren, Alexander, 209
Warren, Benjamin, 207
Warren, Dr. "Ike," 151
Warren, Mathew, 87
Warren, Sam, 151, 162
Warren, William S., 87
Warriner, Eva, 127-28
Warriner, James A., 126
Washington, Sarah (Mrs. William A.), 27-28

Washington, William Augustus, 27-28
Waterloo, town of, 64
Waters, Joe, 192-93
Waters, L. L., 82
Water system, first (Somerset), 168
Watkins, Brit, 95
Watkins, Bishop W. T., 102
Watkins, George, 207
Watthall, Rev. Barclay, 107
Weatherford, Winfield, 87
Weaver, Abraham, 94
Weaver, James, 86
Weaver, Sam, 140
Weaver, William, 141
Webb, Ernest, 140
Weddle, Dr. A. A., 58, 66, 152
Weddle, Dr. Brent, 65, 154
Weddle, Celia Tarter (Mrs. William), 31
Weddle, Claude, 58, 66, 93-94, 158
Weddle, C. V., 141
Weddle, Daniel, 30-31, 64, 66, 209
Weddle, Dr. E. V., 157
Weddle, Elizabeth Spencer (Mrs. William), 30
Weddle, Elizabeth Ware (Mrs. Jacob), 180
Weddle family, 58, 93, 200
Weddle, Grace Waddle (Mrs. Claude), 158
Weddle, Jack, 65
Weddle, Jacob (Jake), 164, 180
Weddle, James S. (Jim), 65, 87
Weddle, John, 31, 209
Weddle, John Milton, 18, 19, 30-31, 54, 58, 64-65
Weddle, J. W., 18
Weddle, L. B., 136
Weddle, Margaret, 54; see Tarter
Weddle, Patsy Tarter (Mrs. Solomon), 31
Weddle, Polly McDaniel (Mrs. John Milton), 30, 58
Weddle, Rebecca, 31; see Phipps
Weddle, Dr. Richard Hunt, 158

Weddle, Sally, 31; see Tarter
Weddle, Solomon, 31, 54, 58
Weddle, Stella, 164
Weddle, Vida, 164, 180; see Allen
Weddle, William 30-32
Weldon, Dr. J. W., 101
Wellington, Sallie, 103
Wellington, W. H., 103
Wells, Robert, 25
Wesley, Elbert, 18, 137
Wesley, Enoch, 16
Wesley, E. T., 102, 127
Wesley, Gladstone, 19, 127
Wesley, John P., 141
Wesley, Mariah Cox (Mrs. James King), 34
Wesley, Parker, 162
West, Isaac, 76
West, James M., 212
West, Jane, 103
West Pulaski County, settlement of, 64-66
West, Wesley, 103
Westerman, Charles, 89
Wetherby, Gov. Lawrence, 63
Wheeler, Mattie, 166; see Cooper
Whiles, Thomas, 21 see also Wiles
Whinnery, Mrs. Elizabeth Crawford, 35, 101, 113
White, Barron and Company, 119
White, Frank J., 84
White, Mrs. Jennie Sandifer, 113
White, Joel, 207
White, John, 207
White, Dr. F. J., 157
Whitley, Captain, 2
Whitley, Rev. Thomas, 31, 66
Wiatt, James, 26
Wiatt, Penelope, 26
Wiatt, William, 26
Wight, Father B. J., 96
Wiles (Whiles), Thomas, 15-16
Wiley, A., 106
Will, first, 23
Williams, ———, 106
Williams, Amanda, 103
Williams, Cecil, 122, 180
Williams, George B., 209
Williams, Irvine, 87
Williams, Col. J. B., 125
Williams, Rev. J. H., 101

271

Williams, Mae Berry (Mrs. Cecil), 122
Williams, M. C. and Son, 162
Williams, Nannie, 202; see Owens
Williams, Ralph (Ralp), 21, 24
Williams, Richard, 125
Williams, Sherrod, 175
Williams, Rev. W. H., 94
Williamson, Rev. W. E., 106, 110
Willis, David, 212
Willis, Henry, 207
Willis, Gov. Simeon, 144
Wilson, Benjamin G., 209
Wilson family, 65
Wilson, Floyd, 127
Wilson, F. B., 138
Wilson, James, 207
Wilson, John, 203
Wilson, Thomas, 27
Wilson, Truesdale, 127, 136
Wilson, W. Clark, 102, 137-38
Wilson, W. F., 136
Wilson, W. S., 141
Withers, Elizabeth, 52, 171; see Shepperd
Witherspoon, Rev. Joseph, 104, 106
Wolf Creek Dam, 63, 104
Wolfe, Abe, 168
Wolford, Col. Frank, 210-14, 217-21
Wolford's Cavalry, 210
Wontland, Thomas, 207
Wood, Amelia, 103
Wood, Ansel L., 87
Wood, Edd, 95
Wood, Rev. W. B., 94-95
Woodall, John, 209
Woodall, William, 212
Woodcock, Green, 59
Woodcock, John, 191
Woodcock, J. H., 125
Woodcock, Mary, 59
Woodcock, Mrs. Mary, 113

Woodcock, Pamelia, 42, 97, 155; see Gibson
Woodcock, Robert, 59, 100, 120
Woodcock, Sallie Zachary (Mrs. Stephen), 59
Woodcock, Stephen, 59
Woodcock, William, 15, 59, 124-25
Woodcock, Willis, 59
Woods, Archibald, 105
Woods, Elgie, 164
Woods, Jim, 95
Woods, Margaret, 105
Woods, Mary, 105
Woods, Peter, 90
Woods, Polly, 28
Woods, Silas D., 33
Woods, William, 22
Woodstock, 60-61
Woolridge, Otilla, 153; see Hughes
World War I, 224
World War II, 225, 228
Wort, Mr., 131
Wright, Ballinger E., 92
Wright, Effie, 41; see Gibson
Wright Fannie, 41; see Gibson
Wright, Gen. H. C., 219-20
Wright, Kate, 41; see Gibson

Yeams, John, 207
Yehning, Dudley, 141
Yoak, Dr. R. J., 101
Young, Gen. Bennett H., 227
Young, Michael, 203

Zachary, Addie Eliza, 59; see Ingram
Zachary, Amanda, 59; see Richardson
Zachary, Benjamin, 58-59, 129
Zachary, Bettie, 59; see Jones
Zachary, Mrs. Betty, 58; see Cundiff

Zachary (Zachery), Judge Charles A., 16-17, 59, 129
Zachary, Elizabeth, 59; see Jones
Zachary, Etta, 59
Zachary, Eva, 59
Zachary, Everett, 59
Zachary family, 58-59
Zachary, Frances Vaughan (Mrs. John), 59
Zachary, Harriett, 59
Zachary House, 129-31
Zachary, James, 59
Zachary, James Brent, 59
Zachary, Jane, 59; see Arthur
Zachary, John, 58-59
Zachary, John Vaughan, 34, 59
Zachary, Louisa, 59; see Cundiff
Zachary, Louise Moore (Mrs. Charles), 59
Zachary, Martha Ann, 34, 59; see Cox
Zachary, Mary Frances, 59; see Collins
Zachary, Matilda, 58; see Fitzpatrick
Zachary, Pamelia Q. Porter (Mrs. John Vaughan), 34, 59
Zachary, Permelia, 59; see Cundiff
Zachary, Polly, 41, 59; see Gibson
Zachary, Sallie, 58-59; see Woodcock
Zachary, William, 27, 58
Zachary, Willis, 58
Zachary, Willis Fields, 59
Zernow, Rev. H. B., 106, 110
Zimmerman, Rev. ———, 100
Zollicoffer, General Felix, 199-200, 212-214, 227
Zollicoffer Park, 227

www.ingramcontent.com/pod-product-compliance
Lightning Source LLC
Chambersburg PA
CBHW020643300426
44112CB00007B/222